Mysterious Skin

To Ian

Mysterious Skin

Male Bodies in Contemporary Cinema

Edited by

Santiago Fouz-Hernández

Published in 2009 by I.B.Tauris & Co. Ltd
6 Salem Road, London W2 4BU
175 Fifth Avenue, New York NY 10010
www.ibtauris.com

Distributed in the United States and Canada Exclusively by Palgrave Macmillan, 175 Fifth Avenue, New York NY 10010

ISBN 978 1 84511 831 0

A full CIP record for this book is available from the British Library
A full CIP record for this book is available from the Library of Congress
Library of Congress catalog card: available

Typeset in Rotis by Dexter Haven Associates Ltd, London
Printed and bound in India by Thomson Press India Ltd

Contents

PART 2: FEELING THE BODY: DISSECTIONS, TEXTURES AND CLOSE-UPS

PART 3: THE BODY, SEX AND SEXUALITY

Illustrations

Every reasonable effort has been made to contact copyright holders in order to acquire the necessary permissions.

Contributors

Nathan Abrams was educated at the Universities of Oxford and Birmingham. He is Director of Graduate Studies and a Lecturer in Film Studies at the School of Creative Studies and Media at Bangor University. He has written widely on Jewish Studies, American Studies and Film Studies. His books include *Jews & Sex* (Nottingham: Five Leaves, 2008), *Commentary Magazine 1945– 1959: 'A journal of significant thought and opinion'* (London and Portland, OR: Vallentine Mitchell, 2007), *Containing America: Production and Consumption in Fifties America* (co-edited with Julie Hughes; Birmingham: Birmingham University Press, 2000) and *Studying Film* (co-authored with Ian Bell and Jan Udris; London: Arnold, 2001).

Chris Beasley is a Reader in Politics at the University of Adelaide, South Australia. She has also lectured in a number of other disciplinary/interdisciplinary areas – particularly Women's Studies, Sociology, Aboriginal Studies and Cultural Studies. Her books include, *Gender & Sexuality: Critical Theories, Critical Thinkers* (Sage, 2005), *What is Feminism?: An Introduction to Feminist Theory* (Sage, 1999) and *Sexual Economyths: Conceiving a Feminist Economics* (Allen & Unwin, 1994). Her analysis of hegemonic masculinity is the centre-piece of a symposium on the subject in *Men & Masculinities* (2008). Chris Beasley's main interests are gender/sexuality studies, social and political theory, cultural studies, international politics, embodiment and ethics. She is currently writing a book on the politics of popular film, continuing shared research (with Carol Bacchi) on global ethics and embodied citizenship, and preparing a co-authored book on heterosexuality.

Robert Davis (PhD, Harvard University; MFA, University of Southern California) is Professor of Film History and Production at California State University, Fullerton. He has written, particularly on Asian Cinema, for *Film Criticism*, *The Journal of Popular Film and Television*, *Film-Philosophy* and *Senses of Cinema*. He is a regular contributor to *American Cinematographer*, for which he has conducted extensive interviews on visual style with dozens of Korean, Japanese, Chinese and Vietnamese directors, cinematographers and production designers.

Santiago Fouz-Hernández lectures in Spanish Cinema at the University of Durham (UK). He is co-author of *Live Flesh: The Male Body in Contemporary Spanish Cinema* (I.B.Tauris, 2007) and co-editor of *Madonna's Drowned Worlds: New Approaches to Her Cultural Transformations* (1982–2003) (Ashgate, 2004). His work on masculinities in contemporary Spanish and British cinemas has also been published in journals that include *Romance Studies, Journal of Iberian and Latin American Studies, Men and Masculinities* and *New Cinemas*. He is reviews editor of the journal *Studies in Hispanic Cinemas* (Intellect) and guest editor of the journal's special issue on the male body (3.3). He is currently preparing a Spanish-language manuscript on representations of the body in European and North-American film, advertising and popular culture entitled *Cuerpos de cine*.

Susan Hunt is a faculty associate at Santa Monica and Pasadena City Colleges. Her essays on the representation of sexuality and the mind/body split in films – co-authored with Peter Lehman – have appeared in *Titanic: Anatomy of a Blockbuster, Enfant Terrible! Jerry Lewis in American Film, Framework, Jump Cut* and the forthcoming *Persistence of Whiteness*. She and Lehman are currently writing a book on the same subject for Rutgers University Press.

Rachael Langford is Senior Lecturer in French at the School of European Studies at Cardiff University. She has published widely on French and Francophone African film, literature and visual culture, and on nineteenth-century French culture. She coordinates a cross disciplinary research network on the representation of migration, mobility and identity in European cultures, and is currently preparing a monograph on genre in Francophone African film, and commencing a research project on representations of the Congo in Francophone textual and visual culture in the pre-Independence period.

Peter Lehman is Director of the Center for Film, Media, and Popular Culture at Arizona State University, Tempe. He is author of *Roy Orbison: The Invention of an Alternative Rock Masculinity* and the revised, expanded second edition of *Running Scared: Masculinity and the Representation of the Male Body*. He is editor of *Pornography: Film and Culture and Masculinity: Bodies, Movies, Culture*.

Vek Lewis lectures in Latin American Studies at the University of Sydney, Australia. He has written on the articulation of gender and sexuality in Latin American literary and cinematic forms, mostly notably with respect to the representation of gender variant homosexual and trans subjectivities. His current line of work examines Mexican media texts and the production of gendered marginality. It centres on how mediatic discourse on contemporary urban minorities from certain locales interacts with the production and establishment of juridical frameworks. While interested in the way multimodal texts function socio-culturally as they produce, circulate and limit dominant knowledges about subjects, Lewis is also concerned with how publics make sense of, use and contest knowledges found in the cultural forms around them. His contribution on Mexican cinema and practices of codification, decodification and viewer spectatorship continues this critical focus.

Tim Maloney is a graduate of Northwestern University and the University of Southern California's School of Cinema/Television. He was director of the ABC–Disney Saturday morning animated series, *Mrs Munger's Classroom*, and his art-animations have been shown in major galleries throughout the world and on *Good Morning, America*. He has published essays on copyright issues, the post-production pipeline and the experimental cinema of Craig Baldwin. He is currently Assistant Professor of Film History and Production at California State University, Fullerton.

Gary Needham is a lecturer in the School of Arts, Communication and Culture, Nottingham Trent University. He is the co-editor of *Asian Cinemas: A Reader and Guide* (Edinburgh University Press, 2006) and has published on Hong Kong Cinema, Italian Cinema, film music, disco and American television. He is the co-editor of *Queer TV* (Routledge, 2008) and author of a monograph on *Brokeback Mountain* (Edinburgh University Press, 2009).

Konrad Gar-Yeu Ng is an assistant professor in the Academy for Creative Media at the University of Hawai'i at Mānoa. Formerly, he was Curator of Film and Video at the Honolulu Academy of Arts and a film programmer for the Louis Vuitton Hawaii International Film Festival. He is author of the exhibition catalogue *Won Ju Lim: In Many Things To Come* (2006) and has published articles on cinema, race and gender in academic and popular journals. He teaches courses on the art, politics and history of global cinema and is currently working on a book about Asian cultural identity, politics and digital media.

D. Cuong O'Neill is an assistant professor at the University of California at Berkeley. He completed his PhD from Yale University in Japanese Literature in 2002. He teaches courses in modern Japanese literature and aesthetics, post-war intellectual history and popular culture. His research interests include the novel in comparative perspective, critical theory and gender/sexuality studies. He has published essays on modern Japanese literature, literary criticism, translation and gender theory in journals including *Japan Forum: The International Journal of Japanese*

Studies (2006) and *Discourse: Journal for Theoretical Studies in Media and Culture* (2008).

Alison Peirse is a Lecturer in Film Studies at the University of Hull, where she teaches Horror Film, British Cinema, Alfred Hitchcock, and Film Theory and Analysis. Her research focuses on representations of gender, sexuality and the body in horror film and cult television. She has recently published articles on postfeminism and horror in contemporary television, and on the 1930s output of filmmaker Edgar G. Ulmer. She is currently writing a research monograph on the male body in 1930s horror film.

Heidi Schlipphacke is an associate professor of German and European Studies at Old Dominion University in Norfolk, VA, USA and she is currently Visiting Associate Professor at Haverford College. She has published widely on the European Enlightenment, family and gender, Critical Theory, and post-war German film and literature in journals including *Camera Obscura, The German Quarterly, Orbis Litterarum* and *The Lessing Yearbook.* She recently completed a manuscript on nostalgia in post-war German literature and film, and she is currently working on a project on masculinity in post-war German cinema.

Aparna Sharma is a film scholar and filmmaker keenly interested in the cultural implications of the cinema and its scope as a historical medium. Her filmmaking deploys a mix between theory and practice, deriving particularly from the disciplines of Visual Anthropology and Ethnography. Her recent PhD submission involves a thesis arguing for a regime of viewing ethnicity by mobilising modernist aesthetic practices such as montage. Her submission is supported by a short experimental documentary, *Crossings in a Beautiful Time*, which surrounds the Gujarati community in Cardiff. The film was premiered as an installation at the Next Wave Festival of Youth Art, Melbourne 2006. Aparna is a critic and reviewer for a spread of publications across the world including Leonardo Digital Reviews (MIT Press) and the Women's Feature Service. She also serves on the editorial panel of the Oxford University Press.

Acknowledgements

This book would not exist without the hard work of the scholars who have contributed with their chapters. I have been extremely lucky to have been able to work with 14 extremely diligent and generous academics who have made the sometimes taxing job of editing an immensely pleasurable and rewarding experience. My main acknowledgement is to them. Peter Lehman deserves a special mention for agreeing to contribute to this collection and for his confidence in this project. His work in this field has been and still is a major source of inspiration for my own research and partly responsible for my drive to put this book together. I also thank all those scholars who submitted excellent proposals for this book, but whose work could not be included here.

Durham University (UK) supported this project with a period of research leave in 2007 which allowed me to research and write my own contribution to this book, as well as to edit most of the manuscript. I conceived this project while working on a previous book on the male body in Spanish cinema. That earlier period of research was supported by AHRC (Arts and Humanities Research Council) and British Academy grants and I would like to express my gratitude to those institutions. I am indebted to my editor Philippa Brewster for putting her trust in me once again and for her constant encouragement and support, and to everyone else who has been involved in the production of this book at I.B.Tauris, especially Gretchen Ladish and Jayne Hill. I would also like to thank Natascha Teunissen for granting me, on behalf of Kasander Film Company, permission to use the cover image (and also the image used in the introduction).

On a more personal note, I would like to thank my partner Christian for his patience and constant support. He also developed my concept for the cover, produced the cover artwork and helped me with formatting issues in the final stages. As always, I thank my close family and friends, especially Mario and Ian, who have been around the longest, and are always there when I need them.

Introduction: Mysterious Skin

Santiago Fouz-Hernández

The representation of the body has been extensively discussed in film studies since the 1970s. Following an initial emphasis on the study of the representation of the female body, the 1990s and 2000s have seen attention turn also to masculinity. In 1993 alone a number of key contributions to the field were published, with monographs by Peter Lehman, Yvonne Tasker and Steven Shaviro as well as edited collections by Cohan and Hark or Kirkham and Thumin. These books were pioneering in their studies of genres (from gladiator epics to comedy, horror, musical, melodrama, pornography, suspense or war films), stars (from Schwarzenegger, Stallone or Willis to Ford, Gable or Hudson) or specific films paying particular attention to masculinity and the male body. What connects these books is their critical approach to the wealth of criticism that, in its attempt to counteract the gender imbalance described in Mulvey's much-discussed essay about visual pleasure and narrative cinema (1975), focused almost exclusively on femininity (the female subject, the female gaze) and left nearly untouched 'the secure and comfortable "norm" of masculinity' (Cohan and Hark 1993: 2). The need for a shift of focus onto men and masculinities was clearly summarised by Lehman: 'only after [...] centring the male body will it be possible truly to de-centre it for it is precisely when the penis-phallus is hidden from view in patriarchy that it is most centred' (1993: 5). Other important studies followed suit throughout the 1990s, notably by female authors. Among the most influential are Jeffords's monograph on 'hard bodies' and masculinity in 1980s Hollywood cinema (1994) or Bordo's (1999) book on the male body, which included a chapter on 1950s Hollywood films and references to the gay male body in more contemporary Hollywood comedies. Journals such as the *Michigan Quarterly Review* also published special issues on the male body in the mid-1990s.[1] The field has been equally productive since 2000. Lehman published a new collection of essays on bodies and masculinities in 2001 (Lehman 2001a); Holmlund a monograph on male and female bodies in Hollywood film in 2002; Powrie, Davies and Babington an edited collection on masculinities (including a section on male bodies) in 2004; and journals such as *Paragraph* and *Men and Masculinities* also published special issues on male bodies in 2003 and 2007 respectively (see Still (2003) and Stephens and Lorentzen (2007a)). While there is no room here for a detailed summary of the ongoing discussions in the field (see Powrie, Davies and Babington for a useful overview (2004: 1–5)), it is crucial to note that, as evidenced in the titles and short descriptions of many of these books, most of the work to date on male bodies in film studies has focused on Hollywood cinema. One of the main aims of this volume is precisely to readdress the balance by offering a wider and more representative picture of the depiction of the male body in contemporary cinema.

This book borrows its title from Gregg Araki's 2005 film, itself borrowed from the Scott Heim's novel on which it is based.[2] Araki's *Mysterious Skin* is the story of two eight-year-old boys who, sexually abused by their high school paedophile sports coach (Bill Sage), find different ways of coming to terms with this memory (or lack thereof). For over a decade, Brian Lackey (Brady Corbet), now a shy and unconfident teenager, still living in the small Kansas town where the abuse took place, suffers from inexplicable nosebleeds and blackouts, struggles to remember what happened at the time of the abuse, trying to find an explanation in an imagined alien abduction. By contrast, Neil (Joseph Gordon-Levitt), faces the harsh reality of a rent boy now living in New York. The 'mysterious skin', seen from Neil's perspective, might refer to the male skin of the mysterious men that he had been sexually attracted to from an early age (the coach, his sister's boyfriend) and now that of his older customers (one of them affected by Kaposi sarcoma asks only for a back massage because he 'needs to be touched'). Brian's own skin conversely, is mysteriously marked with what he thinks may be evidence of his alien abduction but also frequently stained with his nosebleeds. Notably, the more resilient Neil (barely distressed by his various STD episodes) is physically hurt by a client and bleeds for the first time just before his re-encounter with Brian back in Kansas ten years later. Like Araki's previous films, the male body is presented to the viewer as a site of intense desire, pleasure and pain. As in some of the examples from other films discussed in this volume, the camera contemplates the male body in a way that makes us feel it, provoking an enhanced 'carnal' experience in the spectator, to use Sobchack's term (2004). *Mysterious Skin* is thus an appropriate title for this collection of essays on representations of male bodies in world cinema in that, although the male body may have ceased to hide behind its status as 'the norm', it seems nonetheless that there are still many mysteries to resolve; indeed, even in their attempt to deconstruct dominant representations of 'the' male body (one that is markedly 'male', heterosexual, young, white and often Anglo-American), existing studies of masculinities and male bodies in cinema often focus on Hollywood productions.

Figure 1: Ewan McGregor in *The Pillow Book*. Kasander Film Company.

One of the films that I had in mind when conceiving this book was Peter Greenaway's *The Pillow Book* (1996). Appropriately, the film brings together the main three areas that are explored in this collection: national and ethnic identities; the body as a cinematic canvas; and the vulnerability and versatility of those gender and sexual identities usually associated with 'masculinity'. The choice of Scottish actor Ewan McGregor as the male protagonist of that film adds a layer of complexity to his role as an 'English' translator living in Hong Kong. As I have argued elsewhere (Fouz-Hernández 2005), his job as a translator who lives abroad and is fluent in four languages, further resists those identifications with Britain that are suggested elsewhere in the film: he feigns suicide like in Shakespeare's classic *Romeo and Juliet* and he lives in what at the time was still a British colony at a time of flux, just before its return to China. As shown on the cover of this book, his markedly white Anglo-Saxon body is written on with Japanese characters – and later made into the pages of a book inspired by a Japanese text (Sei Shônagon's *The Pillow Book*).[3] The vertical direction of the writing in itself undermines (phallic) Western understandings of linguistic linearity. Indeed, Jerome's (McGregor's) body is also susceptible to other types of deconstruction. While the noticeable size of his penis (even when flaccid) may suggest a phallic type of masculinity, this contrasts not only with the vertical writing on his body, but also with his willingness to have his skin written on by his female lover Nagiko (Vivian Wu) and later inspected by the male publisher (Yoshi Oida) and the calligraphers that transcribe the text. Jerome's posture and gestures when revealing his 'book' to the publisher suggest a willingness to be looked at traditionally associated with female stars (Mulvey 1975) and reminiscent of the female (decidedly not male) strip show and fashion business (see Figure 1). His gender versatility is thus contained in his adaptability as an 'active' calligrapher and a passive canvas which, in turn, is linked to his ambiguous sexuality.

Beyond its deconstruction of national, gender and sexual identities, Greenaway's *The Pillow Book*, also opens itself up to a number of readings of film as a corporeal experience. The narrative calls for a constant inspection of the male body in all shot types while it is shaven, written on, checked by the publisher and calligraphers and so on. The cinema screen, often split in this film, becomes the perfect metaphor for the skin as canvas. Like the screen, Jerome's body will be later split, while his shaved and flawless skin will form the medium on which part of the story is written. As highlighted in the film's press book, the calligraphic style used for Jerome was the most sensual of all the books, applied as if to describe his anatomy and 'caress his skin with words' (Kasander and Wigman 1996). The visual contrast established between the male body in all its beautiful plenitude and its later destruction in death (internally by pill ingestion and externally with razor-sharp cuts into the corpse's skin shown in close-up as the skin is removed from the flesh, dried and made into the pages of an actual book) further emphasise the vulnerability of a male body which is no longer to be perceived as monolithic, hard and invincible.

As mentioned above, the areas exemplified in this short analysis of *The Pillow Book* form the three key themes explored in this book. Inevitably, these areas overlap and there are frequent intersections between all the chapters. Whereas a 'geographical' division of the book might have proven an appropriate way to structure it, it would also have been somewhat deceptive. Despite the wide range of genres, films, directors and stars discussed here, this book makes no claims to global coverage. Whereas the films discussed are to some extent representative of the cinematic traditions of the various countries of origin in the last twenty years or so, the chapters were not conceived as studies of 'national' cinemas. It should also be noted that, although some of the essays in this book draw in part upon studies of Hollywood films to reach nation-specific conclusions, they do so with the aim of opening up debates that will shed new light on future interpretations of mainstream Hollywood productions. Partly due to the global influence of Hollywood, representational politics and conceptions of masculinity and the male body are perhaps less differentiated than one might have expected in the films studied here. Indeed, many of the essays in the first section of the book, about ethnic and national identities, engage in an open dialogue with Hollywood. Abrams, for example, focuses on the representation of the Jewish body in mainstream Hollywood films, while Beasley and Langford refer to Hollywood models of masculinity as an immediate reference point to define those of Australian and Francophone African films. Conversely, Ng reminds us that the norms used to study Hollywood cinema should not be used to measure 'other cinemas' and Sharma's essay makes a point of studying Indian cinema beyond the big Bollywood productions that international audiences have come to associate with Indian cinema.

Nathan Abrams's essay explores the idea that the apparent increase in representation of Jewish male bodies in Hollywood cinema has brought about subtler representations that could suggest that Jews are more integrated into mainstream society. Beyond the traditional two-tiered representations of tough and queer Jews, in its extensive analysis of films that include Spielberg's recent *Munich* (2005) or the *American Pie* and the *X Men* sagas, the chapter identifies a relatively wide range of representations that take into consideration religious subtleties and do not shy away from nudity or discussions of the circumcised penis as a source of laughter as opposed to its most traditional association with suffering and the Holocaust. In turn, Heidi Schlipphacke's essay about the male body in recent German films interestingly focuses on how the memory of Nazism and the Holocaust has affected German male identities. She argues that the success abroad of a particular type of German film that tends to focus on the past and 'the abnormality of Germany' (in particular period films such as *Der Untergang/Downfall* (dir. Oliver Hirschbiegel, 2004) and *Das Leben der Anderen/The Lives of Others* (dir. Henckel von Donnersmarck, 2006)), contrasts with the wish to be 'normal' marked by the German effort to present itself as a friendly and welcoming nation during the hosting of the FIFA World Cup in 2006. Yet, a number of national productions successful at home seem to present what she calls, based on Deleuze and Guattari (1987), a 'schizophrenic' male body that has come about as a result of the necessary break-up from the past and the lack of father figures and appropriate models of masculinity. In films such as *Das weiße Rauschen/The White Sound* (dir. Hans Weingartner, 2001) or *Lola rennt/Run Lola Run* (dir. Tom Tykwer, 1998), the bodies of representative German actors Daniel Brühl or Moritz Bleibtreu respectively often seem lost and disorientated, as shown by their positioning in the margins of the frame or in oppressively enclosed spaces. Beyond the Nazi past, the unification of Germany has also impacted on notions of national identities and the German male body.

The disjuncture between the past and the present also haunts the other chapters in the section. Konrad Gar-Yeu Ng analyses Wong's trilogy of nostalgia films about relationships between men and women in 1960s Hong Kong. Through a detailed analysis of *A-Fei Zhengzhuan/Days of Being Wild* (1991), *Huayang Nianhua/In the Mood for Love* (2000) and, especially, *2046* (2003), the chapter criticises the notion of 'Chineseness' as a single ethnic identity. Using Deleuze as a starting point, Ng argues that the palimpsest Chinese male bodies in Wong's films embody a critical temporality in which the cinematic form of Chinese cultural identity becomes 'a state of permanent crisis'. The use of the same actor Tony Leung and his character Chow throughout the trilogy with ever so slight physical changes in each instalment, further complicates the notion of any fixed identity by association with Leung's own star persona and previous performances.

Chris Beasley's essay on Australian male bodies is equally critical of any notion of hegemonic masculinity. She calls for a revision of what she regards as a monolithic account of the term 'hegemonic masculinity' in Connell's work and proposes the consideration of supra- and sub-hegemonic masculinities, arguing that, even at a local level, understandings of 'the hegemonic' are necessarily plural. Cinematic representations of the Australian male have varied according to their context. She uses Paul Hogan's iconic characterisation as Mick Dundee in *Crocodile Dundee* (dir. Peter Faiman, 1986) as an example. Despite what foreign audiences may perceive as an excessive and even camp representation of the stereotypical Outback Aussie man, in the film, North America becomes feminised (even tamed) by the brutish, nature-wise, idealised Australian man. Elsewhere, the identity of the 'Australian' male body may be determined by his various states of undress. In comparison with the colonial suited 'supra hegemon', the Australian is portrayed as somewhat primitive, sun-weathered working-class 'bloke', revealing his wiry musculature and overall relaxed manners. Yet, as seen in films such as *Rabbit Proof Fence* (dir. Philip Noyce, 2001) or *The Tracker* (dir. Rolf De Heer, 2001), his position with regards the aboriginal male is one of white superiority. He may not wear a suit, but wears some clothes and is usually seen standing up, in contrast with the aboriginal male who is often semi-nude and literally placed lower, closer to the ground, than the white Australian.

Some of these ideas are developed by Rachael Langford in her analysis of the Western genre in Francophone African films. After a useful revision of the main interpretations of the American Western in terms of gender and sexuality (from those that regard the Western as a hyper-masculine and hyper-heterosexual genre, to those that focus on the implicit homoerotic nature of many of these films), Langford discusses gender issues of the French colonial discourse. The core of her essay analyses the representation of the male body in Francophone African films such as *Tilaï/The Law* (1990), *Samba Traoré* (1992) and *Kini et Adams/Kini and Adams* (1997) (both directed by Idrissa Ouédraogo) or Sissako's *Bamako* (2006), and argues that the use of common tropes of the American Western film provides a critical intertext of Western cultural and political domination through an engaging dialogue between America, Africa and France.

As already noted, in the essay on Indian cinema that closes the first section, Aparna Sharma draws the line between Bollywood and Indian cinema to focus on the film *Daayara/The Square Circle* (dir. Amol Palekar, 1996) and explore its subversion of traditional Hindu views of masculinity and the male body through cross-dressing. The film is a love story between two characters, a male transvestite and a young female who has been a victim of rape. The woman, who will have to wear men's clothing herself in order to find work and eventually seek revenge on the men who raped her, frees herself of previous prejudices about cross-dressers, induced by institutionalised Hindu religion. In an analysis drawing on Judith Butler's work on gender performativity, Sharma argues that cross-dressing destabilises dominant notions of masculine identities and the body in Hindu societies, where the transvestite is seen as a pariah with a biological defect. The nomadic experiences of these characters reflect a spiritual journey that is visually emphasised through the use of long shots that integrate the characters in the lush landscape of east coastal India. The film thus 'naturalises' the alternative identities of these characters as it expresses a nostalgia for the rural that, in itself, contains a critique of the urban-oriented Bollywood productions and the heroic image of the Indian male that they uniformly favour.

The second section of the book, 'Feeling the Body' includes four essays that, despite touching on elements of national identities in Vietnam, France, Spain and Britain, discuss the male body in more visual terms. Robert Davis and Tim Maloney analyse three films by Vietnamese director Tran Anh Hung – *Mùi dud u xanh/The Scent of Green Papaya* (1993), *Xich Lo/Cyclo* (1995), and *À la verticale de l'été/Vertical Ray of the Sun* (2000) – where the prominence of the male body is significant. In a close analysis of four key scenes based on Sontag's 'erotics of the art' approach, they argue that Tran's films encourage a heightened sensorial experience in the spectator. This is partly achieved through the use of unusual editing techniques and the tendency to shoot the male body from angels or poses that defy Hollywood conventions.

Gary Needham's essay on the use of the close-up in shots of the penis in contemporary French cinema develops the idea of enhanced corporality in film. He suggests that, whereas international audiences have come to expect nudity from French films, the attention paid to the male body, and to the male genitals in particular, has gained a notable prominence in films not necessarily 'queer' as such but which favour non-hegemonic gazes. Drawing on Mary Ann Doane's (2003) work on the close-up and Laura U. Marks's (2000) on haptic visuality, Needham explores how the filming techniques and props used in films such as Gäel Morel's *Le clan* (*The Clan*) (2004) successfully draw us 'closer' to a male body ideal. Such an 'ideal' can often be deceptive, as in Ducastel and Martinez's

Crustacés et coquillages/Cockles and Muscles (2005), but also pleasurable for the queer spectator.

Some of these issues are also crucial to my essay on the films of Catalan director Ventura Pons. Focusing on three films that span across three decades, my choice of films engages with key tropes of the representation of the male body in Pons's extensive oeuvre. Starting with the documentary *Ocaña, retrat intermitent/ Ocaña, an Intermittent Portrait* (1978) I argue that the approach to male nudity and male bodies in this film is iconic of the Spanish democratic transition. The film not only favours the perspective of a male transvestite, but in the year in which censorship was officially abolished, it encourages explicit discussions of homosexual sex and features male frontal nudity at a time when female nudity was prominent in Spanish film. The vivid descriptions of Ocaña's sexual experiences draw the spectator closer to the male bodies being discussed. In *Carícies/Caresses* (1997) the proximity to the body is achieved through the contrast between scenes of explicit violence and the film's only caresses at the very end. Further to this, the 'fleshiness' of the film is enhanced once again through dialogue and descriptions of sexual organs. Finally, in his English-language film *Food of Love* (2001) the sense of corporality materialises in the visual comparison between the city of Barcelona (often celebrated in Pons's films) and the body of young American tourist Paul (Kevin Bishop), as well as in the comparison established between his body and those of his older lovers, another trope of Pons's cinema.

Alison Peirse's study of the British horror film *Dog Soldiers* (dir. Neil Marshall, 2002) engages with Halberstam's (2007) view that bodies that splatter challenge the gender stability dependent on notions such as the hard and phallic male body. Contrary to what may be suggested at first by the presence of squaddies in a training exercise on the Scottish highlands, the presence of werewolves in the area will undo any preconceptions about the genre. Not only is the werewolf a girl, but, in Peirse's reading, the traditional role of the 'Final Girl' in the horror movie, will be here allocated to a man. Peirse questions gender-specific notions of masochistic spectatorship as well as gendered associations of abjection with the feminine. Perhaps even more intensively than in other films up to this point of the book, the male body will be destroyed and dissected in a visceral disintegration of the phallic male body, even when the most horrid moments of such destruction occur off-camera.

The three essays included in the final section of the book further challenge established conceptions of masculinity and the male body in their respective cultural backgrounds, this time focusing on sex and sexuality. Vek Lewis's study of two key contemporary Mexican films – *Y tu mamá también/And Your Mother*

Too (dir. Alfonso Cuarón, 2001) and *Zapata: el sueño del héroe/Zapata: Dream of a Hero* (dir. Alfonso Arau, 2004) – focuses on the films' deconstruction of the quintessential Mexican macho as seen in the figure of the *charro* in Mexican Golden Age cinema. The strong homoeroticism of Cuarón's coming-of-age story provoked a certain degree of disquiet in Mexican audiences, unaccustomed to facing male nudity on the screen, specially from behind, where the male body is at its most vulnerable, an 'open body' associated with Colonialism and the mythical raped Indian woman (the *Malinche*). Even more controversial was the choice of pop singer Alejandro Fernández to incarnate the iconic revolutionary macho hero Zapata in Arau's version. Not only was the singer-come-actor surrounded by rumours about his sexual orientation, but his performance in the film lacked the physical resilience and sexual prowess associated with the mythical figure.

The Taiwanese film analysed by D. Cuong O'Neill also debunks a mythical symbol of masculinity in its own socio-historical context by queering it in a more contemporary context. Tsai's *Bu san/Goodbye, Dragon Inn* (2003) reinvents the kinaesthetic male bodies of the martial arts film by projecting King Hu's martial arts film *Long men ke zhan/Dragon Gate Inn* (1967) in a decaying cinema theatre in its closing night. The cinema is now used by gay men to cruise in the semi-darkness of the surroundings. As O'Neill points out, although Hu's male bodies were celebrated more for their nobility than their muscularity, the editing and careful choreography of the hyper-masculine supernaturally-moving bodies were associated with some sort of indestructible patriarchal power. Interestingly, some of the actors of the original film reappear here as ageing cruisers in a nostalgic confrontation with the more agile, young and perfected images of themselves projected on the screen. O'Neill's analysis explores ways in which the kinaesthesia of the bodies on the screen contrasts with the awkward movements of the cruisers in the darkness and how the dialogue and soundtrack of the original film acquires a new meaning in Tsai's film, thus further heightening the deconstruction of Hu's celebration of a particular type of Taiwanese male body.

The final essay of the collection is a contribution by Peter Lehman and Susan Hunt. Their analysis of the French–German co-production *Twentynine Palms* (dir. Bruno Dumont, 2002) illustrates their concept of 'the body guy' (usually rivalled by the 'mind guy'). The authors trace this mind/body duality back to 1930s Hollywood, with special emphasis on well-known examples such as *The Piano* (dir. Campion, 1993), *Legends of the Fall* (dir. Zwick, 1994) or *Titanic* (dir. Cameron, 1997) among others. In Dumont's film, David's (David Wissak) masculinity seems threatened by what could be perceived as a penis-size issue and by an unexpected episode in which he is physically humiliated in front of his Russian/French girlfriend Katya (Yekaterina Golubeva), with disastrous consequences for both. By somehow closing the circle opened with the discussion of circumcision in the first chapter, Lehman and Hunt's discussion of the representation of the penis brings the collection to a close by appropriately drawing attention to an issue that should not be taken for granted in studies on the male body (as Lehman himself has argued in his ground-breaking *Running Scared* (1993: 24)).

Although this book is a collection of essays that cover a wide range of genres and national cinemas, the essays have been selected to provide an overview of representations of male bodies in contemporary cinema worldwide. Readers are encouraged to read the entire collection, not just separate essays, and thus discover that, while the differences in representations of male bodies around the world reveal the vulnerability of 'masculinity' and 'the male body' as uniform or incontestable concepts, the similarities can also be surprising.

NOTES

1 The impact of these texts is perhaps best evidenced by their enormous popularity and the frequency with which they are quoted (for example, in this collection, even fifteen years later). Furthermore, the special issues of the *Michigan Quarterly Review* were republished in book format – see Goldstein (1997) and Lehman's influential book was revised for a second edition in 2007. Shaviro, on the other hand, has recently published an article that revisits his own book and outlines what he now sees as the shortcomings of his frequently cited work (see Shaviro 2008).

2 I would like to thank Tom Whittaker (Queen Mary, University of London) for drawing my attention to this film upon its DVD release.

3 I am grateful to Jo Lumley (Newcastle University, UK) for his help deciphering the Japanese writing.

Part 1

The Body and Ethnic/National Identities

1

From Jesus to Jeremy: The Jewish Male Body on Film, 1990 to Present

Nathan Abrams

I. INTRODUCTION

Representations of the Jewish male body in mainstream Anglo-American cinema have traditionally fallen into four categories: invisible; idealised – replaced by the gentile body playing the Jewish one; stereotyped; and victimised and humiliated. Recently, however, representations of the Jewish male body on film have entered a new phase. Not only have they multiplied, they have also taken on different forms, marking a radical rupture with the past. Cinema and television have witnessed a shift towards more subtle, nuanced, playful and even outrageous representations of the Jewish male body. In contrast to earlier representations, the male Jewish body is not just as a site of suffering, humiliation, victimisation, stereotyping, idealisation and sexual inadequacy but has also become a site of identification, pride and sexual prowess where male Jewish bodies, in all their variety, are openly and proudly identified as Jewish. Although there has been a trickle of such representations over the course of the twentieth century, recently it has become a veritable flood, and the list of films is numerous and continuing.

Certainly, the Jewish male body has become almost ubiquitous on present-day screens. One need only mention Sandler and Stiller, as well as Jack Black and Steven Berkoff to prove the case. This essay will survey these changed and changing but recent representations of the Jewish male body in recent mainstream cinema. However, I propose not to look at Israeli cinema here. In addition I will only discuss those *characters* (whether real or fictional) who are identified as Jewish in their films regardless of their *actual* ethnic status. This is because Ashkenazi Jews (those of Eastern and Central European descent) are now, in the main, considered *white*. Combined with the prevalence of circumcision, particularly in America, Jewish men are thus harder to identify, particularly in contrast to those who, by dint of their skin colour, cannot hide their ethnic and/or racial origins.

II. A HISTORY IN BRIEF(S) OF THE CINEMATIC JEWISH MALE BODY

In general self-images of the Jewish male have fallen into two opposing categories: the 'tough' Jew, that is the idealised hyper-masculine, militarised and muscled, though not very intellectual, Jew of the Zionist project (Yosef 2004: 2; Brienes 1990) and the 'queer' Jew: the effeminate, gentle and delicate Jew of traditional Eastern European Jewish culture who devoted his life to the study of the Torah (Boyarin 1997: 23). Both models of masculinity were 'openly resistant to and critical of the prevailing ideology of "manliness" dominant in Europe' (Boyarin 1997: 23). Cinematic representations of the Jewish male body in American cinema have navigated distinct paths between these two dichotomous poles. As mentioned at the outset, these responses can be divided into four very rough categories since the beginning of the twentieth century, according to the different stages of Jewish life in America. Of course, these distinctions are not watertight and we see exceptions in every period. The first category is that of the 'Invisible Jews', c. 1900–47, the period, as described by Neal Gabler in his *An Empire of Their Own* (1988), in which Jews were hidden on screen both literally and figuratively. Jewish actors changed their names, as their Jewish bosses considered that their predominantly white and working-class audiences did not want to watch Jews on screen. This period encapsulated what Sander Gilman has called 'the desire for invisibility, the desire to become "white"' (1991: 235). The two major exceptions to this general invisibility were *The Jazz Singer* (1927) and *Crossfire* (1947). Yet, even here, in the former film's depiction of Al Jolson playing an Orthodox Jew seeking to assimilate into the wider American culture by rejecting the ways of his cantor father and adopting the profession of singing jazz in blackface, it is the desire to become hidden that is noticeable. While in the latter, the Jew is largely concealed: as a murder victim, his actual screen time is minimal since the film devoted itself to exposing the roots of racism and bigotry rather than its consequences.

The second category was that of the 'Idealised Jew', c.1947–67. The post-war period has been described as a 'golden age' in American Jewish history. Hitler had been defeated, overt and explicit anti-Semitism had been made unfashionable to be replaced by the more 'gentleman's agreement' type which itself was slowly being eroded. Restrictive practices in hiring, university entrance and the professions were being destroyed. Yet, this did not make Jews any more visible on screen. Instead, rather than being hidden, the Jewish body was idealised, de-Semitised and played by non-Jews. The major examples include Gregory Peck as Philip Schuyler Green in Elia Kazan's *Gentleman's Agreement* (1947) – Hollywood's other post-war movie about anti-Semitism alongside *Crossfire* but ironically made by the only Jewish studio not headed by a Jew, Twentieth Century Fox – Charlton Heston as Moses and Ben Hur in *The Ten Commandments* (1956) and *Ben Hur* (1959) respectively and Paul Newman as Ari Ben Canaan in *Exodus* (1960).

By 1967 the 'golden age' had come to an end and, if *Commentary* magazine is to be believed, then it had been replaced by an age of anxiety, stirred by Jewish reactions and non-Jewish reactions to the Six Day War which led to the respective growth of what has been called a 'Holocaust consciousness', as well as anti-Zionism often allied with anti-Semitism. The result was the period of 'Stereotyped Jews', c.1967–89, in which representations of Jews, according to Elliot B. Gertel, 'became more aggressive, more pointed. There was a determined and concerted effort to stand up for Jewish identity and to throw Jewish practices back into the face of a film culture that had ignored them or shunted them aside' (2003: 2). But this 'explosion of Jewish references, associations, and even ambivalences' (Gertel 2003: 2), betrayed a contradictory impulse: a retreat into affectionate nostalgia as symbolised by *Fiddler on the Roof* (1971), versus neurotic, anxious stereotypes as mastered by Woody Allen whose richest period was from 1971–89, or a combination of both as depicted by the films of Mel Brooks.

Overlapping with all of these previous periods and reaching its zenith in 1993 with *Schindler's List* is that of the victimised and humiliated Jew, the site of suffering most usually during the Holocaust. In direct contrast, however, stood the criminal gangster and killer. Rarely, however, were these Jewish male bodies presented as spectacle or erotic. Furthermore, underlying these visual characterisations of the male Jew on screen were certain recurring stereotypical physical tics, particularly in American cinema, which David Desser has listed as fast-talking intelligence, physical weakness small stature and sexual entanglement with non-Jewish female bodies (2001: 269, 275, 276).

Since 1990, however, representations of Jews have not only multiplied but also taken on a new form, which, within the context of a century of Anglo-American cinema, marks a radical rupture with the past. There had been a trickle of such representations hitherto but from 1990 onwards, it became a veritable flood. It is marked by the advent of *Seinfeld* in 1990 – which, according to the Nielsen ratings, was the most popular sitcom of the 1990s – a show about nothing which featured four nasty, selfish, self-serving, venal characters. Since then, the list is numerous and continuing. These representations both play with and debunk the underlying stereotypes listed by Desser, as well as the poles of the East European/Zionist Jewish self-image.

III. SOLITARY, NASTY, BRUTISH AND SHORT

Since *Seinfeld* the number of mean, nasty and venal Jews has proliferated on screen. These Jewish bodies are often also represented as physically unattractive and un-erotic: short, ugly, fat, balding, frequently with brutish, self-serving and selfish characteristics to match. Such physical drawbacks are not ameliorated by wit, intelligence or sense of humour. Walter Sobchak (John Goodman) in *The Big Lebowski* (1998) is a complete reversal of the previous stereotypes, Sobchak is not only a slightly deranged Vietnam veteran (most likely suffering from undiagnosed post-traumatic stress disorder), he is – atypically – a convert to Judaism, having done so at the request of his wife; and even though he has since divorced from her he still maintains his religious identity and is very proud of it: he claims insistently, 'Three thousand years of beautiful tradition, from Moses to Sandy Koufax...[shouting] You're goddamn right I'm living in the fucking past!' and 'I'm as Jewish as fuckin' Tevya!' He quotes Theodore Herzl, the founder of Zionism. He even maintains a level of Jewish Orthodox practice. He explains that he can't bowl ('roll') or drive on Saturdays because he is '*shomer shabbos*' and absolutely refuses to do so unless it is an emergency. Walter is proud of his Jewishness and does not mind shouting about it. At the same time, however, he is an unattractive figure both physically and mentally. He is overweight, given to frequent profanity ('This is what happens when you fuck a stranger in the ass,' he frequently warns) and is close to unhinged – he waves his gun in the face of an opponent whom he believes is cheating at bowling. The irony here is that size and beard apart, he couldn't be farther from *Fiddler on the Roof*'s cute, cuddly, kitsch, aphorism-spouting Tevya, itself merely a fantasised, Americanised image of *shtetl*-dwelling Jewry.

Another figure who fits into this category is Ron Jeremy. Although Jeremy is known predominantly as a porn star, he has made a number of crossover appearances into mainstream cinema such as *52 Pick-Up* (1986), *Killing Zoe* (1994) and most significantly *Pornstar: The Legend of Ron Jeremy* (2001). If his viewers did not already know it, the latter film outted Ron as a proud Jew. His longevity in the adult industry aside (he began his porn career in the 1970s), Jeremy is a highly unusual porn star in that he is not conventionally attractive: described in *Pornstar* as 'small, fat and very hairy', his overweight and unkempt body has earned him the nickname 'the Hedgehog'. Although presented in erotic scenarios, his body is the obverse of the normative models of masculine sexual attractiveness. One scholar has gone as far as to describe him as 'repulsive' (Shelton 2002: 119). Nonetheless, this very repulsiveness has helped Jeremy's cinematic Jewish body to achieve iconic status. In part this is due to his positioning in erotic filmic texts, his longevity in the industry as well as his above-average penis (this will be discussed in more detail below), but no doubt it is mainly due to his collapsing of the boundaries between porn's hyper-masculine excess and the average, everyday male physique. As Gill's film states, he is 'a hero for the common man'.

IV. JEWS IN SPACE

At the end of his *History of the World, Part 1* (1983) Mel Brooks offers up a humorous sequence depicting an alleged sequel to his preview of 'Hitler on Ice' entitled 'Jews in Space', a sci-fi spectacular featuring Star-of-David-shaped spaceships, flown by obviously Orthodox Jews, singing of the glories of 'defending the Hebrew race' (Desser 2001: 267). But where Brooks offered up such a vision for parody, recent cinema has actually realised such visions seriously. In *Serenity* (2005), Mr Universe (David Krumholtz), is a reclusive techno-geek who lives alone on a moon with his love-bot 'wife', Lenore. He has a great affinity for data, and is capable of intercepting nearly any transmission or recording in the universe. He is also identified as Jewish when seen stepping on a cloth-wrapped glass while wearing a yarmulke in a video clip of his wedding and after his death, stones are placed on his grave in the Jewish tradition. Likewise *Independence Day* (1996) features what Rogin calls a 'neurasthenic hysteric' Jewish character (Rogin 1998: 48) in David Levinson (Jeff Goldblum). Stereotypically, like Mr Universe, and building upon his previous roles in *The Fly* (1986), *Jurassic Park* (1993) and *The Lost World* (1997) Goldblum is an intellectual, a scientist, a 'Jewish computer whizz' (Rogin 1998: 49). He is a talker or 'Jew is mouth as nervous brain' as Rogin has put it (Rogin 1998: 49) who marries his non-Jewish wife not once but twice (the Jew–Shiksa relationship is a key part of Desser's typology). Thus, *Serenity* and *Independence Day* feature smart nerdy, weak, Jewish bodies, defined only by their intellectual rather than physical capacities – both are scientists. Neither is shown nude which stands in clear contrast to *Independence Day*'s Captain Steven Hiller (Will Smith), the fast-talking, wise-cracking black fighter pilot, whom we first meet semi-naked in bed. It says much that Hollywood has not yet considered reversing the roles that Goldblum and Smith play so that we see the Jewish fighter pilot and the black scientist.

Goldblum and Krumholtz are both still 'queer Jews', whose bodies are reinforced by the presence of further 'queer' Jews. David's father, Julius (Judd Hirsch), is a Yiddish-speaking male hysteric Jewish mother stand-in and Harvey Fierstein is Levinson's panicked and somewhat effeminate sidekick, Marty Gilbert, who not only calls his mother from under his desk but also his psychoanalyst 'Dr Katz' from his car phone. Indeed, 'queer' Jewish male intellectual rather than bodily values are valorised by both films, as it is '*Yiddishe kopf*' or 'Jewish brains' that brings salvation (Gertel 2003: 132). This is most notable in *Independence Day* for it is Jewish hypochondria – a key device of Jewish cinematic queerness – that becomes a key plot device as when David's dad asks him if he's getting a cold, he gets the idea for using a computer virus as a weapon (Rogin 1998: 57). Yet, the sense of the 'tough Jew' also creeps in, for as David and Steven prepare to go into orbit together, a black lab assistant rushes up with a yarmulke and prayer book for the religious ceremony that will consecrate their journey into space, and some of the warplanes which help to destroy the alien invasion bear not only the American flag but also the Star of David, consequently invoking the State of Israel and its alliance with America. Incidentally, brief shots of Israeli fighter pilots standing in front of an Israeli flag and jets invoke the 'tough Jews' of the Zionist project. Furthermore, ultimately, a shift has taken place for while both Mr Universe and Levinson are contemporary incarnations of Dr Spock they, unlike him, have come out of the ethnic-religious closet to unashamedly assert their Jewish ('queer') values. Where William Shatner and Lenoard Nimoy could only refer to their Jewishness by submerging it into allegory (see Shandler (1999) for more on this), Goldblum and Krumholtz are open about theirs.

V. JEWS AS JAWS

In contrast to erstwhile depictions of the Jew as victim, recent cinema has represented the Jew as assassin. Although this is not a new development, in terms of Jewish manhood such films present contradictory sentiments. In *Munich* (2005), Spielberg's dramatised reconstruction of the Israeli government's response to the murder of eleven Israeli athletes at the 1972 Olympic Games, three of the five members of the assassination team sent to exact revenge – all but one of whom are played by non-Jews – are killed. On the other hand, the team reverses the traditional paradigm of the Jew-as-victim in having the Jews as killers driven by bloodlust (Jews as Jaws perhaps), as well as vengeance. Steve (Daniel Craig), the South African driver, articulates these sentiments unambiguously: 'Don't fuck with the Jews.' The team is seen killing in cold blood and sometimes taking intemperate and undisciplined revenge. Jewish violence is presented as brutal, heartless and methodical, not the expression of individuals willingly sacrificing themselves for a just cause but the coldly mechanical and calculated product of the intelligence apparatus of an aggressive state. While some of the individual agents on the team may have moral qualms about their task, their bosses are presented in no such way. Jewish officials are shown to be zealous, chilly and clearly using the team who are instructed 'You'll do what the terrorists do. Do you think they report back to home base?' At the same time, the film taps into enduring ethnic slurs concerning Jews and their relationship to money, for they are presented as nearly obsessive on the subject, suggesting a cavalier attitude towards human life. The team leader Avner (Eric Bana) needs to obtain receipts for every expenditure no matter how trivial and his fellow team members fret over such things as the price per kill; their first target, one of them notes ruefully, 'cost us, by my calculations, $352,000'. They are thus clearly the 'tough Jews' of the Zionist project.

Furthermore, the assassination team and the larger organisation of which it is a part are not simply represented by intellectual values as they are not as efficient as its global reputation suggests. Mistakes, blunders and errors recur throughout the movie. The bomb maker played by Mathieu Kassovitz is recruited without anyone realising that his actual skill was in *dismantling* such devices. One bomb he makes is so large that an Israeli honeymooning with her Lebanese husband in the next room to the target is blinded by the explosion. He later dies when a bomb he is creating (accidentally?) explodes (although, interestingly, we never see his dead body). Throughout the film, Avner and his team show an undue reliance on a shadowy French outfit for their logistics, weapons, intelligence and safe houses which leads to one mix-up when both Israelis and Palestinians share a room for the night. Undoubtedly, this sequence was deliberately engineered by Spielberg and the screenwriter Tony Kushner in order to produce an (artificial) meeting between the two sides in the Israeli–Palestinian conflict. But, it serves to undermine the competence of the Israelis. Finally, only two of the original five members survive and one of those is killed by a female mercenary. The death of a male at the hands of a female not only problematises his masculine identity but also in death his body is represented as passive and hence feminine, submissive and impotent.

In an echo of the 1950s the film resorts to using non-Jews in the lead roles. The team could be described as handsome, scrupulous, exceptionally well-mannered Jewish agents and, as played by Eric Bana, Avner is certainly a fine-looking and loving husband (even if he does abandon his family and home for the greater cause of his homeland). As the only member of the team depicted naked, he is the fulfilment of the Zionist project of a 'Jewry of muscles'. His body is toned, taut and fit. Yet, in general, *Munich* shied away from revealing the musculature of its protagonists, with the exception of Avner on rare occasions. He is virile and shown having lovingly flushed sex with his beautiful pregnant wife (Ayelet Zurer) and even endangering himself by flying home illicitly from his secret mission to see the birth of his child which, in itself, proves his potency as a father even while he is not so proficient as a killer. Ultimately, Avner is presented as a good father (he takes his family to the relative safety of pre-9/11 Brooklyn), but a bad killer (although one wonders if he was cast for his previous incarnations as psychos and killers from *Chopper* (2000) through to *Black Hawk Down* (2001), *The Hulk* (2003) and *Troy* (2004)) – in the end he and his team are ineffectual against the hydra-like rise of terror – and a bad Israeli as he abandons his homeland for the United States.

Another tough Jew is the antagonist in a completely different genre of film. Ian McKellen plays the mutant leader Erik Magnus Lehnsherr, aka Magneto, in the *X-Men* trilogy (2000, 2003, 2006) and is presented as both victim and victimiser. The opening scene of *X-Men* (2000) depicts him as a young boy being separated from his parents at a Nazi death camp in Poland during the Second World War. Via this sequence we are then led to believe that like many others his entire family was murdered. He is thus scarred and seemingly no different from the millions of other Holocaust victims. His status as victim/survivor is reinforced both in narrative terms ('I have heard these arguments before. It was a long time ago') and visually/physically by a glimpse of the tattooed number on his arm. At the same time, however, Lehnsherr/Magneto is a mutant who possesses special powers – in his case, as the name implies, a telepathic ability to generate a magnetic field which can bend or deflect metal objects such as guns and bullets. While the mutant powers is a new twist on the representation of the Jewish male body, particularly as the protagonist superhero is openly Jewish and not hyper-masculine (unlike say Superman or Spiderman), he confirms existing stereotypes by having his mutant power derive from his mind rather than his body which, in contrast is physically weak.

Furthermore, Magneto is superficially represented as an evil body (although by no means in a stereotypically anti-Semitic way). He grows up with an obsession to supplant humankind with a race of mutants like himself. In the trilogy's diegesis, as the leader of the Brotherhood of Evil Mutants whose aim it is to overthrow mankind, he is seemingly the villain, positioned against the hero, Dr Charles Xavier, who, in contrast, founded a school to teach mutant teenagers 'to learn to use our powers for the benefit of mankind'. As Lawrence Baron points out, in its representation of a man confined to a wheelchair whose special power is mind-reading, the film has created 'a Gentile hero who fit the traditional stereotype of Jewish males as intellectuals with weak bodies' (Baron 2003: 47). Furthermore, it is Xavier, and not Magneto, who is pursuing the traditional Jewish social justice agenda of *Tikkun Olam* (healing the world). However, a subtler reading of the film suggests that both are heroes who, like contemporary Jewish Democrats and Republicans in America, use Jewish tradition and religion to achieve their different political objectives. While Dr X is unequivocally 'good', using his powers for the benefit of mankind, Magneto is not his binary opposite nor represented as unequivocally 'evil'. Indeed, in its insistence on depicting events from his childhood in 1944 and constantly reminding us of the Holocaust through a series of visual and aural signifiers, the film gives Magneto genuinely understandable motives, summed up by the words 'Never Again'. Magneto wants to prevent another Holocaust, albeit this time against mutants. In this light, then, it is the non-mutants who are evil in their desire to locate, categorise and demonise others simply because they are different. Furthermore, perhaps it is Dr X and his optimistic Panglossian naiveté (for which he pays the ultimate price) that is the true albeit unwitting villain of the films, for he seeks to protect humanity. Overall, then, Magneto presents an interesting combination: the queer Jew with tough values.

VI. HARD JEWS

The modern (if retrogressive) religious epic *The Passion of the Christ* (2004) presents yet another version of the male Jewish body on screen. Replicating the Biblical films of the 1950s, Jesus is played by a non-Jew (Jim Caviezel) and within the terms of the film clearly does not derive from the same world as the first-century Palestinian Jews. In multiple sequences, he is visually contrasted with his co-religionists and even though he speaks the same language as them, he shares nothing in common physically. The gulf is further reinforced in that Mel Gibson's Jesus speaks Greek thus aligning him with the Greco-Roman world in comparison to the male Jews who speak Aramaic and are clearly depicted, in dress, speech and mannerism as proto-Muslims. Furthermore, as Scott Bartchy points out, Jesus is a 'hunk', with 'abs', and essentially an amalgam of the director Gibson's previous roles in *Braveheart* (1995) and the *Lethal Weapon* series (1987, 1989, 1992, 1998) and more: a man who can 'take beating, flogging, flaying, even filleting, and finally crucifying' (2006: 80, 85). The film's use of lingering slow motion to capture the beating, flagellating, raking, ripping, dislocating and piercing of Jesus' flesh fetishises the Jewish male body and its ability to withstand torture. It is an irony here that Gibson, whose views of Jews are dodgy at best, has unwittingly produced a cinematic Jewish male body which fulfils the Zionist vision of a muscled Jewry.

VII. GANGSTERS

From Jewish crime czar Hyman Roth (Lee Strasberg) in *The Godfather II* (1974) through to Abraham 'Cousin Avi' Denovitz (Dennis Farina) in *Snatch* (2000), there have been many extremely violent male Jewish gangsters, criminals, killers and corrupt bookmakers on screen such as those in *The Long Goodbye* (1973), *Lepke* (1975), *GoodFellas* (1990), *Bugsy* (1991), *Casino* (1995) and *Inside Man* (2006). But few present as interesting a take on the male Jewish body as *Lucky Number Slevin* (2006). The film presents much paradoxical juxtaposition which plays on the traditional cinematic representations of Jews. Shlomo 'the Rabbi' (Ben Kingsley), is the neurotic leader of a Hasidic criminal gang. He is a rabbi who would rather be a gangster and a gangster who would rather be a rabbi. Although he is a *soi-disant* 'bad man', like Walter he is also a practising Orthodox Jew who will not answer the telephone on Shabbat. Nor will he contemplate premeditated murder as it is proscribed by Jewish law, but he will act in self defence, as this is permitted, and as such is armed with a shotgun for his personal protection. The representation of the rabbi as Orthodox is not just signified in narrative terms but is reinforced by the film's use of mise-en-scene. Deploying the traditional symbols of Judaism, the rabbi is shown wearing a yarmulke and reading from the Torah. His office, which he never leaves, is adorned with the Star of David and its entrance gates are wrought from Hebrew lettering.

The rabbi's bodyguards are Hasidic Jews who wear the traditional garb of that sect: long black coats, hats, yarmulkes and side curls. Unlike traditional characterisations of that group, however, these Orthodox Jews are violent. Thus, the 'queer' Jewish scholar has paradoxically become hard and, within the film's narrative, brutal, too. Although the concept of the male Jew as gangster is neither new nor innovative in either reality or art, the representation of an evil and *Orthodox* Jewish gangster is and one would be hard pressed to discover any similar vision elsewhere. Indeed, cinema rarely treats the male Jewish body in a religious sense, preferring to code it ethnically. Thus, in this respect, the film's depiction of religiously Orthodox Jews as cruel, which in the film they undoubtedly are, is a breakthrough cinematically.

Two further characters play on the depiction of the cinematic male Jewish body and code the poles of Jewish masculine self-image. The Rabbi's son is gay (a fact of which the rabbi is, presumably and therefore blissfully, unaware): Yitzchok the fairy is the epitome of the weak, effeminate, homosexual Eastern European Jew. He is unable to protect himself, is constantly accompanied by two ex-Mossad bodyguards and in a unique use of a traditional Jewish sign even wears a panic button around his neck in the shape of a Star of David. In direct contrast stands the protagonist, the eponymous Slevin Kelevra (Josh Hartnett). He is a cold, calculating and ruthless Jewish killer who, unusually, spends a good proportion of his screen time wearing only a bath towel, revealing, like Avner, his toned and muscled upper torso. Although he is superficially similar to the Mossad assassination squad in *Munich* in his profession, unlike them, he has no moral qualms about his vengeful actions *and* is completely and lethally successful, suffering no reverses or humiliations that he does not himself intend. Indeed, he is presented as disciplined, controlled and ordered, fully in control of his destiny, as encapsulated in his very surname (*kelev ra*) which in Hebrew translates as 'bad dog'.

These images are tempered by more traditional ones, in particular, the Jew as victim. There is a body count of at least eleven Jews during the course of the movie and many shots depict these Jews either dead or dying. Yet, many of these Jews have been killed by one of their co-religionists and this proves to be a highly unusual development in the recent depictions of the Jewish male body on screen. Typically, Jews are shown as victims of non-Jews in cinema and rarely, if ever, are they victims of each other. Again, unlike much traditional and even recent cinema such as *Munich*, this Jewish killer is shown as coming out on top as he successfully avenges the murder of his parents, and not only has no regrets but gets the girl at the end, too. Thus, the film clearly takes sides in which representation it prefers as the secular tough Jew kills the transgressive, tough and queer 'Eastern European' Jews. It must be said, though, that the film cannot escape cinematic stereotyping in that not only is Kelevra played by a non-Jew and hence harking back to the era when gentiles played Jews, but also the paradigm of the Jew–Shiksa relationship is maintained as it is highly implausible that his girlfriend (Lindsey) played by Lucy Liu is in any way Jewish.

VIII. THE SCHMOK[1]

Ever since Abraham and Isaac, a key signifier of Jewish masculinity has long been the circumcised penis. It sets the male Jew apart as Jewishness is literally inscribed on his body (Gilman 1991: 91). And this is also true on screen. To take but two recent examples: in *Hostel* (2005) and *The History Boys* (2006), the Jewish characters in the films are identified by references to their circumcisions. In his extensive (albeit Holocaust-focused) survey of the Jew in film, Omer Bartov concludes that the circumcised penis is 'a focus of identity, danger, and fascination' (2005: 341, n. 33). Typically, as Peter Lehman and Susan Hunt (2007) have pointed out, the Jewish penis is the nub of suffering, and representations of male Jewish nudity, with particular reference to the Holocaust, have 'exposed' the

Jewish penis in all its 'passivity', namely, 'femininity'. Often, the Jewish penis is the focus of this representation, as the site of suffering. Recent mainstream cinema, in constructing Jewish masculinity, can not help but allude to the Jew's genital organ; however, it has been played with (both literally and figuratively) in a number of contradictory ways. While films such as *Schindler's List* (1993) and *Sunshine* (1999) clearly maintain the equation of the Jewish penis as locus-of-suffering paradigm, these and other films seek to turn that notion on its head. Even as it depicts the Jewish male in death, *Munich* also symbolises almost the exact opposite: the reversal of the Holocaust paradigm from Jews who are killed to Jews who kill. Although the Mossad agent's death is depicted as humiliating, particularly given that he is seduced and killed by a female agent, the image stands against the narrative trajectory of the film which is a projection of Jewish potency. Indeed, the love-making sequences are clearly a vindication of Avner's sexual prowess which, unusually for film, is endogamous.

What is more, Ron Jeremy's naked, sweaty, sexual body, in particular his penis which itself is renowned for its size, is displayed and celebrated in explicit, perpetually hard close-up on film. The Jewish penis is no different here either and hence it provides a contrast to those images *of the penis* which project male Jewish humiliation, vulnerability, suffering, victim-hood and death. And they clearly explode Hunt and Lehman's assertion that 'The Jewish penis is always shown in situations of humiliation, vulnerability, and death – never sexuality – never as potent; always as impotent' (2007: 160). Indeed, Jeremy in particular is celebrated across America by Jews and non-Jews alike for the use of his penis. Although the prevalence of circumcision in the genre of pornography confuses the Jewish/non-Jewish penis distinction given its prevalence among gentiles there, such representations present a counterpoint to Lehman and Hunt's focus on the humiliation of the Jewish male.

The nebbish (an unfortunate simpleton; an insignificant or ineffectual person; a nobody; a nonentity) in which the Jewish male body is represented as a site of fun, laughter and most usually ridicule is also nothing new on screen but it is the use of sexual prowess and the penis as the locus of this laughter which is. Interestingly, cinematic depictions of circumcision as a source of laughter have been few and far between when compared to television. The distinctively Jewish protagonist of the *American Pie* trilogy (1999, 2001, 2003), James Emmanuel Levenstein aka Jim (Jason Biggs), is also the only character to feature in several sequences that focus (literally) on his (unseen) penis as the source of ridicule. In the first film, he fails (twice) in his public (they are depicted over a webcam) attempts to seduce the visiting student Nadia and he is caught red-handed by his father (Eugene Levy) while making love to the eponymous American pie. By the second instalment, Jim has graduated from tarts to women and is caught mid-coitus by his father again. In yet another sequence he manages to glue his hand to his member when he mistakes a tube of superglue for lubricant. Although these scenes superficially resemble those of suffering and Jim is indeed humiliated by his efforts, unlike the films identified by Bartov, Hunt and Lehman, we see no close-ups of Jim's penis; the genre is clearly comedic rather than serious and, in the final analysis, Jim always comes out on top and is clearly represented as the filmic hero. One only need to compare him to the quite obviously gentile Stifler to demonstrate this point: despite the suggestion implicit in his name that he is a symbol of hyper-masculine potency, Stifler suffers a series of humiliating reverses when he unwittingly drinks semen, eats dog shit and has to live with the fact that his mother was willingly seduced by his archenemy.

Likewise, Ben Stiller's various Jewish characters suffer in ways similar to Jim. In *There's Something About Mary* (1998), which replicates the older Jew-chasing-the-blonde Shiksa pattern, he is so nervous that he catches his genitals in a zipper, and, later in the film, a dog, and a little one at that, attacks his crotch. In *Meet the Parents* (2000), his father-in-law (Robert De Niro) keeps bursting in on him and his girlfriend as they are about to make love, and, in the sequel (*Meet the Fockers* (2004)), it is still only his parents who get to make love and live up to the promise of their surname. In doing so, we see a rare cinematic depiction of endogamous coupling as compared to both Stiller and Biggs, who maintain the filmic tradition of either sleeping with or marrying non-Jewish women. Nonetheless, the cinematic depiction of their bodies occupies the interstice between the hyper-masculine Zionist Jew and the callow Talmudic scholar, being neither one nor the other.

IX. CONCLUSION

'There is more than one way to be Jewish,' said Israeli novelist Sami Michael, opening a gay pride rally in Jerusalem in 2006. Nowhere has this been more convincingly demonstrated than in mainstream cinema's depiction of the Jewish male body since 1989 where we have seen nasty and brutish Jews, tough Jews, gay Jews, Jewish criminals, Jewish porn stars, Jewish assassins, rebellious Jews and Jews in space. Restrictions have not permitted me to mention every film or even every category. To the above can be added: Jewish cowboys, Jewish skinheads, Jewish transsexuals, Jewish superheroes and deviant and dysfunctional Jews. This shift towards more subtle, nuanced, playful and even outrageous representations signals that Jews feel more comfortable, particularly in America, that they have arrived. It says much that there are so many examples of this trend in recent film that not all of them could be listed or treated here. It is also in part a cinematic fulfilment of the dream of the first prime minister of Israel, David Ben Gurion, who said 'We will know we have become a normal country when Jewish thieves and Jewish prostitutes conduct their business in Hebrew'.

Furthermore, many of these cinematic narratives are not marked by invisibility or the desire to become 'white', but rather celebrate the Jewish (albeit Ashkenazi) male body in all its guises. And in that many of these films include religious factors, namely Judaism, in their representation of the Jewish male body on screen, they break the predominant paradigm in the field of film studies, which has largely tended to focus on Jewish identity as an ethnic rather than a religious category. Yet, this essay must end by saying that although the use of non-Jewish actors or what is known in Jewish culture as 'the goy' – 'the hypermale gentile' (Yosef 2004:18) – only serves to reinforce the musculature of filmic Jewry by collapsing the real non-Jewish body with the imaginary Jewish one, Anglo-American Jewish cinema can only really perhaps be said to have succeeded when it can film Jews as Jews on screen. In this last respect, in its creation of a new paradigm, the Jew playing the Jewish character that falls into neither category of the tough nor queer Jew, this has been achieved.

NOTE

1 The *Yiddish Dictionary Online* defines schmok as 'jerk, fool, idiot, contemptible person; naive person, person easy to deceive; (vulg. penis, dick, asshole) (American Jewish)', <http://www.yiddishdictionaryonline.com> Last consulted in April 2007.

2

Fragmented Bodies: Masculinity and Nation in Contemporary German Cinema

Heidi Schlipphacke

In recent years, a discourse of 'normalisation' has entered mainstream discussions about national identity, history and art in Germany. The notion of a 'normal' Germany, one no longer defined by its abnormal past, is simultaneously desirable and unnerving to Germans. The histories of Nazism, the Holocaust and the division of Germany have fundamentally defined German national identity since 1945, placing it always in an anomalous position vis-à-vis its Western peer nations. The left/right divide that had distinguished discussions of German normalisation among historians and literary scholars in the 1980s and 1990s seems to have all but vanished in the twenty-first century. The goal of being normal, just like the others, cuts largely across the contemporary German political spectrum so that both Gerhard Schröder, the Social Democrat, and the Christian Democrat Helmut Kohl have expressed their commitment to the national goal of normalcy. Schröder's embrace of the new German *Unbefangenheit* (unselfconsciousness) (Taberner and Cooke 2006: 10) mirrors a national fantasy of being blissfully average as articulated by Helmut Kohl. Asked by Serge Schmemann of *The New York Times* at the transformative moment following the fall of the Berlin Wall about his goals for Germany, Chancellor Helmut Kohl expressed the desire that 'things will normalize. That's the most important thing for us, that we become a wholly normal country, not "singularized" in any question [...] that we simply don't stick out. That's the important thing' (Brockmann 2006: 17). Germany's path to prosperity and global acceptance is imagined as the path of the Average Joe, a national identity that would appal patriotic Americans, French or British citizens. And this intensely modest German patriotism has, to my mind, profound repercussions for conceptions of gender and, in particular, models for masculinity.

In this chapter, I will explore the link between the national desire for normalcy and contemporary German masculinity. As George Mosse shows, the masculine body has stood in for Western and, specifically, German conceptions of nation since the eighteenth century (see Mosse 1996: 3–16). Visual representations of masculine beauty have symbolised national ideals as manifested in the neoclassical revival of the German Enlightenment and its perverse re-appropriation by the Nazis in the twentieth century. I will focus on contemporary filmic representations of masculinity because the medium of film, I suggest, contains both the weight of Germany's tortured history as well as the dream of a global future. I will argue that many contemporary German films reflect the desire for normalcy via a proliferation of 'average' male types. Indeed, three of the most popular and critically acclaimed German male film stars – Moritz Bleibtreu, Daniel Brühl and Jürgen Vogel – embody the ideal of 'averageness'. They are neither truly beautiful nor unattractive; they are often weak, but never entirely bad. And they are often insecure, lost and alienated. Indeed, their lack of orientation – what is sometimes depicted as psychic and physical fragmentation – is a product both of the type of stars currently *en vogue* in Germany as well as the narrative and stylistic techniques that frame their characters. What is imagined by Helmut Kohl as an ideal – the dream of being normal, of not standing out – is then dramatised in a number of films as a new crisis of masculinity and nation.[1]

During the summer of 2006, when Germany hosted the FIFA World Cup, Germans seemed to be obsessed with proving to the world that they could be 'normal', a gracious, relaxed host to the world, a host who could simultaneously cheer on the home team and party with the fans from other nations in the streets of Berlin. Indeed, one could say that the dream was almost realised; within Germany, one had the sense that the visitors were enjoying themselves. German flags were more prominent than ever before since the end of Nazism, yet these flags were generally not perceived as symbols of a Nazi threat. Here, many claimed, was the arrival of German normalcy, of the new unselfconsciousness ('*Neue Unbefangenheit*'). Yet how would this normalcy be defined? So many articles were written at the time about the new, relaxed Germany by the Germans that it would be difficult to support the claims of unselfconsciousness. To be 'normal', it seems, is to be unselfconsciously average – to accept one's past with a shrug, with some level of pride and to enjoy the present. The fantasy of normalcy was quickly shattered in the autumn of 2006, when the moral compass of the nation, Günter Grass, admitted to having served in the *Waffen SS*, an especially brutal arm of the Nazi military machine, unleashing a nation-wide debate about the relevance of the Nazi past for present-day Germany. Lightness and normalcy do not come easily to Germans, and perhaps this is how it should still be. Yet the desire to be average, not to stand out, remains reflected in contemporary film heroes who are alienated and 'clueless', to use Horst-Eberhard Richter's (2006) term to describe German masculinity in the twentieth century. And the lack of orientation on the part of these figures is not surprising, for the goal of 'averageness' is ultimately anathema to notions of national and, indeed, of masculine identity.

The cultural embrace of the ideal of normalcy has unleashed a new kind of national identity crisis. If Germany were no longer to stand out by virtue of the horrors of its past, then who would it be? Worldwide repulsion and attraction to Germany has long been predicated upon its indelible link to its abnormally atrocious recent history. If the nation were able to achieve its dream, to shed its villain's mantel for the slicker of an average guy, would the world still be interested? And how would one slip into the new identity without repressing the past, a gesture generally scorned in German culture today? I believe that these contradictory desires are reflected in contemporary German films which present alienated and lost male protagonists. In particular, I will focus here on films that have been well received in Germany but which have not had great distribution outside of the domestic market. In general, heritage films like *Der Untergang/Downfall* (dir. Oliver Hirschbiegel, 2004) and *Das Leben der Anderen/The Lives of Others* (dir. Henckel von Donnersmarck, 2006) have grabbed all the attention outside Germany. The former, nominated for the Best Foreign Film Oscar, is a costume piece dramatising the last days of Hitler, and the latter, the winner of the 2007 Oscar for Best Foreign Film, depicts the lives of an East German Stasi officer and the GDR citizens he observes. Hence, as Paul Cooke, has pointed out, in using 'the difficult topics as a "selling point"' the success of German films abroad 'paradoxically, resides in their ability to reaffirm, through their choice of theme, the *ab*normality of the nation and its continuing need to address aspects of its past' (Cooke 2006: 225). The drama of the average post-wall boy, it seems, is of interest to no one but the Germans themselves.

The elusive desire for a 'normal' national identity ironically cements Germany's particularity within Europe and the West. What other Western nation shares this fantasy? Indeed, Germany's desire for unselfconsciousness is a product of years of unresolved confrontations with the nation's history. The utopian view on Germany's anomalous historical position is that nationalism might be re-imagined within this nation, that nation might be conceived as always already split, fragmented and aware of its own split. Stephen Brockmann articulates the unique potential within contemporary Germany along these lines: 'In this sense Germany, precisely because of the singular horror of the Nazi dictatorship, is well positioned to attempt the creation of a non-conventional national identity, an identity based as much on self-questioning as on self-affirmation' (Brockmann 2006: 28). Yet while Germany exhibits symptoms of fragmentation, the cultural splitting reflected in contemporary German cinema is, to my mind, rarely articulated as utopic freedom.

I. THE SCHIZOPHRENIC BODY

The impasse reached at the juncture of 'normality' and national identity may be described as particularly German. This fractured state resembles the fragmentation characteristic of the schizophrenic body. The desire to be 'normal' and 'average' is ultimately akin to a negation of the self. The desired and the 'real' self do not match, and an irreparable rupture follows. Hence, the post-rational mode of schizophrenia could be said loosely to define the current state of German national identity and, in consequence, German masculinity. Representations of masculinity in films such as *Das weiße Rauschen/The White Sound* (dir. Hans Weingartner, 2001), *Lola rennt/Run Lola Run* (dir. Tom Tykwer, 1998), *Agnes und seine Brüder/Agnes and His Brothers* (dir. Oskar Roehler, 2004), *Goodbye Lenin!* (dir. Wolfgang Becker, 2003) and *Ein Freund von mir/A Friend of Mine* (dir. Sebastian Schipper, 2006), among others, are either literally or figuratively schizophrenic. These films dramatise the schizophrenic split that follows from the attempt to achieve identity without wholeness, without the past or usable models for masculinity. In *Anti-Oedipus: Capitalism and Schizophrenia*, Gilles Deleuze and Félix Guattari (2000) lauded schizophrenia as the antidote to fascism, as an escape route via 'schizoanalysis'. Schizophrenia is 'anti-ego as well as anti-homo' (Seem 1983: xx) and, hence, liberatory, beyond the rigid thought structures of the Cartesian ego. In the films discussed here, German male figures seem indeed to have a tenuous grasp on the ego as they unconsciously reject the fascist past through their utter lack of sovereignty.

All of the films discussed in this chapter represent contemporary German masculinity as schizophrenic, whether in the form of frustrated fragmentation and disorientation or elated escape from the self. Yet the film that most explicitly pictures masculine schizophrenia is Hans Weingartner's *Das weiße Rauschen*, starring the boy next door, Daniel Brühl. In appearance, Brühl has achieved the look of 'normalcy'. He has a sweet if not beautiful face, medium brown hair, and an average body that is not too buff and not too weak. Even in his most unsympathetic roles, he never seems truly dangerous. In *Das weiße Rauschen*, Brühl plays Lukas, a young man about to begin his studies at the University of

Köln but whose university career is interrupted by the onset of schizophrenia. Lukas leaves his grandparents in the country to live with his sister, Kati (Anabelle Lachatte), and her drug-obsessed hippie boyfriend, Jochen (Patrick Joswig), in their chaotic playground of an apartment. The film begins with Lukas arriving at the train station in Köln, and already here his exaggerated disorientation is apparent. The abruptly moving hand-held shots render enough of Lukas's state of loss and heightened anxiety to hint that something is wrong. Kati is late, and Lukas almost loses his sense of reality while waiting for her. However, all is seemingly well after she arrives and takes him to the communal apartment he will now share with her and Jochen. Lukas is initially elated by the freedom this space offers, the ready drugs and possibilities, but he is soon overwhelmed by the lack of structure.

Although Lukas's schizophrenia is not caused by the lack of structure in his new home, the paucity of any positive authority figure in Lukas's life contributes to his feelings of disorientation. Kati is quite loving, but childish, interested in taking drugs with her boyfriend. And Jochen is anything but an authority figure for Lukas. When Lukas is overwhelmed by the labyrinthian nature of the administrative buildings and neglects to sign up for university courses, Jochen shrugs off the importance of the university and invites Lukas to take drugs with him. Throughout the film, Jochen never seems to hold any kind of job; Kati occasionally goes to work, and when she returns, they party together. A drug-inspired trip to the country during which the three take hallucinogenic mushrooms together may serve as the catalyst for Lukas's psychotic break, but his inability to navigate the spaces around him is apparent from the beginning of the film. He is likewise unable to interpret meanings in basic conversations, and his date with a woman he meets at a party is abruptly aborted when the women selling tickets at the theatre informs him that *Taxi Driver* (dir. Martin Scorsese, 1976), the film they planned to see, will not be screened until the following week. In response, Lukas is unable to accept the schism between his own understanding of the world and the one offered by the ticket seller, and he flips out, repeatedly insisting that he wants two tickets for *Taxi Driver*, finally resorting to paranoid accusations that the woman doesn't want him to see the film. Lukas's interest in *Taxi Driver* is a sly reminder on the part of the director of the ways in which films can represent shifts of perspective and paranoid schizophrenia. However, Lukas's interest in *Taxi Driver* is rather derivative; he chose it, he tells his date, because his sister said it was good. Lukas's identity seems, even when lucid, to be strangely unformed and indistinct. He is simultaneously 'average' and without character.

Das weiße Rauschen is, in my view, both a sensitive depiction of a young man's fall into the nightmare of schizophrenia and an allegory of contemporary German national identity and masculinity. Lukas's radical lack of orientation, his indistinct identity and the lack of male authority figures who might offer a usable model for 'normal' masculinity parallel the schism I have described in the German desire for normalcy. Lukas's state of fragmentation is beautifully portrayed in scenes in which Lukas alternately resists and embraces 'the white noise' of schizophrenia. In German 'Rausch' means 'noise' but also intoxication and ecstasy. Hence, 'Das weiße Rauschen' is conceived by Lukas as both the nightmare of insanity and the ecstatic release from reason. Along the lines articulated by Deleuze and Guattari, schizophrenia contains here also the potential for release from the ego and the tyranny of Enlightenment reason (which Deleuze and Guattari link to fascism). Hence, while the film depicts Lukas's intense suffering as he hears voices and experiences a radical split between possible realities, the film nevertheless always maintains the tension between the goal of normalcy and the dual potential beyond reason: the potential for a post-fascist utopia beyond subjects and, alternatively, the regression manifested in the anti-rational mania of German fascism. Brühl's Lukas and Weingartner's film embody all possibilities in one body, providing a hyperbolic picture of a new crisis of German masculinity, a masculinity that attempts to achieve identity while preserving fragmentation and eschewing history.

Das weiße Rauschen places the spectator in uncomfortable proximity to the fragmented psychic state of its protagonist. Liberal use of hand-held shots creates an atmosphere of confusion so that the spectator, like Lukas, is often unsure of the location of the shot without the larger space depicted in the film. Likewise, the camera frequently alternates between a perspective closely allied to that of Lukas's to one slightly distanced from him. At other times, long shots are used that depict Lukas's body out of sync with his environment; he rarely inhabits the screen in a sovereign manner but rather often occupies the periphery of the frame, his bodily stance denoting insecurity and anxiety. Here, the spectator experiences Lukas's body as fragmented and small. One of the most memorable shots of the film is a high-angle one that shows Lukas lying naked in the shower in a semi-foetal position, flooded in a golden light, a variety of shampoo and soap bottles near his feet (Figure 2). The 'white noise' of the shower provides an escape for Lukas from the voices that hound him, and he remains for hours in this fragile position. The image cements Lukas's vulnerability and utter helplessness; indeed, his body is highly androgynous here and in stark contrast to idealised images of masculine strength and beauty. The position of the camera nears that of a bird's eye, so that the spectator is forced to view Lukas's body coldly, almost clinically. The golden light simultaneously envelops and entraps Lukas and provides a bright light for the clinical eye of the observer.

Yet this sovereign perspective is juxtaposed with shots that provide little distance from Lukas's perspective. The spectator is privy not only to Lukas's mad paranoia, but also to the voices he hears, voices inaudible to the other figures in the film. In this sense, the film never offers a viable space for reflection outside of Lukas's world. Beginning and ending with a voice-over of Lukas's thoughts about 'the white noise', thoughts themselves highly ambivalent, the film circumscribes the experience of the spectator within this logic and hence avoids taking a stance on which form of masculine identity would be desirable: some semblance of medicated 'normalcy' or a form that embraces the white noise beyond reason. In the end of the film, having left the more restricted cultural space of Germany, Lukas sits alone at the sea in Spain and reflects on the trappings and potential of the 'white noise'. In this way, the film never entirely alienates the spectator from Lukas and refuses to take a position on a desirable mode of masculinity for the new Germany. The shifting perspectives of *Das weiße Rauschen* dramatise both Lukas's schizophrenia and the schizophrenic nature of contemporary German masculinity.

Another recent German film that represents German masculinity as symbolically schizophrenic while refusing to prognosticate or moralise is *Der freie Wille/The Free Will* (dir. Matthias Glasner, 2006). The film stars Jürgen Vogel (who also co-wrote the script), another 'average' male type with a somewhat goofy, but generally attractive appearance. Like *Das weiße Rauschen* the film has received a great deal of critical acclaim in Germany (Jürgen Vogel won the Silver Bear at the Berlin International Film Festival). This relentlessly intense film focuses on the damaged lives of Theo (Jürgen Vogel), a rapist, and Nettie (Sabine Timoteo), a multiply abused woman who falls in love with him. Theo emerges from years of treatment desiring only one thing: to be 'normal'. Although the film depicts Theo ruthlessly

Figure 2: Daniel Brühl in *Das Weiße Rauschen*. X Verleih AG. Germany.

raping two women, it nevertheless refuses to demonise the character entirely. The spectator is radically alienated from this figure, but the film consistently presents moments in which we see the world from Theo's perspective or from that of the woman who loves him, and it is especially this latter perspective – a brilliant device on the part of the filmmakers – that rescues Theo, despite his despicable behaviour, from pure villainy. In the first scene of the film, he pursues a victim and then consistently resists his urges, finally giving in to them in a brutal rape. Following the rape, the woman runs away and injures herself, and Theo then follows her with a first aid kit. This first vignette depicts a masculine subject who has given in to the most brutal of urges and who, nevertheless, has simultaneously retained a shred of humanity and pity. These qualities render Theo from the outset, like Lukas, a split subject – split between the crimes of the past and the desire to be 'normal'. Here again, the split male body mirrors the national German body. And when Theo cries, his worked-out body seems to be literally fragmented. In the final scene of the film, Theo has escaped to the sea, and Nettie, the masochistic woman who loves him, watches as he literally cuts into his body, slitting his wrists with a razor blade. Here, escape and entrapment seem to meet while no clear 'line of escape' (Seem 1983: xvii) is posited.

II. AFTER FASCISM: POST-CLASSICAL MALE BODIES

The disarming image of the brutal man in tears is repeated numerous times throughout *Der freie Wille*. Here we have what might be called the post-classical body – a masculinity which is not whole. In the desire to be 'normal', figures such as Theo and Lukas have no male role models at their disposal. In this and other recent German films, there is a paucity of father figures, and those few figures who might temporarily stand in for a father are usually damaged '1968'er' types (the sons of Nazis who grew up rebelling against their fathers and the repression of history) who have become disillusioned with rebellion or are simply disengaged from any political or cultural mission. In *Die fetten Jahre sind vorbei/The Edukators* (dir. Hans Weingartner, 2004), Daniel Brühl plays Jan, an anarchist who demonises the rich capitalists in Berlin, until he and his friends kidnap one, learning that this father figure of sorts was a rebellious 1968'er in his own time. More often than not, though, father figures are absent. In *Das weiße Rauschen* the actual father is never mentioned. Lukas has been living with his grandparents, and the grandfather speaks of the mother's suicide, but no one mentions the father; it is as if he never existed. This gap is significant, I believe, for there are no figures in the film who come close to taking the place of a paternal signifier – not the child-man

Jochen, nor the hippies with whom Lukas travels to Spain, nor the psychiatrist who discusses Lukas's illness in a cool and detached manner and prescribes him medication. In this sense, the entire structure of the film is post-oedipal, a stage ripe for schizophrenia. Likewise, the only father in *Der freie Wille* is Nettie's father who has presumably sexually abused her for years, but this figure is strangely detached and lacks power. He represents the sick remains of fascist masculinity.

Thomas Elsaesser has argued that the films created by the directors of the New German Cinema (Fassbinder, Herzog, Wenders, et al.) can be interpreted as products of an oedipal crisis, as these filmmakers struggled to distance themselves from the filmmakers and fathers who preceded them (Elsaesser 1992: 289). In the case of contemporary German cinema, however, one does not have the sense that these films stage an oedipal revolt. Rather, with the absence of authoritative father figures, the new German men are one more step removed from the oedipal conflict. In 1967, Alexander and Margarete Mitscherlich published their psychoanalytic study of post-war Germans (translated as *The Inability to Mourn* in 1975), and psychoanalytic readings of German *Vergangenheitsbewältigung* (coming to terms with the past) have been ubiquitous in German studies ever since. The work of coming to terms with the past was conducted, many argued, via this oedipal revolt. As Eric Santner has noted, it is through the father, Lacan's paternal signifier, that 'all mourning must pass' (Santner 1990: 101).[2] Yet what happens when the father is absent, either literally or as a figure who embodies paternal qualities? This seems to be the place where male figures find themselves in contemporary German cinema: desirous of a normalcy that would give them a new identity, but unable to imagine this alternative identity without the presence of history.

In this sense, the problem that confronted German filmmakers after 1945 – how to represent history without wholeness – has reached a new level of crisis in contemporary German cinema. Films by New German Cinema directors such as Fassbinder observed an unspoken taboo on the representation of an unfragmented masculinity, for these films were explicitly concerned with rejecting concrete models for masculinity that they deemed abhorrent. In the case of contemporary German cinema, the representation of fragmented male bodies stems less from a taboo on wholeness than from the absence of intact masculine models.[3] The break with the naïve representation of masculine wholeness in German cinema, however, began with the fall of Nazism. The Allies declared a moratorium on filmmaking in Germany for one year following the end of the war, for German cinema had been the ultimate propaganda tool used by the Nazis. As Linda Schulte-Sasse has argued, Nazi films provided illusion and spectacle that gave the impression of 'imaginary wholeness' (1996: 33 – see also Rentschler (1996) and Hake (2001) on

Nazi cinema). In her reading of Veit Harlan's infamous anti-Semitic propaganda film, *Jud Süß/Jew Suss* (1940), Schulte-Sasse shows how the Jew Süß's body is feminised, punished and fragmented (in the end the camera focuses only on his hanging feet) while the film reconstitutes an identity of wholeness in the figure of the Aryan hero Faber and the German nation itself.

The Nazis embraced an 'adopted' neoclassical aesthetic (Fotis 2007: 16) in architecture, art and in their worship of the beautiful 'Aryan' body. Leni Riefenstahl's film *Olympia* (1938), the infamous documentary of the 1936 Olympic Games in Berlin, famously links the neoclassical art and ideals of Ancient Greece to the model of masculine beauty prevalent in Nazi Germany. The original rebirth of classical aesthetics in Germany is generally linked to the Enlightenment figure of J.J. Winckelmann, whose worship of Greek statues culminated in the phrase 'noble simplicity and quiet grandeur' ('*edle Einfalt und stille Größe*'), a phrase that captures the dialectic of power and restraint Winckelmann associated with ideal masculinity. According to Anthea Collen, the Apollo of Belvedere embodied 'competing fantasies of unyielding domination and exquisite desirability' that characterised the masculine ideal (Collen 1998: 612). As George Mosse (1996) argues, manliness and nationhood become inextricably linked in eighteenth-century Germany – a time when theories of physiognomy were becoming popular and when Winckelmann's writings on neoclassicism provided an aesthetic and masculine model for a national ideal. It is also in the eighteenth century, Mosse points out, that European culture becomes visually oriented. Hence, it is at this time that what he calls 'the masculine stereotype', an ideal encompassing the dialectic of power and self-restraint, is born (see Mosse 1996: 3–16). What is more, the national ideal, as embodied in figures such as the Apollo of Belvedere, is a homoerotic and homosocial one. Women do not play a significant role in Winckelmann's ideal neoclassical society.

By adopting a perverted model of neoclassical masculinity as their aesthetic and national ideal, the Nazis effectively tainted the Western masculine stereotype of strength and beauty. In 1998 the historians Heide Fehrenbach and Uta Poiger wrote about the difficulty of forging a masculinity in post-war Germany that counters the stereotype of the aggressive Nazi male. Fehrenbach has described the 'demasculinisation' (Fehrenbach 1998: 109) that characterised the German defeat after World War II. Men were scarce in any case, and those who were around were humiliated by their inability to find work. What is more, the fact that many Allied soldiers fathered the children of German women was seen as a double victimisation: of German woman and of German men. The period following the war engendered, according to Fehrenbach, 'the death of native masculinity' (Fehrenbach 1998: 111). She then suggests that 'remasculinisation', a term she borrows from Susan Jeffords (1994), coincided in Germany with rearmament in the 1950s. Fehrenbach argues that films from the period such as *Das doppelte Lottchen/Two Times Lotte* (dir. Josef von Báky, 1950) (which received the first Federal Film prize awarded by the West German Ministry of the Interior) reflect a new model for German patriarchy – one that rejects fascism and American materialism but which attempts to forge a 'new style' of *Vaterland* in West Germany 'where "might" is tempered by "moral accountability"' (Fehrenbach 1998: 126). The rejection of models of masculinity represented by the American occupiers dovetailed with the fear of duplicating a fascist model of an overly aggressive man (Poiger 1998: 148).

III. GLOBALISATION AND GERMAN MASCULINITY: 'THE HEROES ARE CLUELESS'

A post-9/11, post-Wall, and globalising Germany has not provided a path out of the aporia of masculine subjectivity. In a recent interview with the magazine *Spiegel* psychoanalyst Horst-Eberhard Richter posits that German women have developed in the past decades, becoming more and more hermaphroditic in their abilities to adapt to various cultural changes. Men, on the other hand, have remained the same. They continue to be victimised by an 'inability to suffer' – 'die Unfähigkeit zu leiden' – a nod to the Mitscherlichs – (Richter 2006: 150) that afflicted German men after World War II. Suffering the guilt of their parents, those sons born after the war 'were forced to serve as replacements for their fallen fathers' (Richter 2006: 154, my translation). Yet this task is also ultimately an impossible one, one at which the sons can only fail. Hence, for Richter, 'the heroes are clueless' (Richter 2006: 150, my translation):

> Men have become superfluous in the role of head of the family, and they are still searching for their role as modern partners and fathers. They are no longer needed in order to support the family nor, in the age of sperm banks, as he who provides the sperm. What now? (Richter 2006: 150, my translation)

Despite dramatic cultural changes in Europe and Germany due to the formation of the EU, the fall of the Berlin Wall, and the forces of globalisation, a certain placelessness and stagnancy continues to characterise German masculinity.

One of the most striking images of alienation and vulnerability, depicting both entrapment and lack of orientation, is the shot of Daniel Brühl lying in the shower in *Das weiße Rauschen*. Another powerful image depicts Moritz Bleibtreu as Manni in the phone booth in Tom Tykwer's explosively popular *Lola rennt*.

Figure 3: Moritz Bleibtreu in *Lola rennt.* X Filme. Germany.

Manni is a small-time crook who is in dire need of 100,000 Deutschmarks within 20 minutes. For much of the film, Manni waits in a phone booth, calling Lola and everyone else he knows, begging for money (Figure 3). While Manni waits, Lola famously runs. Manni's body is trapped within the small phone booth, and he is 'clueless', unsure what to do as he waits for help from others. In fact, the phone card he is using is borrowed from a blind woman played by Monica Bleibtreu, Bleibtreu's mother in real life. In this sense, he is doubly infantilised here, trapped and dependent upon the blind and the maternal. Although he carries a gun and wears leather and tattoos, he chews on his thumb in a manner that emphasises his boyishness and lack of maturity. Here is another example of the split male subject – simultaneously potentially violent and weak, inconsistent in character and lost.

Moritz Bleibtreu is another German star whose 'average' good looks and general likeability make him a perfect vehicle for the particular constellation of 'normalcy' and fragmentation that tend to characterise contemporary representations of German masculinity. In *Im Juli/In July* (dir. Fatih Akin, 2000) he plays an 'average,' clueless German schoolteacher, Daniel, who is 'lost' in contemporary Germany. His disorientation is beautifully rendered via numerous high-angle and long shots in which Daniel is unable to negotiate his environment – trapped in a field in Romania or entering a multi-cultural party in Hamburg. His fascination with Istanbul is sparked by his infatuation with a beautiful Turkish woman, Melek (Idil Üner) and by the impetus of 'Juli' (Christiane

Paul), the globally savvy German woman who leads him to the border of the Orient. On the way, there are two scenes in which Daniel is given drugs by women, scenes shot and edited in a manner to emphasise the distortions of perspective. Drugs play a prominent role in contemporary German films (the earlier mentioned *In Juli, Das weiße Rauschen, Die fetten Jahre sind vorbei* and also *Solino/Solino* (dir. Akin, 2002)), and these scenes offer another window into the placelessness, disorientation and desire for escape on the part of the protagonists. Within a globalising Germany, escape is sought via drugs, travel and foreigners (on fantasies of travel in *Im Juli* see Göktürk 2002: 254–55).

In essence, though, contemporary male German film protagonists are truly only concerned with the drama of the split male subject. Theo's literal performance of self-destruction in *Der freie Wille*, though witnessed by Nettie, ultimately has nothing to do with her. A kind of self-hating narcissism informs these male performances of fragmentation, for femininity is seemingly not in crisis. Rather, in many new German films the narratives take on a homosocial, and even homoerotic tone. In *Nichts bereuen/No Regrets* (dir. Benjamin Quabeck, 2001), Daniel (played by Brühl) engages in erotic play and kisses with his mentor/friend, the Italian Dennis (Denis Moschitto). *Ein Freund von mir* focuses on the friendship between Karl (Brühl) and Hans (Jürgen Vogel), two men from dramatically different social milieus. The friendship between the two is far more important to these men than is the woman they both love. In one scene, they race each other naked in their cars, a sexually charged and juvenile pleasure.[4]

The mode of homoeroticism and homosociality that characterises a number of contemporary German films once again sets these representations of masculinity off against the masculine/national neoclassical ideal. For these men do not embody the dialectic of self-control and heroism associated with the Apollo of Belvedere (Mosse 1996: 32). Far from this ideal, contemporary male film stars consistently break down, cry and lose control. The narcissistic wound that festers, that allows for neither the attainment of 'normalcy' nor escape, repeatedly brings Brühl, Bleibtreu and Vogel to tears and affective excess in German films. Indeed, tears and hysteria seem to have been co-opted by these fragmented male figures. And as we know from Winckelmann and G.E. Lessing, loss of control is not beautiful to the neoclassical eye. In his analysis of the Greek statue group *Laocoon*, Lessing argued that were Laocoon to open his mouth wider in anguish at the imminent death of his sons, this passion would produce 'the most hideous contortions of the face' that would throw 'the body into such unnatural positions as to destroy all the beautiful lines that mark it when in a state of greater repose' (Lessing 2005: 12). Yet it is precisely this passion that is expressed repeatedly in the films discussed here.

The symptoms of hysteria – tears and emotional excess – abound, although they are rather products of the kind of fragmentation described in this chapter than the repression that is at the root of Freud's hysteria.[5] In the first scene of *Nichts bereuen*, Daniel describes his own behaviour as 'hysteric', but his affectively excessive behaviour is clearly not a product of repression, for the spectator is privy to the gamut of his contradictory thoughts and feelings. Here is perhaps another reason why the feminine is marginalised in a number of contemporary German films: the crisis is purely masculine in nature and not, as had been the case in earlier decades, a product of the increasing threat and power of women.[6] The female body is not actively repressed; it is simply no longer the primary object for projection in German cinema. Despite their literal inability to occupy the centre of the screen, the bodies of German stars such as Bleibtreu, Brühl and Vogel constantly call attention to themselves, begging for empathy even in their utter lack of heroism. The fragmented, wounded and traumatised male body that dominates the German screen today is, in this sense, not a 'feminised' one. As in the Enlightenment, the male body stands in for an imagined national body. Yet the German national body can seemingly no longer be imagined in dialectical terms. Hence, the split pictured in the male bodies described in this chapter cannot be understood along the lines of a strict gender binary; these bodies are rather schizophrenic, sometimes ecstatically so, and sometimes in a manner that causes narcissistic self-pity. They stubbornly embody a kind of post-oedipal purgatory. Hence, despite the presence of Germany's first female chancellor, the crisis on the national stage in today's Germany has little to do with the feminine. It remains, rather, between men: between the masculinities of the past, the present and the future.

NOTES

1 To date surprisingly little academic work has been done on masculinity in contemporary German cinema. In his highly useful collection on post-war German masculinity, Roy Jerome and his contributor Klaus-Michael Bogdal point to the paucity of men's studies and gender studies in the German academy in comparison to the popularity of these fields in the USA (Jerome 2001: 9 and 26). Jerome's volume primarily focuses on sociological analyses and literature and contains no essays on film. The essays collected by Hißnauer and Klein (2002) engage exclusively with masculinity in film, but, with the exception of a piece on the actor Götz George, the volume contains very little discussion of German cinema.

2 A number of the essays in Jerome (2001) use the psychoanalytic notion of 'trauma' to analyse contemporary German masculinity. See, for example, Jerome's Introduction to the volume and his interview with Tilmann Moser, as well as Moser's essay. While this

approach is fruitful, in particular for the analysis of the children of Nazi perpetrators, I attempt in this chapter to analyse along post-psychoanalytic lines what I see as a new crisis of masculinity reflected in contemporary German cinema.

3 A fascinating exception to this model is the 2003 hit *Das Wunder von Bern/The Miracle of Bern* (dir. Wortmann, 2003), a film celebrating the 1954 Football World Cup which the Germans won. This film engages in an almost defiant aesthetics of insistent wholeness and patriotism. Interestingly, the film was partially funded by FIFA, the international football federation, presumably to create excitement about the World Cup games in Germany in the summer of 2006.

4 In my view, the earlier mentioned and critically celebrated film *Das Leben der Anderen* likewise turns on a homoerotic desire: that of the Stasi captain Gerd Wiesler (played by Ulrich Mühe) for the dramatist he observes, Georg Dreyman (played by Sebastian Koch). Here, too, Dreyman's actress girlfriend is a figure primarily functionalised to further the homoerotic narrative.

5 Bogdal makes the point that what he sceptically calls the 'New Men' of advertising and film are largely 'freed from the function of *producer-protector-provider* [...] and they are freed as well from the requirement to discipline their bodies and passions' (2001: 37; emphasis in original).

6 In *Männerphantasien* Theweleit (1977) famously showed how modern German masculinity is constructed via the exclusion of women, though I believe that this kind of exclusion is predicated upon a feminine threat that is missing in the films discussed here. See also Stephan (2003).

3

Hong Kong Cinema and Chineseness: The Palimpsestic Male Bodies of Wong Kar-wai

Konrad Gar-Yeu Ng

In a world now characterised by multiple forms of narrative and aesthetics, instances of transnationalism, transculturalism, diaspora and assertions of the regional and the local, Hollywood models of film studies and the emphasis on national cinemas requires re-thinking. The recognition that the cultural disjuncture and difference of the present calls for new approaches to cinema studies is being explored in the 'ethnic' sub-fields of film studies where suspicions are surfacing around the tendency to measure 'Other' cinemas according to norms of Hollywood cinema.[1] In this regard, Rey Chow's work on Chinese identity in literature, film and pedagogy is instructive. Chow's commentary on the elements of what defines Chinese cultural identity or simply, 'Chineseness', highlights the issues emerging from the study of Chinese cinemas. Rather than treat Chinese cultural identity as a geopolitical or ethnic given, Chow reads formations of Chinese subjectivity as a discursive practice. She notes that, if the ideological dimensions of evaluative criteria in area studies are left unaddressed, the establishment of a 'Chinese' area of study often becomes an 'ethnic supplement' for existing disciplines in a way that 'stigmatize[s] and ghettoize[s] non-Western cultures' (Chow 2000: 3). Similarly, she contends that a 'myth of consanguinity' (Chow 1993: 24) haunts Chinese studies in how Chineseness is mapped as a conflation of race, nation and language. Chineseness can act as a 'coercive mimeticism' that demarcates people and territory according to degrees of fidelity to China. In this process, exactly who is being included/excluded and according to what criteria? Chow states that the problems of Chineseness are 'not likely to be resolved simply by way of the act of pluralizing [Chineseness...] powerful and necessary as it is, [pluralizing] is by itself inadequate as a method of reading' (Chow 2000: 18). She argues that the study of Chineseness should reveal how the definition and mapping of Chinese cultural identity is an ideological practice rather than a straightforward description of identity. To read Chineseness as a singular geopolitical and ethnic referent offers a crude point of departure for cultural study; it neither recognises the multidimensionality of contemporary cultural flows nor the multiple affiliations and sites of Chineseness.[2]

Chow's work outlines some of what is at stake in the study of Chinese cinemas and the importance of disentangling race, nation and language in the formation of Chinese subjectivity. Recent work in Chinese cinema studies supports Chow's call for a more nuanced cultural method and a move away from an 'expressive model of national cinemas', an analytic that Chris Berry and Mary Farquhar describe as the study of film according to 'something called "traditional Chinese culture" or "Chinese national culture," or even some characteristics constituting "Chineseness"' with the idea of seeing 'how these things were "expressed" or "reflected" in Chinese cinema as a unified and coherent Chinese national identity with corresponding distinctly Chinese cinematic conventions' (Berry and Farquhar 2006: 3). In *China on Screen: Cinema and Nation*, Berry and Farquhar argue for 'the abandonment of the national cinemas approach and its replacement with a larger analytic framework of cinema [...that] puts the problem of what the national is – how it is constructed, maintained, and challenged – at the centre' (Berry and Farquhar 2006: 3). In part, Berry and Farquhar address the recognition that Chinese cinemas emerge from a broad and uneven cultural field that can be understood through resemblance, connection and disjuncture as opposed to being discrete expressions of national identity. The Chineseness of films, they suggest, is composed of real and imagined communities that find full expression in selected films and not just through the citizenship of the film.[3] The idea is that Chinese cinemas re/produce Chineseness in a way that attends to the discourses that compose its representation, including discourses of the nation. Chinese cinemas are a 'paradox of discourses that declare the national subject as fixed and transcendent yet are marked by contradiction, tension, multiple versions, changes over time, and other evidence of contingency and construction' (Berry and Farquhar 2006: 8). Berry and Farquhar contend that Chinese cinemas should be studied as performative instances that locate each film and each representation of Chineseness in a specific space and time.

I. CHINESENESS, CINEMA AND MALE CORPOREALITY

This chapter explores Chinese cultural identity and the cinematic male body as a way to contribute to the globalisation of contemporary film studies. In addition, it follows Chow's critical engagement with the politics of Chineseness and its conflation with race, nation and language. Rather than explore the meaning of the male body through gender, sex and/or sexuality, my premise is that the meaning of Chinese male corporeality in Chinese film is indexical of other discursive formations; the male body in Chinese cinemas exceeds its own cinematic representation of masculinity and framework for 'ethnic' identity. I am concerned with how a specific conception of the male body in cinema provides a counter-narrative to the coercive mimeticism of consanguineous Chineseness.

This line of argumentation has been thoughtfully explored in a number of ways. In *Embodied Modernities: Corporeality, Representation, and Chinese Cultures*, Larissa Heinrich and Fran Martin remind us that body representations provide an exceptional measure of Chinese modernities and a link between the idea of Chineseness and lived experience: whether the representations are in 'popular fiction, film, print journalism, contemporary art, or digital video serials [...] we are able to view the structures of body knowledge that, to a large extent, *produce* the very bodies that modern social subjects experience in everyday life' (Heinrich and Martin 2006: 5, emphasis in original). Writers such as Andrew Grossman (2000), Julian Sandell (1997), Julian Stringer (1997) and Yvonne Tasker (1997) use frameworks of genre, auteurism, gender and queer theory to explore aspects of Asian male corporeality in cinema. The broad work of Chris Berry (2006, 2000) on Chinese cinemas reads cinematic representation of Chinese masculinity in relation to cultural tenets such as Confucianism, modernity, or as bodies caught within transnational debates about masculinity. A vigorous discussion about the Asian male body has emerged in the field of Asian American studies. Writers such as Jachinson Chan (2001), David Eng (2001), Richard Fung (1996), Darrell Hamamoto (2000) and Sheng-mei Ma (2000) examine the conflation of Asian male bodies with discourses of emasculation, Orientalism, the model minority, or 'action' genres in Western popular culture.

I want to further the discussion on the male body and Chinese cinemas by considering the cinematic male body as a form of philosophy. Taking the insights of Gilles Deleuze as a point of departure, I suggest that the Chinese male body in film can embody a critical temporality in which the cinematic form of Chinese cultural identity becomes 'a state of permanent crisis' (Deleuze 1989: 112). For Deleuze, media such as cinema, music, art and literature embody expressions that correspond to modes of philosophy to suggest new connections between fields of knowledge and practice. The medium of cinema is not simply a vehicle of representation, but a form of thinking. Cinema's narrative associations between story events and the aesthetic rendering of such associations, reveal states of affairs in the world. Deleuze states that the study of cinema 'is not simply a question of film-content: it is cinematic-form [...] which is capable of revealing [...a] higher determination of thought, choice [...and] link with the world' (Deleuze 1989: 178).

To develop this argument for the cinematic male body as critical philosophy, I turn to Hong Kong cinema and selected films by Wong Kar-wai – both provide exceptional sites to explore Chineseness, cinema and the male body. This chapter joins Laikwan Pang and Day Wong's recent scholarship on the longstanding 'masculinity tendency' of Hong Kong cinema. Pang and Wong (2005) argue for the recognition of the 'multiple meanings and manifestations of masculinities in Hong Kong cinema that compliment, contradict, and complicate each other' and the importance of 'the social, cultural, and theoretical environments that make these representations possible and problematic' (Pang 2005: 7). Although it has been a decade since Hong Kong's handover to China, the region's sense of Chineseness continues to be a matter of negotiation. Against the backdrop of globalism, the cultural anxieties prompted by the handover have been sustained by the uncertainty of Hong Kong's status as a Special Administrative Region (S.A.R.) and agitated by the influx of migrants from the Chinese mainland and elsewhere. Abbas (1997) contends that the region's incessant negotiation of Chineseness is indirectly expressed in selected Hong Kong films and particularly, in the films by Wong. Wong's critically acclaimed work engages themes of affectivity, dislocation and concepts of space and time to act as mnemonic activities that are emblematic of Hong Kong's elusive identity.

Following Abbas, Kraicer (2005) suggests that identity is the central theme in Wong's films. For Kraicer, commentaries on Wong's films tend to reflect two camps: Wong's films are poetically atmospheric works of art or enigmatic, literary-minded, commercially savvy, art-house philosophy. Kraicer contends that the distinction between art and philosophy does not fully reflect what is at the core of Wong's cinema: the re-evaluation of the concept of identity. He argues that Wong's films propose 'a porous sense of self-in-other and other-in-self whose boundaries are not policed like well-behaved analytic categories, but are rather blurred, permeable, malleable, illusory [...and] epitomise an identity without stable boundaries' (Kraicer 2005: 15). While he is right to highlight identity as an additional analytic native to Wong's work, it is important to situate the theme of identity in relation to the milieu from which Wong's films emerge: Hong Kong. When read within the context of Hong Kong's cultural ethos, Wong's cinematic male bodies open up a realm of thought that extends beyond being counter-instances to stable characters and singular identifications. In Wong's films, the male body comments on broader anxieties of Hong Kong cultural identity and the discourse of Chineseness.

On the topic of male bodies and Chinese cultural identity, Wong's acclaimed, *Chunguang Zhaxie/Happy Together* (1997), is usually the film of note. The film was Wong's first feature film not set in a Chinese location and features two gay Chinese men trapped in Buenos Aires.[4] While *Chunguang Zhaxie* is an important film, I am interested in developing a different trajectory in Wong's filmography. I want to trace the politics of the cinematic male body in relation to Wong's trilogy of nostalgia films about the melancholic relationships of young men and women set in 1960s Hong Kong: *A-Fei Zhengzhuan/Days of Being Wild* (1991), *Huayang Nianhua/In the Mood for Love* (2000) and *2046* (2003). Wong doesn't explicitly treat *A-Fei Zhengzhuan*, *Huayang Nianhua* and *2046* as a trilogy, but the films are generally considered a trilogy because all three films set their stories in the 1960s, share similar themes, tropes and feature some of the same characters played by the same actors. What interests me is how the films, and specifically *2046*, depict the male body as a palimpsestic figure who haunts the present. In particular, the transformations of Tony Leung's character, Chow Mo-wan throughout the films, gestures to a sense of agency that is always in flux. Through the use of voice-over, multiple dialects of Chinese, stylised editing, expressive cinematography, disjunctive, overlapping storylines and the morphing of characters played by the same actors, Chow's male body is a composition of associative layers that enable a palimpsestic visualisation of identity. To read the body of Leung/Chow in this way is to recognise that the narratives involving the character and his presence have surface appearance in a classical film sense, but there are sub-surfaces where meaning emerges from metaphoric and symbolic association. Through this optic, the male body in Wong's nostalgic film world presents Chinese identity as a superimposed corporeality with multiple cultural meanings existing simultaneously. This enables a suspension of the present and by doing so, opens up new possibilities for speaking about Chineseness.

Overall, my objectives here are similar to Olivia Khoo's (2006). Khoo explores how *Huayang Nianhua* addresses the cultural enclosure linked to ethnically marked Chinese spectators of Chinese film. That is, how can the Chinese body in film 'function as "visible" without at the same time "trapping" it – in the sense of providing a fixed representation that ethnic spectators cannot escape from[?]' (Khoo 2006: 236). Following Chow's critical analysis of Chineseness, Khoo suggests spectral corporeality as a way to avoid the traps of ethnically embodied spectatorship in which Chinese identity is fixed. She contends that the bodies in

Chinese cinemas can 'no longer be regarded as a dependent marker of [Chinese] identity, whole and fully present, since Chineseness also appears today in increasingly fragmented forms tied to diasporic experience' (Khoo 2006: 235). Khoo develops her argument of spectrality in relation to the female body of actress, Maggie Cheung, whereas I use the male body of actor, Leung, as a palimpsestic cultural cartography for the anxieties of Hong Kong's relationship to Chineseness.

To this end, I want to develop this line of thinking in two stages. First, I expand on the Hong Kong cinema, Chineseness and the politics of nostalgia to sketch the cinematic-cultural context of Wong's male bodies. The idea is to link the critical temporality of nostalgia with the meaning of male corporeality. Second, I discuss the filmic representations of male corporeality to demonstrate how these depictions encourage a palimpsestic Chinese subjectivity. While I comment on the depiction of the male body in *A-Fei Zhengzhuan*, *Huayang Nianhua* and *2046* and trace the body throughout the trilogy, my analysis will focus primarily on *2046*, the last 'Chinese' film made by Wong.[5] Substantive commentary on *2046* is limited and while *A-Fei Zhengzhuan* and *Huayang Nianhua* are known for their nostalgic treatments of the past, *2046*'s dystopic world is the first Wong film to gesture to the temporality of possible futures. The presence of a future world enables new sets of thinking and meaning.

II. IMMINENT CHINESENESS, HONG KONG CINEMA AND NOSTALGIA

When the Sino-British Declaration was signed in 1984 to finalise the transfer of Hong Kong from British colonial rule to S.A.R. under China in 1997, Hong Kong entered a period of profound social, political and economic anxiety. What was the future of Hong Kong as a S.A.R. going to be like? What kind of lived experience was to emerge in the post-handover period of 1997 to 2046, the fifty-year interval during which Hong Kong is to become fully incorporated ('back') into mainland China and Chinese culture? And if the Hong Kong way of life was to simultaneously begin and end in both 1997 and 2046, what, exactly, is the identity and life that is subject to repeated eulogy and inauguration, departure and 'homecoming'? In a sense, the events pose questions about how to deal with the imminent Chineseness of being (re-) absorbed into the narrative of mainland China. For Hong Kong, the handover was not wholly celebrated as a consanguineous reunification, rather, as Abbas suggests, the handover forced Hong Kong to recognise its colonial, global and capitalist specificities; Hong Kong realised its cultural distinctiveness and resistance to China's discourse of reunification. As a S.A.R., Hong Kong continues to be a (neo-)colonial site of Chineseness, one that is embedded in a global-capitalist nexus that provides material benefits for the region while remaining under the rule of an external authority. In response to the cultural transformations initiated by 1997 and 2046, a unique sense of cultural identity took form in cinema, one that invented a form of Chineseness yet implied the mortality of that formation. The feeling was that there was a way in life in Hong Kong that would simultaneously end and begin. The temporal rupture implied in cultural mortality creates a unique mutative colonial ethos that Abbas describes as a 'culture of disappearance' (Abbas 1997: 7). Abbas contends that cinema was the ideal expression of this attitude. Film's aesthetic and narrative properties enable a 'form of visuality that problematizes the visual' (Abbas 1997: 8) and by doing so, 'intervene in political debates more effectively [...] than by advancing direct arguments about identity' (Abbas 1997: 48). For Abbas, certain Hong Kong films expressed 'the elusiveness, the slipperiness, the ambivalences of Hong Kong's cultural space [...] in their explorations of history and memory, in their excavation of the evocative detail' (Abbas 1997: 24). Hong Kong's cultural mortality was represented by 'the introduction of new kinds of cinematic images or in the rewriting of film genres' (Abbas 1997: 28).

While Abbas will argue that the manifestation of disappearance in films by directors such as Wong is suggested through stylised visuality, multiple storylines, ensemble casts, disaffection, anachronism and the denial of genre expectations, other scholars cite the prevalence of nostalgia as a response to the cultural anxieties of impending Chineseness. Wong's *A-Fei Zhengzhuan*, *Huayang Nianhua* and *2046*, films set in the 1960s, are part of a larger movement of Hong Kong films that locate stories in the past to fabricate a nostalgic audiovisuality. For Natalia Chan Sui Hung, Hong Kong's nostalgia films use melancholic affection for a 'past' to rewrite and revise history, identity, collective memory and offer speculation on an uncertain future. She states that the 'nostalgic past that is stylized in the films shows the audience who they are, what they are about, and whither they go [...] to rewrite or reinvent the history of the past in cinematic form, in this respect, is to reconstruct the collective identities and memories of the society' (Hung 2000: 265). Hung's claim is instructive. In its sentimentalisation of the past, Hong Kong nostalgia cinema becomes a form of 'counter discourse of the official history, composes a different story about the colony' with some films being the 'antithesis to the official documentation of national unification between Hong Kong and China [...and revealing what] has been suppressed in the national discourse of historical writing' (Hung 2000: 266). The nostalgia cinema of Hong Kong responds to the temporal and affective dislocations of 1997 and 2046 by providing a structure of feeling for processing Hong Kong's negotiation of

Chineseness. In this sense, Hong Kong's nostalgia films act as an index of the region's cultural identity and provide a cinematic world in which formations of Chineseness are predicated on feelings for an imaginary past. Consequently, Wong's trilogy of nostalgia films, *A-Fei Zhengzhuan*, *Huayang Nianhua* and *2046*, all highly stylised films about the relationships between melancholic young men and women during 1960s, can be read as expressions of feeling about Hong Kong's negotiation of imminent Chineseness set in (e)motion by the deadlines of 1997 and 2046.

III. PALIMPSESTIC MALE CORPOREALITY AND *2046*

In the context of cinematic nostalgia, the notion of a palimpsestic body expresses the simultaneous narrative associations at work – layers of past, present and future overlap with each sheet suggestive of an alternate trajectory. Through the body of Leung/Chow, the cultural composition of Chineseness can be understood as an identity of expressive superimpositions similar to the illusionary visual depth of *trompe l'oeil*; the claim is that the surface of the body may correspond to the notion of a coherent and singular character in a classical film sense, but sub-layer meanings exist and suggest more than one identity. Each layer of identity, I contend, is a Deleuzian time-image. Deleuze (1986 and 1989) argues that aesthetic properties of cinema, like editing, cinematography, sound and mise-en-scene, incubate philosophical concepts and forge critical connections between different fields of knowledge. Rather than measure cinema according to principles of classical film form in which the cinematic experience is based on the promotion of continuity, linearity, resolution and realism, the Deleuzian time-image describes the analytical possibilities of cinematic discontinuity and non-linearity. Deleuze claims that stylised instances of aesthetic and narrative techniques such as flashbacks or *mise-en-abyme* initiate the recognition that there are multiple forms of narrative. The time-image characterises how sheets of past, present and future can be layered in film to convey new and 'untimely' affectivities and affiliations and by doing so, de-naturalise the normative structures of the present. The time-image introduces a provocative dimensionality to cinematic form that is no longer motivated by the singular, narrative causality characteristic of classical film form, but rather by evocative images and overlapping narratives.

I want to trace the palimpsestic corporeality of Tony Leung and his character, Chow. The claim is that, throughout the trilogy, nostalgia's counter-memory is embodied in the arc of his body. Beginning with his appearance in the last scene of *A-Fei Zhengzhuan*, to his transformation from restrained lover/dutiful husband/writer in *Huayang Nianhua*, to a womanising gambler/science fiction writer in *2046*, the corporeality of Leung/Chow is a canvas of overlapping on- as well as off-screen roles that resist the notion of a singular identity. That is, the arc of the fictional character Chow is tied to the cultural embodiment of Tony Leung. Throughout Wong's films, the actors generally appear on screen looking physically similar to how they appear in actuality; very little is done to augment the identity of actors while they are in character. The transparency adds an additional layer of meaning to Wong's characters that is tied to the actor's previous cultural work. An actor's performative history affects the lens of meaning through which characters are viewed and how films are understood.[6] In this sense, the Chineseness of Chow's body in *2046* is tied to the Chineseness of Leung as a film star, music star and citizen of Hong Kong; Leung's multiplicity adds sheets of meaning that extends the scope of Chineseness and its possibilities.

In Wong's 1960s trilogy, the critical arc of Leung/Chow's palimpsestic body begins in *A-Fei Zhengzhuan* and *Huayang Nianhua* and finds its fullest expression in *2046*. *A-Fei Zhengzhuan* and *Huayang Nianhua* introduce tropes, styles and other bodies that surface in *2046* and become characteristic of the trilogy – together, the films and the male corporeality of Leung/Chow express nostalgia cinema's resistance to a consanguineous myth of Chineseness and cultivate alternate narratives for identity. In the hypnotic *A-Fei Zhengzhuan*, a film about the relationships between aimless young people, the lives of two main characters, the womanising Yuddy (Leslie Cheung) and the naïve, Su Li-zhen (Maggie Cheung), intersect randomly and what emerges is a cluster of lives that offer disjointed parables about time, chance and affectivity. Yuddy courts Su, only to break her heart, and he finds himself on a self-destructive hunt for love and reconciliation. Wong faithfully reconstructs the mood of the 1960s in *A-Fei Zhengzhuan* through the soundtrack and mise-en-scene. For Abbas, *A-Fei Zhengzhuan*'s fragmented sense of affectivity embodies Hong Kong's cultural anxiety (1997: 27). Similarly, both Hung and Chow contend that the film 'highlights not only the nostalgic feeling of love during the 1960s but the social insecurity of the 1990s' (Hung 2000: 267) and belongs to the group of films that 'collectively exhibit a nostalgic tendency in their explorations of alternative times and alternative values' (Chow 1998: 147). At the end of *A-Fei Zhengzhuan*, Leung makes his first appearance as Chow in a dialogue-less long-take in which he is grooming himself meticulously with some period music set over the scene. There is no clear narrative motivation for his inclusion at the end of *A-Fei Zhengzhuan* but his appearance after the death of the main protagonist, Yuddy, suggests a rebirth of identity as the story of one male body ends and another one is resurrected.[7] This hard break suggests indirectly, that Chow's narcissistic, well-groomed body is significant.

Mirroring the anxieties of pre-1997 and post-1997 break, Leung/Chow's body inaugurates a trajectory of self-reflection in Chinese cultural identity, the theme that, I suggest, will run throughout the films.

In the sublime *Huayang Nianhua*, Su (reprised by Maggie Cheung) reappears and is married to a man who is having an affair with their neighbour's wife. Chow (reprised by Tony Leung) reappears as the husband of the woman who is having the affair with Su's husband. While realising that their spouses are having an affair, Su and Chow find themselves in an intense, passionate, but seemingly unrequited relationship. Chow moves to another building and takes residence in room 2046 to begin his career as a writer. Chow then asks Su to leave with him to Singapore and she refuses, but she secretly visits Chow briefly. Their relationship ends, and in the final scenes of the film, Su and Chow revisit their old apartments separately and inquire indirectly about each other. *Huayang Nianhua* ends with Chow whispering a secret in the ruins at Angkor Wat. Similar to *A-Fei Zhengzhuan*, the melancholic affair between Su and Chow unfolds to a 1960s art direction and soundtrack and their relationship is based on a disjointed sense of affectivity and narrative. But the film introduces the dynamics of the palimpsestic image. In *Huayang Nianhua*, Cheung and Leung appear to reprise their roles from *A-Fei Zhengzhuan*, but the similarity and continuity of their characters across the films is deliberately ambiguous. The characters have the same name and are played by the same actors, but Cheung and Leung portray Su and Chow differently and there are only oblique references to a uniformed character arc across the films. The effect treats meaning as something that is overlapping. Similarly, a palimpsestic dimension of *Huayang Nianhua* resides in how Su and Leung/Chow pretend to be each other's spouses as they rehearse confrontations about the affair. Wong presents the rehearsals ambiguously by using off-screen space and jump cuts to obfuscate the identity of the characters. While embedded in tropes of nostalgia such as music, clothing, hairstyles, buildings, *Huayang Nianhua*'s instances of character/actor sameness/difference in relation to *A-Fei Zhengzhuan* and spousal impersonations challenge the privileging of a singular filmic identity by treating the body as a text to be overlaid with multiple characterisations.

Traces of *A-Fei Zhengzhuan* and *Huayang Nianhua* appear in *2046*. The film *2046* begins after Chow has left Hong Kong for Singapore in *Huayang Nianhua*. Chow is now leaving Singapore to return to Hong Kong where he will rent a room to continue his vocation as a writer. The film's narrative is loosely composed of four sub-plots that intersect and overlap with Chow and his room, 2047 (room 2046 was unavailable). One story is about Chow and his volatile relationship with a young courtesan named Bai Ling (Ziyi Zhang). Another story involves Chow and his relationship with Wang Jing-wen (Faye Wong), the daughter of his landlord.

Chow helps Wang continue her relationship with a Japanese man (Takuya Kimura) despite disapproval from Wang's father. Eventually, Chow and Wang collaborate on writing a science fiction serial called '2046' and set in the same year as the title. A third story is Chow's fictional world of the serial, '2046', a timeless yet futuristic place served by female android concierges who have expiration dates. Chow writes himself into the story world of '2046' as a Japanese man travelling by train to the year and fictional world of 2046, but along the way, he falls in love with an android that resembles Wang. As Chow's '2046' serial develops, he uses the storylines of other characters from his everyday life. A fourth story depicts Chow's time in Singapore before he leaves for Hong Kong. In this story, Chow meets a woman named Su Li-zhen, but this Su, played by Gong Li, is much different from the Su character in *A-Fei Zhengzhuan* and *Huayang Nianhua*. While the Su played by Cheung appears in a brief, dialogue-less scene in *2046*, the Li/Su character is a professional gambler and Chow's companion in Singapore before he returns to Hong Kong.

The stories that compose *2046* contain the same forms of nostalgia as those that are present in *A-Fei Zhengzhuan* and *Huayang Nianhua*. Story arcs are told in a fragmented, non-linear fashion with story events included for melancholic effect rather than for narrative closure. But *2046* differs from *A-Fei Zhengzhuan* and *Huayang Nianhua* in how part of the film is set in the future and as such, it visualises a time and world that has yet to materialise. Echoing the palimpsestic cinema, the meaning of the film operates on multiple levels. First, the title holds a double meaning. On one gloss, the numerical title refers to a space and a time, the hotel room used by Chow and Su in *Huayang Nianhua* during their time together. On a second gloss, the title holds political significance as the year of post-colonial Hong Kong's final integration into China after fifty years of being a S.A.R. In this sense, the film's title inflects the meaning of the film to be an indirect mediation on the meaning of Chinese cultural identity. Through nostalgia and the layered body, Wong reflectively explores Hong Kong's 'Chineseness' defined by 1997 and 2046.

A publicity still for *2046* (Figure 4), shows how Chow continues to resemble his character across the trilogy but it also suggests how he is also different. A 'Clark Gable' moustache now adorns Chow's face and the pictures suggests that he comports himself according to a sharper, more solemn attitude. The image also makes reference to the multiple meanings of 2046. While the moustache appears to be the major physical difference of Chow across the trilogy, we shall see that his character has changed dramatically. In *2046*, Chow is far removed from his appearance as a mysterious well-groomed young man in *A-Fei Zhengzhuan* and from his role as restrained lover/dutiful husband in

Huayang Nianhua, to become a womanising, hard drinking, gambling, science fiction writer.

The disjuncture between characters conveys the transformation of Chow's body from coherent, singular character to a body that is composed of layered meanings. This palimpsestic subjectivity is sustained by the story itself in how Chow writes himself and the lives of others around him into the serial '2046'. Chow uses composite characters based on the people around him to express his alternate personas with the same actors playing Chow's characters. The actions and thoughts of the characters in the serial '2046' mirror his own thinking about time, which is grounded in Chow's present, a moment defined by Hong Kong's turbulent riots in the 1960s and represented as such in the film. As in *Huayang Nianhua*, Wong occasionally includes in his films what appears to be footage of historical events experienced by former colonies. In the film *2046*, brief footage, ostensibly of the Hong Kong riots of the 1960s, is included in the film. While the 'historical' footage assists in crafting the nostalgic mood of the film, it also grounds Chow's consciousness and the film itself in a specific layer of colonial history. Given that the protests were against British colonial rule by pro-China/pro-communist demonstrators, the inclusion

Figure 4: Tony Leung in *2046*. Sony Pictures Classics.

of the events into the film remind viewers of Hong Kong's negotiation of Chinese identity.

Stylistically, *2046* resembles many of Wong's other films with its fast and slow-motion cinematography, vivid imagery, poetic camera movement, jump-cuts, use of off-screen space, mise-en-scene, elliptical editing, among other techniques. There are also scenes in *2046* that restage scenes of significance from *Huayang Nianhua*. One such motif involves taxicab rides as the opportunity for Chow to express his affections, only to be rebuffed. Shot in slow motion and black and white, these scenes stand out in how their repetition adds a self-referential dimension to the trilogy and presents an opportunity to contemplate additional layers of meaning to the films. Another aspect of the film's style that assists the palimpsestic dimension of Chow is the element of sound and specifically, the role of language and voice-over. Given the fragmented nature of Wong's films, the use of voice-over narration helps guide the narrative, sustains an overall, but minimal sense of continuity, and develops a degree of insight and/or empathy for the characters. However, the use of Chow's voice-over throughout *2046* does not always provide coherence to the film – there are times when his commentary is discontinuous with the imagery on the screen and tells a different narrative arc. In this sense, Chow's narration is an activity that overwrites the cinematic image and adds an additional layer of meaning to his corporeality. The voice-over problematises the notion that there is a single way to identify with the film. Instead, Chow's role as narrator suggests a multi-perspective engagement with the actions on the screen.

Similarly, dialect plays a significant role in the films. While Chow generally speaks Cantonese and Leung is a Cantonese star, the other characters in *2046* speak different dialects of Chinese or other languages that are generally and mutually unintelligible. However, Chow remains conversant with characters who do not speak the same dialect of Chinese or language. From vernacular Cantonese, Shanghainese, Mandarin to Japanese or English, all the characters engage with Chow using a different language, but are able to communicate with each other. The notion of the Chinese language as being composed of multiple dialects is often lost on non-Chinese speakers, but those who are cognisant of Chinese languages can recognise that aspects such as dialect and accent, (re)locate characters in different Chinese cultural geographies. Each dialect of Chinese language adds an additional gloss of Chineseness. Leung/Chow's body walks through the film in constant engagement with different Chinese identities. In this sense, language adds a sub-surface of identity to the film.

In *2046*, Chow reconfigures the worlds of his present into the timeless future of the fictional world of '2046'. The nostalgic narrative world of the film *2046*

– including the ethos of the 1960s, the dystopic vision of the year 2046 and the arc of its characters – is constantly overwritten by other times, narratives, characters, voice-overs and languages. The film switches between the fictional serial about 2046 and the story world already represented in 2046 with stories, characters and temporalities retaining a semblance of its counterpart. In this, the film argues against definitive senses of time, space or identity. By being the corporeal thread between *A-Fei Zhengzhuan*, *Huayang Nianhua* and *2046*, Chow's body becomes the site of palimpsestic visuality and the play of identity.

IV. CONCLUSION

Earlier in this chapter, I mentioned that my argument complements Khoo's concept of the spectral body in Chinese cinemas. To avoid the confinement of a singular self-identification, spectrality, as I understand it, loosens the demands of cultural fidelity by suggesting a more porous corporeality on film. The notion of a palimpsestic cinematic embodiment operates similarly but locates the practice of self-identity back with spectatorship. When one views the Chinese male body in Wong's nostalgia films, Leung/Chow is not a singular subject, his body is composed of different narratives that run throughout the individual film, the trilogy and into off-screen lived experience; spectatorship is an activity of discerning multiple attachments to cinematic bodies. In Figure 5, we can read a gesture towards this trajectory of thinking. In the image, Chow has lost a bet where he must shave half of his moustache. In the preceding scene when Chow flirtatiously confronts Bai Ling about his loss, Wong frames Chow in two side profile headshots to show Chow with and without a moustache, directing the audience to consider Chow's different looks. While the scene plays a small role in the film, its inclusion playfully reveals that Chow's body holds more than one identity. The overall multiplicity inherent to the cinematic male body of Leung/Chow resists the reading of the film as a narcissistic sign of Chineseness wherein Chinese cultural identity is presented as a monolithic and transcendental entity rooted in a national homeland. The claim is that a critical attitude towards imminent Chineseness of 1997 and 2046 in Hong Kong nostalgia cinema forms the context from which palimpsestic forms of male embodiment reveal the composition of Chineseness as a layered identity rather than a consanguineous practice.

To paraphrase Deleuze on the possibilities of cinema, the palimpsestic male body of Leung/Chow in Wong's nostalgia films is not about 'addressing a people, which is presupposed already there, but of contributing to the invention of a people' (Deleuze 1989: 217). My analysis of *A-Fei Zhengzhuan*, *Huayang Nianhua*

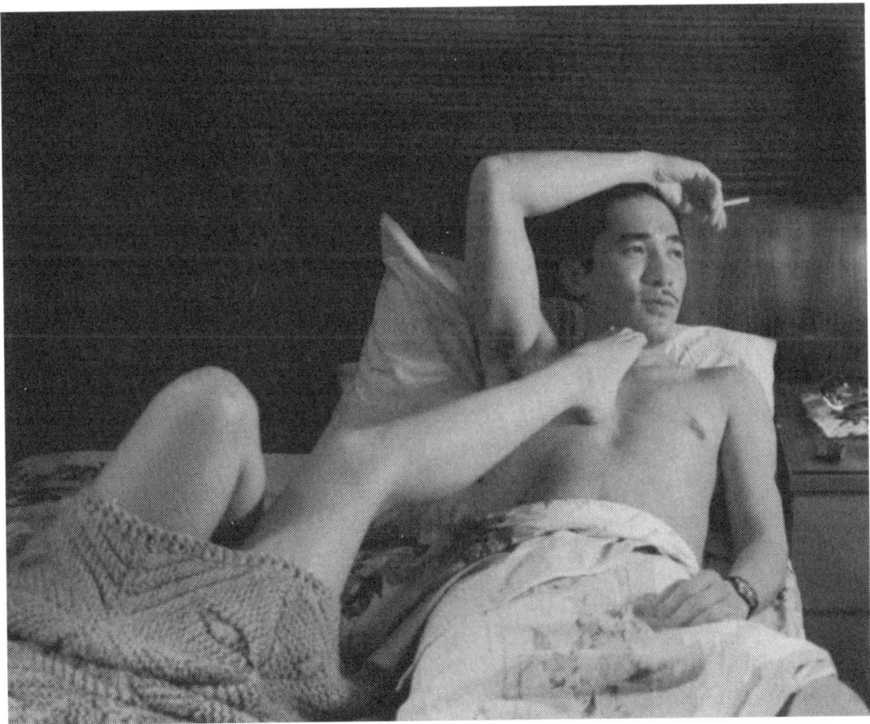

Figure 5: Tony Leung in *2046*. Sony Pictures Classics.

and *2046* can be applied to Wong's other films such as *Chongqing Senlin/Chungking Express* (1994) and *Dongxie Xidu/Ashes of Time* (1994); these films are similar in terms of narrative and aesthetic style and both explore themes of identity through the palimpsestic male body. However, what is striking about Wong's *2046* is how the film suggests that the discourse of Chineseness continues to haunt Hong Kong in the post-1997 era. The film's beautiful rendition of unsettled identities treats Chineseness as a concept to be explored, rather than as a national, ethnic and linguistic given. Overall, the palimpsestic male bodies of Wong's films are inventive vehicles for detailing the multiple forces that shape identity and by doing so, his films can express relief for those whose identity remains in contention.

NOTES

1 I take 'disjuncture and difference' from Arjun Appadurai (1996) and his insightful work on the cultural dimensions of globalisation. He suggests that the cultural kinetics of the present must now be tracked along ethnoscapes, mediascapes, technoscapes,

financescapes and ideoscapes. The transmission of bodies and forms along these scapes disrupt territorial anchors for experience and prompt new ways of defining 'the local'.

2 Ien Ang (2001) ruminates on the tension between Chineseness as a monolithic identity defined by race, nation and language and its multiple formations beyond the scope of those geopolitical markers of identity. She argues for Chineseness as an ontology of hybrid and syncretic encounter that problematises bounded notions of identity.

3 Recent texts that explore the transnational, diasporic, regional dimensions of Chinese cinemas include: Lu and Yeh (2005); Morris, Li and Ching-kiu (2005); Marchetti and Kam (2007) and Yau (2001).

4 Tambling (2003), Berry (2000: 187–200) and Siegel (2001: 277–94) offer instructive interpretations of *Chunguang Zhaxie*. Tambling's work, *Wong Kar-wai's Happy Together*, is part of the excellent *The New Hong Kong Cinema Series* edited by Wimal Dissanayake and Ackbar Abbas, and offers a comprehensive overview of the film. Berry reads *Chunguang Zhaxie* as part of a movement of Chinese films with gay themes to suggest that the emergence of the homoerotic trope of the moody and lonely young man is a prism for the global displacements facing contemporary Chinese identity. Siegel unpacks the relationship between visuality, space, sexuality and global movements in *Chunguang Zhaxie* to suggest how the film is an index of new forms of intimacy.

5 Wong's two film projects that follow *2046* are US co-productions featuring talent who are considered part of the Hollywood industry: *My Blueberry Nights* (2007) and *The Lady from Shanghai* (in production).

6 The *New York Times* film critic Manohla Dargis, makes an interesting comment on this phenomenon in her review of *A Mighty Heart* (2007) with regards Angelina Jolie's role. Dargis argues that 'even when he's showing you the back of Ms. Jolie's corkscrew-curly head, which he does repeatedly, you never forget whom you're watching. And, really, why should we? [...] Like all big movie stars, she can't disappear into her role for long; rather, she bobs to the surface of our consciousness, recedes, bobs to the surface, recedes' (Dargis 2007).

7 According to some reports, Chow's story was not in *A-Fei Zhengzhuan*, because Wong ran out of money to finish the film (see Teo 2005a).

4

Male Bodies at the Edge of the World: Re-thinking Hegemonic and 'Other' Masculinities in Australian Cinema

Chris Beasley

Studies of masculinity ubiquitously employ the concept of 'hegemonic masculinity'. This chapter initially focuses upon this term, and considers possible problems within it, in order to offer some directions for the as yet relatively undeveloped study of masculinities (including representations of masculinities) in a globalising world. The critique and refinement of the concept hegemonic masculinity is then employed to explore differentiated masculinities and relations between them in contemporary Australian film. A cultural studies approach informed by post-colonial theorising is used in conjunction with an emphasis on bodily 'repertoires' to consider cinematic representations of embodied Australian masculinities.

I. HEGEMONIC MASCULINITY AND ITS DISCONTENTS

The term hegemonic masculinity is currently used in Masculinity, Feminist and International Studies to stand in for a singular monolithic masculinity, a global hegemonic form 'on a world scale' (Connell 2000: 46) and is understood to refer to 'transnational business masculinity', to an elite group of socially dominant men. However, this conceptualisation offers an account of globalisation as a singular and one-way, top-down process in which the political legitimating function of hegemonic masculinity in the gender order is eclipsed by an emphasis on economic power. What if however gendered globalisation is not so simple and more a question of particular interactions between embodied masculinities in different contexts? What if masculinities located at the periphery of global politics cannot be understood only from the perspective of the global metropole? Later in the chapter I use Australian film to pursue this question. However, at this point I will briefly outline how a re-thinking of the term hegemonic masculinity permits a more detailed unpacking of relations between masculinities in the global/national nexus and, in particular, a more detailed assessment of hybrid post-colonial masculinities (Beasley forthcoming).

R. W. Connell developed the term 'hegemonic masculinity' in the late 1970s/early 1980s and it is now virtually omnipresent in Masculinity Studies literature, as well as being very widely employed in Feminist, Sexuality and International Studies writings (see Beasley 2005: 192). The term is most importantly a means to recognising that 'all masculinities are not created equal' (Kimmel 1997: 189). Hegemonic masculinity holds an *authoritative* positioning over other masculinities and will 'dominate other types in any particular historical and social context' (van Kriekan et al. 2000: 413). However, at this point, as a number of writers within Masculinity Studies have indicated, the term becomes more slippery. Michael Flood (2002) has noted, for example, that Connell's own usage of the term slides between several meanings. In short, I suggest that these may be summarised as a slippage between its meaning as a political mechanism tied to the word 'hegemony'– referring to cultural/moral leadership to ensure popular or mass consent to particular forms of rule – to its meaning as a *descriptive* word referring to *dominant* (most powerful and/or most widespread) versions of manhood,[1] and finally to its meaning as an *empirical* reference specifically to actual groups of men, and often to particular personality characteristics (see Beasley and Elias 2006).

This slippage produces certain problems (see Flood 2002). Nevertheless, the problem of a slide towards a usage that refers to socially dominant types of men reoccurs in Connell's work – including his work on the global context (see Connell and Messerschmidt 2005: 846, 852–3). As is the case with the account of local Western hegemonic forms, the political legitimating meaning of hegemonic masculinity in the global arena quickly slides in Connell's analysis towards its meaning as the 'dominant' masculinity and how an actual group of businessmen 'embodies' this dominant positioning, including how this group exhibits particular personality traits. Connell specifically describes 'transnational business masculinity' as definitively occupying the position of 'a hegemonic masculinity on a world scale – that is to say, a dominant form of masculinity that embodies, organises, and legitimates men's domination in the world gender order as a whole' (Connell 2000: 46).

Yet it is not clear why Connell is so adamant that transnational business masculinity occupies world hegemonic status. Connell does not engage with those writers who question the very notion of economic globalisation or with those who propose multiple, uneven and contradictory globalisations (for example, Mann 2001). Moreover, as Connell himself notes, many men who hold significant social power do not embody hegemonic masculinity (see Connell and Messerschmidt 2005: 838). Think of accountants. Even accountants with considerable authority are scarcely deemed the mobilising model of manliness to which all men should aspire. They may exercise power, but are not able to legitimate it. By the same token, but in reverse, while actual working-class men may not wield institutional power, muscular working-class manhood is sometimes employed as a highly significant mobilising cultural ideal intended to invoke cross-class recognition and solidarity regarding what counts as a man. This is especially relevant, as I will argue shortly, in relation to Australia and representations of embodied masculinity in Australian cultural forms. The notion of an idealised working-class-inflected 'every-bloke' may work in certain contexts as a generalisable representation of proper, honoured manliness – that is, as a form of hegemonic masculinity. Working-class 'blokes' may not actually wield power, but they can provide the means to legitimate it.

Both the example of actual accountants (who are usually not venerated) and the venerated ideal of the working-class 'every-bloke' indicate that it is a matter of some importance to be able to distinguish merely dominant men at this moment in time, from *hegemonic* (legitimating) forms of masculinity. If dominant and hegemonic masculinities are not equated, this has a significant impact on the focus of political work to achieve gender equality (on counter-hegemonic strategies see Gould 2006) because then there is no reason to presume, as Connell does, that the global gender order is necessarily and monolithically legitimated by elite transnational businessmen in a top-down fashion. If there is no equation of actual social power with the legitimating function of hegemonic masculinity, it becomes possible to consider a continuum of modes of legitimation with more or less authority and scope and relatedly to consider the significance of forms of masculinity within national locations that may both be implicated in and resistant to a globalising gender order. The significance of hybrid post-colonial masculinities becomes open to view with this de-massification of Connell's rather monolithic account of hegemonic masculinity. Such a clarification enables us to acknowledge the hegemonic significance of working-class-inflected models in sites like Australia.

Current approaches in Masculinity Studies have multiplied the term 'masculinity' but have tended to retain the notion of 'hegemonic masculinity' as a singular monolith. Connell and Messerschmidt in their recent clarification of the term reassert the singular character of hegemonic masculinity, as precisely about that which is deemed *the* pinnacle of a pyramid of masculinities (2005: 845). By contrast, I consider that the term 'hegemonic' does not require an indivisible mono-type. Following Judith Halberstam's 'taxonomical impulse' (see Halberstam interview with Jagose 1999), I propose instead that more terms may be required, enabling recognition of what I would call '*supra*-hegemonic' and '*sub*-hegemonic' masculinities. As an illustrative instance here, I would suggest that my discussion of the working-class-inflected 'every-bloke' presents a local *sub*-hegemonic masculinity, invoking as it does masculine solidarity and complicity even though it lacks institutional power. The significance of such a form of masculinity in Australia is reflected in the mobilisation by the two major political parties of a language of 'mateship' as the core of national identity, a language which historically draws upon working men as its exemplars – that is, manual workers, bushmen and ordinary soldiers (Johnson 2006; Brett 2003). The iconic status of the 'every-bloke' has a long and established history in Australian culture (Elder 2007: 3–5). Importantly, this is a legitimating ideal shaped against *and* in concert with more global forms. This example reveals why taxonomical expansion matters. Contra the tendency of Connell's employment of the term, taxonomical expansion suggests there is not one single hegemon on the global scale. Rather, hegemonic masculinity, even at the local level, may be seen as hierarchical and plural.

For the purposes of this chapter, disentangling political legitimisation from actual social power is perhaps especially important when considering the cinematic representations of masculinity and particularly those representations emerging from national cinemas ambiguously located in relation to the global metropole.

II. HEGEMONIC MASCULINITY AND THE AUSTRALIAN 'EVERY-BLOKE'

Mark Gibson notes that employing a cultural studies approach involves a concern with both culture and power, such that cultural forms are considered in the context of relations of power such as gender and sexuality, rather than solely aesthetically or in terms of their formal elements (2007: 1–5). It is in this light that I now consider a range of Australian films produced over the last twenty years or so – between 1986 and 2006 – as providing a field of illustrative instances relevant to my clarification of the concept of hegemonic masculinity, a concept central to current analyses of gendered power.

In re-thinking the concept of hegemonic masculinity, I asserted the advantages of focusing the term hegemonic masculinity on its *political* function – the intention was to *narrow* the characterisation of the term – and, secondly, I proposed undertaking a taxonomic *expansion* of its forms to include *supra*- and *sub*-hegemonic forms in order to resist constituting hegemonic masculinity as all of a piece. This re-thinking allows for a more nuanced analysis that can attend to the unevenness of globalisation in different settings and highlight the complex ways in which different hegemonic masculinities are negotiated, and even resisted. In the context of Australian film, such a re-thinking enables consideration of a plural and hierarchical continuum of legitimating masculinities such that local Australian hegemonic forms can be seen in relation to more global forms. Examination of a range of Australian films reveals certain 'thematic regularities' (O'Regan 1996: 7), certain iconic reiterations of masculine embodiment, representing modal forms of national preoccupation with 'proper' Australian manhood. Typically this proper form of honoured manhood is centrally located as the legitimate sub-hegemonic 'middle way' by being placed against and compared with foreign overlords (the 'hyper-' or supra-hegemonic) and the marginalised domestic 'other' (the 'hypo' Aboriginal).

Here I am employing analysis of Australian films to demonstrate why elaboration of the term hegemonic masculinity is likely to be helpful in discussion of contemporary gender relations and of a range of politically significant masculinities. In distinguishing what I have called '*supra*-hegemonic' and '*sub*-hegemonic' masculinities, from marginalised 'other' (Aboriginal) masculinities in a variety of Australian films, I am outlining a broadly 'post-colonial' and embodied taxonomy (Kimmel, Hearn and Connell 2005; Morrell and Swart 2005; McKay, Mikosza and Hutchins 2005; Gerschick 2005; Ang 2003; Loomba 1998; Bartky 1990: 64, 75). The location of Australian masculinities in a settler colony in between the metropolitan First World and the Third World of occupied colonies produces particular responses to gendered globalisation which are likely to be different from those even in other English-speaking countries (Johnston and Lawson 2000: 361; Kiernan 2000: 12). In this setting a number of Australian films more or less explicitly connect Australian national identity, being located as an Australian, with a central masculine citizen/subject.[2] This (white Anglo-Celtic) rough-diamond 'every-bloke' occupies an ambiguous location, at once the local 'native' – *the colonised* – in relation to the authority of globalised supra-hegemonic masculinities and *the coloniser* in relation to Indigenous native masculinities. In a range of Australian films, from 1986 to 2006, this doubled location is presented in reiterated bodily styles and gestures.

The Australian 'every-bloke' in such Australian films is a local sub-hegemonic masculinity in that this representation offers a powerful Australian ideal (though similar to other working-class-inflected manifestations in other countries – Benwell 2003; Kimmel forthcoming), invoking as it does masculine cross-class solidarity and complicity through its constitution as the quintessential national identity, even though it lacks actual domestic institutional power and is explicitly located as distant/differentiated from global authority/power. The Australian 'every-bloke' is presented as that which *is* Australia, that which distinguishes Australian-ness and as authentic masculinity. His 'in-between' location is an ambiguous ambivalent identity and yet somehow centralised, both peripheral and yet more real than the supra-hegemon of the (external) metropole. By contrast, globalised supra-hegemonic masculinities are frequently presented as simultaneously more powerful but lesser, less masculine, while Indigenous masculinities are typically located as outsiders, as strangers whose masculinity is unknowable. By this means, the uncertain ambiguity of the Australian ideal is oddly re-installed as centre-stage on the continuum, even when depicted negatively.

Importantly, this representation is a legitimating ideal shaped against and in concert with more global forms. The Australian 'every-bloke' is thus situated *against* the colonising authority of more powerful models of masculinity from outside Australia (and sometimes in sympathy with the 'other' local – Indigenous masculinities), but also as *complicit* with/culturally aligned with such colonising supra-hegemonic masculinities in the sense of being at a distance from marginalised Indigenous 'others'. This form of sub-hegemonic masculinity in Australian film presents a post-colonial hybrid occupying a space 'between – or in-between – two cultures' (Hayward 2006: 297) and in the process depicts a domestic form of hegemonic masculinity as entailing complex forms of accommodation and resistance to global forces.

My intention is to indicate that masculinities are not only 'relational' in terms of hegemonic masculinity subordinating multiple non-hegemonic masculinities and femininities, but additionally that hegemonic masculinity itself may be de-massified as pertaining to a relational hierarchy of *hegemonic masculinities* – some of which are associated with a more global reach, while others are more national/regional/cultural specific. In order to pursue this analysis concerning relations between what I have called globalised 'supra-hegemonic', national/domestic 'sub-hegemonic' and marginalised domestic 'other' masculinities, I will consider 'thematic regularities' in representations of embodied masculinities in a range of Australian films. I have suggested that an honoured form of Australian manhood is placed centre-stage, even when this sub-hegemon is not treated uncritically. The focus upon embodied masculinities is intended to flesh out Connell's account of the 'relational' character of gender (Connell 2002; Connell and Messerschmidt 2005). Not only are gender identities/masculinities embodied (as Connell points out), but their relational character is also precisely to be understood as *inter-corporeality* – that is, their hierarchical relations are expressed through an interplay of bodily 'repertoires'.[3] I therefore approach cinematic representations of masculinities in Australian film through the lens of articulating them as a scene of 'social flesh', as embedded in a thoroughly embodied sociality.[4]

In order to undertake this analysis, I will initially outline a brief comparison of representations of idealised masculinity in contemporary Hollywood film – in a global film production system – as against those representations of idealised masculinity that are found in the decidedly more localised Australian film industry. That brief comparison then enables a more focused consideration of a range of Australian films from 1986 to today and, in particular, discussion of those in which the Australian 'every-bloke' is explicitly placed in relation to the global metropole and the utterly peripheral (Aboriginal) 'other'. These films include *Crocodile Dundee* (dir. Peter Faiman, 1986), *Dirty Deeds* (dir. David Caesar, 2002), *Spotswood* (dir. Mark Joffe, 1992), *Rabbit Proof Fence* (dir. Philip Noyce, 2001), *Black and White* (dir. Craig Lahiff, 2002), *Japanese Story* (dir. Sue Brooks, 2003) and *Dead Heart* (dir. Nick Parsons, 1996).

III. HOLLYWOOD AND AUSTRALIAN HEGEMONIC MASCULINITIES

Scholarly debate about cinematic representations of idealised masculinity in contemporary Hollywood movies has tended to outline a development from the 1980s from a spectacular hyper-masculinity associated with action and embodied by actors like Arnold Schwarzenegger, Bruce Willis, Mel Gibson and Sylvester Stallone in the *Terminator*, *Die Hard*, *Lethal Weapon* and *Rocky* series (see filmography). Arguably these hyper-masculine models gave way in the 1990s to more emotionalised action men exemplified by John Travolta in *Face/Off* (dir. John Woo, 1997) (see Jeffords 1994; Tasker 1993; Hanke 1999; Hunter 2003). In more recent times, it is possible to suggest that we are witnessing the re-emergence of 1980s-style hyper-masculinity, as evidenced by films like *Live Free or Die Hard* (dir. Len Wiseman, 2007). However, whether or not idealised masculinity in global Hollywood has currently been provided with more or less emotional range and a more or less impermeable physicality, there are certain continuities in these representations.

Depictions of the most highly desirable, most honoured masculinity are remarkably, if disappointingly, in keeping with Kimmel's listing of four key requirements associated with 'traditional masculinity' originally described in the 1970s, including a capability to face anything no matter how dangerous without signs of weakness, a presentation as powerful, authoritative, competitive and aggressive, and a predilection for physical risk-taking involving a potential capacity for violence. Kimmel's shorthand for these requirements is, 'no sissy stuff', 'be a sturdy oak', 'be a big wheel', and 'give 'em hell' (Kimmel 2001). Indeed, these characteristics are typically heightened to the point of extremity. For example, where Schwarzenegger's portrayals present this literally through the medium of extreme muscular bulk, Willis offers extreme physicalised, indeed unrelentingly violent tenacity. By contrast, femininity remains marginalised as not-male and hence subsidiary for the most part, such that although there are signs of some greater diversity in representations of women in Hollywood movies, these are typically located in comedy (as a joke, campy, not serious) or in sci-fi (not realist) (Inness 1996; Lumby 1997; Hopkins 2002). In general women in Hollywood movies remain cast as handmaidens to the central masculine subject. Most importantly, in Hollywood film the centrally privileged idealisation of the over-the-top hard-bodied action man is depicted as the universal story, not as a culturally specific American representation. Even not-ideal (non-hegemonic 'lesser') men (in, for example, *American Beauty* (dir. Sam Mendes, 1999) or *Falling Down* (dir. Joel Schumacher, 1993)) are still located in what are constituted as universal, axiomatic, not-particular stories (Hunter 2003).

In Australian films the representation of an idealised centrally privileged masculinity, is at a distance from the US model. Most particularly, the form of masculinity that is presented as highly desirable and that which stands for proper manhood is precisely not cast as extremity or as universal. Instead, I suggest, a peculiarly Australian sub-hegemonic masculinity appears and is presented as occupying a 'middle ground' – as precisely neither overblown pugnacious hyper-masculinity, nor marginalised hypo-masculine – and most definitely as culture specific – speaking for a national/cultural identity rather than as a universal, non-specific honoured masculine subject. What is crucial to the appeal of this Australian middle-ground national subject is his cultural distinctiveness which bespeaks his evident distance from Hollywood and other global supra-hegemonic representations. This distinctiveness can be more closely demonstrated by shifting from broad comparison between Hollywood and Australian films to his presentations within Australian films.

IV. AUSTRALIAN MALE BODIES ON FILM: RELATIONS BETWEEN GLOBAL SUPRA-HEGEMON AND NATIONAL SUB-HEGEMON

In a wide array of Australian films, forms of masculinity associated with global power, with a supra-hegemonic gender positioning, are regularly cast as culture-specific 'excessive' – embodied as either 'hyper-swagger' in the case of US masculinity or 'hyper-pinched' in the case of British and (less often depicted) Japanese global hegemons. In contrast, that which is cast as the Australian 'every-bloke', as the Australian who is recognised as properly manly is culture specific but Goldilocks-style is also 'just right'. Rather than the excessive overblown boastful wise-cracking US model or the constrained politeness schooled in deference to hierarchy associated with the British/Japanese model, Australian hegemonic masculinity is presented as displaying a very different bodily repertoire, a repertoire which asserts him to be a 'working man', a 'real' man. He is therefore lean, shows the wiry musculature of a sun-weathered working-class 'bloke' rather than a 'built' (narcissistic) body or one that can ever be imagined as primly 'suited'. He has the narrowed eyes appropriate to a shrewd, laconic man used to the outdoors. Rather than wise-cracking smart-arse, his bodily presentation is understated confidence, a relaxed confidence that is not showy or demonstrative, but ironic, self-depreciating and refuses social hierarchy. He is precisely neither bombastic nor prissy. The Australian idealisation is locatable as a hegemonic masculinity, as an honoured mode of manhood, but more specifically as a *sub-hegemonic* mode which is 'in-between', shaped as a legitimating ideal of masculine authority alongside global forms but also at some distance from them.

This Australian sub-hegemonic masculinity is clearly evident in many Australian comedies, including that most successful of all Australian films, *Crocodile Dundee*, as well as in 'smaller' films like *Dirty Deeds*. In the former film, the global hegemon is New York itself, a character which is interestingly feminised by comparison with the authentic masculinity of the Australian outback bloke, Mick Dundee. Importantly, Dundee is played by Paul Hogan, a comic actor known to Australian audiences in terms of his origins as a working-class labourer. Mick Dundee seduces the global figure of New York by winning the heart of a sophisticated beautiful New York journalist. He is presented in this Australian fantasy of the entrancing authority of Australian manhood as a real man who can show global America a thing or two. This is never more clearly evident than in Dundee's memorable encounter with the dangers of the big city (shorthand for America itself) in which, when threatened with a knife, he calmly pulls out his own, intoning 'you think *that's* a knife, THIS is a knife'. Dundee simply IS the bigger 'knife', even as he represents the 'primitive' marginal nation of Australia. In this setting he is depicted – in *King Kong* fashion – as parting the skyscraper labia of New York, the image of America and its global mastery, fingers pressing down on the Empire State Building, in a poster for the film (Figure 6).

Dundee's authenticity as a MAN, as against mere American power, is on display in a bodily presentation as leanly muscular, semi-naked, tanned by the harsh Australian sun and bedecked with hunting 'trophies' from the wilds of 'the bush' – the teeth of crocodiles for whom he is named. While American masculinity studies writer, Michael Kimmel, has in conversation with me described Dundee as 'camp', to an Australian audience this is far from the case. Rather Dundee is an ironic play upon a much cherished exemplar of rugged national character. A genuine 'leading man'.

A remarkably similar presentation of relations between global supra-hegemonic and Australian sub-hegemonic manhood arises in the comedy *Dirty Deeds*. This Australian film depicts an excessive swaggering American – a Mafia boss – arriving in Australia with the intention of throwing his weight around and taking over from a local Australian (crime) boss. The self-importance of this naked (and corrupt) American power is embodied in the florid face and substantial size of the actor

Figure 6: Paul Hogan in poster for *Crocodile Dundee*. Rimfire Films.

John Goodman who at one point sports an ostentatious bow tie. Once again, the lead Australian man is precisely not an overblown bully, nor exactly an underling, but occupies an in-between 'just right' location as understated manliness, as lean, weather-beaten, self-depreciating and smart. He is that favourite of many Australian films – the knowing underdog that should not be underestimated by those who revel in their undisputed authority, the canny underdog that shrewdly bites back. The Australian actor Bryan Brown presents a rugged laconic physicality in this 2002 film that is very like that found many years earlier in *Crocodile Dundee* in 1986. Indeed he is Mick Dundee's urban cousin and, like Dundee, he is more than a match for the overconfident Americans.

This presentation of a recognisably Australian desirable masculinity that is available for comparison with and against other masculinities apparently even has some global resonance. In the Hollywood romantic comedy *Along Came Polly* (dir. John Hamburg, 2004) a nerdy American man (Ben Stiller) – an anal-retentive accountant who is obsessed with safety and over-cautious assessment of risk – must learn to be a real man and therefore capable of real love. He is shown how to become manly and hence appropriately sexual/emotional by an Australian bloke. Bryan Brown once again provides the particularly Australian idealised masculinity that I have already outlined, but importantly here he is also the exemplification of virile manhood per se – even if at the full-blooded end of the continuum. It would seem that not only in Australian comedies is the Australian 'every-bloke' presented as 'the man', but that this nationalist self-gratifying fantasy is at least somewhat accepted and reproduced in global American cultural forms.

Bartky (1990: 64) has argued that normative gender is produced as bodily repertoires and specifically embodied by three types of practices: the production of certain body size and configuration, along with the development of a certain kinesic range, and a particular mode of displayed surface. Bryan Brown's Australian manhood for a global audience in *Along Came Polly* offers a salutary instance of the ways in which these bodily repertoires present a legitimating model of masculinity – a hegemonic model – which is both particularised/different from global masculine authority and yet affirmed as a desirable/proper masculinity in a global context. The Australian 'every-bloke' manifests its sub-hegemonic modality in an upright leanly muscular body which is physically hardy and capable. This body is largely oblivious to and grins at risk; it is weatherworn, tanned and craggy, not beautiful or smooth-skinned metrosexual. The face is that of a man who has 'been around', a lived-in face, and therefore a face that is almost never permitted for women on screen. His stance, movements and gestures are not those of grace or delicacy but of strength and unreflective confidence, a recognisably masculine body physically at home in the natural landscape. Hence, he wears relaxed, casual and/or functional clothing, typically open at the neck, displaying chest and forearms, offering manifestly male bodily signs.

Once again the continuity between this bodily ideal and that of Paul Hogan's Mick Dundee character is evident. The Australian idealised man is cast as having largely localised authority and significance, and yet as a powerful masculine model. Significantly, this ideal is presented as having a potentially global appeal which may be set against the less attractive features of men with global authority. The ideal gains credence from its reiteration. Dundee is merely one exemplary instance of this honoured form of Australian manhood presented in a range of films and set against the Imperial 'Other'. Earlier examples include the ordinary soldiers ('diggers' in Australian parlance) played by Mel Gibson and Bryan Brown respectively in *Gallipoli* (dir. Peter Weir, 1981) and *Breaker Morant* (dir. Bruce Beresford, 1979).

In this context, just as in *Crocodile Dundee*, *Dirty Deeds* and *Along Came Polly* the globalised/universalised figure of America/American man is subject to a critical eye and found wanting compared to the charms of an idealised Australian manhood, so too in an earlier Australian comedy *Spotswood* (1992) we see the imperial English equivalent subjected to similar critical comparison. The supra-hegemon is again cast as mired in hubris, but here hubris is not the 'hyper-swagger' of US hegemonic masculinity. Instead it is physically constituted as stiff-necked, as 'hyper-pinched'. Anthony Hopkins is cast here as Wallace the upper-class English 'efficiency' expert, the harbinger of global economic change, who arrives in Australia with the intention of pulling into shape a small Australian shoe factory in a working-class Australian suburb, largely by firing many of its workers. Australia and its declining manufacturing industry are thus depicted as confronting the imperatives of globalised production.

Hopkins speaks quietly, with the pinched 'excessive' formality, politeness and clipped accent of imperial authority. He wears dark uncomfortable suits, a tie always tightly around his throat, and appears the epitome of emotional and physical restraint. In contrast, those cast as the Australian 'every-bloke' evade, undermine and sometimes explicitly resist the authority of the English 'boss'. They are loud, boisterous, constantly joking and untidy. In a word, unruly. In keeping with the story of relations between the outsider supra-hegemon and local Australian manhood in Australian *comedies*, the representative of imperial mastery is largely won over, is seduced. Just as in *Crocodile Dundee*, so too in *Spotswood*. Hopkins begins to do what he can to assist the Australian workers. Australian masculinity is revealed yet once more as the better model, as desirable while precisely not claiming or craving advancement/power. Australian sub-hegemonic masculinity in these comedies expresses the post-colonial 'in-between', idealised as neither (global) master nor (local) entirely mastered servant. He is his 'own man', and the better for it.

Whereas in these comedies the Australian 'every-bloke', the idealised masculine, is presented as the best man, in Australian dramatic films he is more likely to be cast as deeply compromised and/or mastered. Nevertheless, even in dramas he is always centralised, placed in-between global hegemon and marginal others. In dramas he is more clearly implicated in the reach of global masculine authority (in the company of the colonisers), yet all the same he remains at a distance from and typically somewhat uncomfortable with this authority (colonised/over-ridden). Significantly, unlike in Australian comedies, in Australian dramas the local hero typically does not, is unable to win over the global hegemon. He, alongside utterly marginalised others, is 'done over' and usually cast as comparatively emasculated, as lacking the power to diminish the imperial master by seducing or otherwise thwarting the master's authority. Interestingly, the global hegemon is more likely to be British in these more negative and socially critical dramatic stories.

The earlier mentioned Australian film *Rabbit Proof Fence* (2001) provides a paradigmatic instance here. The film, set in 1931, outlines the colonising policy of forcibly rounding up children of mixed Indigenous and European descent to relocate them in white assimilationist institutions with the aim, over time, of erasing a distinct Indigenous culture deemed to be a primitive relic. Despite the efforts of their mother, three young girls are captured and sent to an orphanage far from their home. The girls escape with the aim of walking over one thousand miles home by following Australia's 'rabbit proof' fence, and are tracked down by a white police officer and a black 'tracker' who can 'read' the country. As in the comedy *Spotswood*, the overseer – in this case, Chief Protector of Aborigines – is a starched, upright upper-class Englishman, played by Kenneth Branagh. Branagh's character is presented as emotionally/physically repressed, as a pedantic paternalist obsessive, determined not to let the Indigenous girls escape his control. Like Hopkins in *Spotswood*, Branagh embodies a tightly contained, disciplined demeanour, one which in military fashion covers any vulnerability with a besuited carapace sharply at odds with the untrammelled heat and dust of the Australian desert landscape (Figure 7). By contrast, a range of Australian white men located as representing local authority are at home in the desert, informally and loosely dressed, unbuttoned at the throat/chest, sweaty, dusty and hard-bitten. They physically 'belong' in the landscape, while Branagh appears to be a pursed-lip transplant who is frequently filmed peering disdainfully downwards. But all the same the Australian men do his bidding, even if often with discomfort.

Similar relations between imperial/global hegemons and local masculinities are also played out in films like the earlier mentioned *Black and White* (2002) and *Japanese Story* (2003). In both cases the supra-hegemonic is expressed in stereotypic physical terms as either British or Japanese bodily constraint, excessively formal dress and arrogant superiority expressed through formal polite behaviours. In both cases Australian national character is constituted around a more 'natural', direct and informal style of masculinity at home in the physical world, a masculinity uncomfortable with strict hierarchical authority, rules of etiquette and 'indoor' clothing. The Australian sub-hegemon is precisely a working man, not given to airs and graces, an idealised model invoking cross-class solidarity about what constitutes genuine manhood but which precisely lacks substantive social power.

V. RELATIONS BETWEEN NATIONAL SUB-HEGEMON AND MARGINALISED 'OTHER' MASCULINITIES

Australian films reiterate the desirable masculinity of the Australian 'every-bloke' by regularly representing and typically idealising the authenticity of (the racially unmarked but actually white) Aussie rough-diamond man as against the hubris (swaggering or uptight) of the global hegemon. Though the Australian every-bloke is *the colonised*, he is, it seems, a 'real' man. However, on the other hand, this sub-hegemon is also presented in embodied terms as the

Figure 7: Kenneth Branagh and Garry McDonald in *Rabbit Proof Fence*. Olsen/Levy Productions/Rumbalara Films.

coloniser in relation to marginalised 'other' masculinities, in particular as against Indigenous men.

I do not have the space here to develop the comparison between national sub-hegemon and marginalised 'other' masculinities and will outline this in more detail elsewhere. Nevertheless, it is useful to give an indication of this relational aspect of hegemonic masculinities by noting very briefly some relevant features of it that arise in a range of Australian films, such as the earlier mentioned *Rabbit Proof Fence*, *Dead Heart* or *Black and White* and also *The Tracker* (dir. Rolf De Heer, 2001). In these films the Australian 'every-bloke' is evidently not every bloke at all after all, but definitively white. Yet he stands in the Australian setting for the neutral, universal, axiomatic Man, whereas Indigenous men are particularised as exotic/mysterious/marginal/other/oppressed. In *Rabbit Proof Fence* and *Dead Heart* the laconic, weather-beaten and white model is clearly differentiated as proper manhood – as against 'white-collar' men who stand for centralised authority, whether global or local – but is also distinguished from Indigenous men. This differentiation marks the latter as non-hegemonic – as native locals, yet outsiders.

Several bodily tropes signal distinguishing features which once again assign the Australian white 'every-bloke' as the central middle-ground. If the global/imperial hegemons are depicted as excessive (as too 'full of themselves') in relation to that middle-ground, then Indigenous men are presented as hypo-masculine, as partial, not fully present. Where global/imperial masters are overdressed and Australian every-blokes are informally and loosely clothed, Indigenous men in Australian film are frequently barely clothed, unstructured and even looser in their mode of dress. If the colonisers are excessively overbearing (full of swagger or overly starched) and Aussie blokes are animated and informal, Indigenous men are remote/impenetrable/mysterious, their expressions unreadable (see for example Figure 8).

The spatial physicality of the three hierarchically organised forms of masculinity is also differentiated – colonisers are large scale, presumptuous and do not belong in nature, Aussie blokes are at home in nature but they are typically filmed standing up – above it. Indigenous men by comparison are often literally located 'lower than' white men. They are 'of nature', and in keeping with their connection with the land, they *sit down* much of the time directly upon the soil. This location in physical space is evident in *Dead Heart*. Bryan Brown, once again the laconic lead, plays a tough bloke, a police officer comfortable out in the bush, but he and the other whites of the remote desert community that is the focus of the film often remove themselves indoors as if to find respite from the unconquerable vastness around them. The Aboriginal men who have stayed in touch with their community and with whom Brown has equivocal relations, sit down outside, in the desert to which they are inextricably bound.

In sum, the Australian every-bloke is an idealised working-class-inflected masculinity located between the colonised and the coloniser, between the global centre and the utterly peripheral 'other' and as such may be considered as a sub-hegemonic model of manhood. Analysis of Australian films indicates the reiterated status of this ideal, and supports my assertion that the notion of hegemonic masculinity should be de-massified to allow analysis of a range of hegemonic masculinit*ies*.

VI. CONCLUSION

At present there are few analyses which link masculinity to global matters (Connell 2005), and there are few analyses connecting masculinity with post-colonial theory (Kimmel, Hearn and Connell 2005). Explicit investigation of the relationships between elite transnational men, local white male settlers and Indigenous men is even rarer in global and post-colonial scholarship. In addition, representations of men's bodies are significantly less commonly discussed than other topics concerning masculinities, and it is most unusual for material discussing men/men's bodies and mass media to appear in texts on masculinities.

However, the main focus of this chapter is to offer an argument – which is relevant to studies of masculinity, film and globalisation – regarding the term hegemonic masculinity and the ways in which embodiment provides the means to reconsider such an important terminology. Like Connell, I believe, it is timely to

Figure 8: David Gulpilil and Gary Sweet in *The Tracker*. Globe Films Australia/ Vertigo Productions.

reconsider the term (Connell and Messerschmidt 2005). In order to undertake this analysis, I initially considered certain theoretical issues associated with the concept and followed this with discussion of a range of male bodies in Australian films. The discussion of Australian male bodies on film indicates how a de-massified account of hegemonic masculinity may be understood. It enables an understanding of relations between hierarchically organised hegemonic masculinities. In particular, the analysis of male bodies in Australian films indicates the ways in which the Australian 'every-bloke' occupies an embodied location in-between the global metropole and the utterly peripheral (Aboriginal) 'other', and hence is placed as a sub-hegemon.

The comparison of representations of male bodies, and interactions between them – between hegemonic and other masculinities placed beyond the centre of the global metropole, ambiguously at the metropole's edge – confirms that the pervasively used terminology of hegemonic masculinity is presently rather a blunt instrument. Re-thinking the term hegemonic masculinity, in particular by investigating representations of male embodiment, is necessary to produce a more nuanced understanding of privileged forms of manhood and of relations between masculinities in the global/national nexus. Such an analysis provides a means to re-think global politics, to re-think how globalisation – as both gendered and embodied – may be conceived.

NOTES

1 Hearn notes this distinction between powerful and widespread in his analysis of notions of dominant or pre-eminent masculinity (1998: 1749–51).

2 This analysis is in keeping with Hughes's perception that liberal nation-states have a 'special relationship' with identity (2004).

3 Such an analysis may be seen as expanding the recognition of social embodiment in Judith Butler's (1993) notion of 'performativity' and Elizabeth Grosz's (1994) account of 'corporeal feminism', in that both of these frameworks are inclined to delineate social embodiment through its play upon 'the (singular) body', rather than through relations among bodies.

4 For a detailed account of the term, 'social flesh', as a means to considering the embodied character of relational social life, see Beasley and Bacchi (2007).

5

The Post-Colonial Cowboy: Masculinity, the Western Genre and Francophone African Film

Rachael Langford[1]

American Westerns have long been present and popular in Africa. Many of the films screened to African audiences in the post-war period, both before and after European decolonisation, have been American Westerns (Emeagwali 2004: n.p.; Gotteri 2005: 6–8; Burns 2006: 73). In Francophone African culture, the embedding of the Western imagination is due in part to the popularity of the Western in French metropolitan popular culture; in visual culture, the high status of the *Bande Dessinée* or *BD*, whose Westerns strips include the ever-popular *Lucky Luke*, as well as *Jerry Spring*, and latterly *Blueberry*, plays an important role. The Western *BD* can be understood to act as a crossover point for Francophone African versions of the Western, in a manner similar to that of Country and Western music in the popular culture of rural Anglophone Africa (Thompkins 2007).[2] Thus the Western imagination, present for many decades in both Anglophone and Francophone Africa via the cinema, is expanded and to some extent also naturalised, by its links with other cultural expressions of the Western – music, the *Bande Dessinée* – which have a 'crossover' status in different African popular cultures.

This practical situation of the transcultural re-activation of the American Westerns' tropes in African contexts points to an interesting pattern which challenges notions of Western culture as obliterating or effacing other cultures where they meet: the *Lucky Luke* albums, for example, themselves parody the heroic masculinity of the cowboy hero and his bodily attributes, as well as the narrative conventions of the Western genre. And so Francophone African visual culture receives the Western via marginal routes, through a Belgian Western which is a parody of American Western values and narrative and cinematic conventions, written by expatriate Francophones working in post-war America; at the same time, *Lucky Luke* is a Francophone cultural product carrying embedded within it another Francophone European worldview. In this case there is a further generic twist, due to the *Lucky Luke* films and television series, through which this Western *BD* 'becomes' the Western cinema whose narrative conventions it both apes and derides.[3]

All this gives the Francophone Western in African contexts a great deal of interpretative instability, affording African filmmakers a range of creative possibilities. But the ambivalence of these subversive potentialities should be recognised, for the Francophone metropolitan Western as instanced in the *Lucky Luke* series parodies the discourse of one hegemonic culture while itself being part of hegemonic cultures (France and Belgium in Africa) troubled in the post-war period by the loss of their spheres of influence to the Superpowers. Moreover, the *BD* and the Western in Francophone metropolitan cultures belong to low status sectors of the cultural field, often on the margins and outside the academic canon, for all their popularity with highbrow audiences and readers. So the Francophone African director who takes on the Western turns to a genre that is filtered through a very particular set of cultural coordinates, beyond those that pertain to the American Western in American cultural contexts.

Therefore, the historical situation of the Western in African popular cultures frames it as a product from elsewhere which spins ideal visions and undercuts them, and which, although expressing images of alien rural and city lives, adapts easily to become a vehicle in which audiences identify relevance to elements of their own material and emotional lives. Moreover, simultaneously as it provides all audiences with the ideological pleasures of participating in the elaboration of imperial culture and borrowing a hegemonic culture's eyes for the space/time of a screening, the American Western when screened in Africa can be understood as always already enmeshed in dialogues of parody and expropriation of hegemonic cultural forms, both consciously and unbeknownst to itself. In this essay I will explore this idea further by considering some of the ways in which masculinity and the male body are interrogated in Francophone African film variants of the Western genre.

I. THE AMERICAN WESTERN AND MASCULINITY

As a starting point, it is helpful to outline the coordinates of masculine identities that critical literature identifies in the American Western film. A number of critics have argued that the Western is a genre fundamentally structured around depictions of gender and around gendered depictions of socio-political realities (Tompkins 1992; Stanfield 1998; McGee 2007). Significant studies of the genre have examined its exclusion and delimitation of women and the coherence of the masculine identities that classic American Westerns propose (Mulvey 1981; Peak 2003).

Critics reading masculinity in American Western films invoke three paradigms. The first is that of the Western as a hyper-masculine and hyper-heterosexual genre, where women are absent or ejected as agents from the filmic universe, but present in objectified form as things to be protected, directed and dominated, albeit often paternalistically. In such readings, the landscape is interpreted as taking on female attributes, so that the male body's struggle to pacify, traverse or simply survive brute nature becomes a visual allegory for the struggle of masculinity to prevail, and to pervade filmic and social space (Tompkins 1992). In the Westerns that Tompkins discusses, the hysterically expressive female body is devalued by its excesses while the hermetic male body is prized for its minimalism and singular existence: the positive male protagonists figure as silent bodies guided by internal instinct, at one with nature in the form of the horse and the landscape. Following Tompkins, it is plausible to read the silent male body functioning in certain Westerns as the narrative's master object. For in films such as *Shane* (dir. George Stevens, 1953) and its revisiting in Clint Eastwood's *Pale Rider* (1985), the male body is not just one among a series of natural objects, but 'The One' on which the camera focuses until it is long out of sight. The emphasis on singularity and mastery in the visual economy of the films is an extension of the narrative of the cowboy hero's exclusive, elite status. To take a well-known example, *The Lone Ranger* (dir. Heisler, 1956), despite his faithful horse Silver and his faithful native friend Tonto, is still always Lone, not only because he is singular, elite and exiled by his hyper-masculinity from domestic society, but also because the power relations between him, Silver and Tonto mark him as the undisputed master of them both, as well as of the natural world of which they are narrative extensions.

The second major interpretative paradigm for studying masculinity in the Western reads the hyper-masculine narrative universe of Western films as one essentially of homoeroticism, placing overtly homosexual inflections of the genre on a continuum which includes the Gene Autry 'singing cowboy' films of the 1930s, 1940s and 1950s, and pointing to the homoerotic subtext that can be traced in a great many classic Westerns, Westerns that others would read as instancing the hyper-masculine. Peter Stanfield points to complex patterns of identification and desire shaping the narrative of the singing cowboy films, so that we might see Autry's work as attempting to evacuate desire and the sexually female from the frame, through the location of male and female attributes in the same character, at the same time as appealing to acceptable norms of domesticated behaviour and drawing in a female audience (1998: 110–11). To some extent this is the case also in *Brokeback Mountain* (dir. Ang Lee, 2005), which presents Ennis and Jack as hyper-male in their mastery of nature (in the form of horses, landscape and the elements), guns, contained aggression and silence; but also shows them acting mothering roles with the livestock and each other, and domestic roles of washing, cooking and tidying in the camp. Homosexuality is presented as a bodily practice rather than an existential essence. It is noteworthy that the desiring male bodies in Lee's film can only consummate their desire in natural surroundings, from the initial pastoral on the mountain, to the later years of 'fishing trips'. This naturalises homosexual desire in the film, but contains it, marking it always as provisional and taking place beyond the boundaries or at the margins of society.[4]

The third critical paradigm for reading masculinity in the American Western charts a passage between the extremes of reading all Westerns as hyper-masculine heterosexual narratives, or all as coded narratives of male desire. This third mode of reading brings the classic Western hyper-male hero into juxtaposition with his feminised variant, and sees these as parts of a wider defining feature of the genre, in which the success of the Western hero is more important than any affirmation of essential masculine traits. The main proponent of this critical insight, Wendy Chapman Peak, argues that the quintessential Western hero, particularly in the post-war period, is the male who uses a variety of strategies to ensure his ultimate success, if necessary by deploying both male- and female-gendered attributes. She contends in particular that masculinity is secondary to Westerns because they are so wholly about men, and that the thoroughgoing masculinity of the Western universe allows Westerns to 'become a "safe space" [...] to explore the pleasures and perils of male bonding' (2003: 209–10). Peak also stresses the extent to which Western masculinities are structured by 'behaviour that is ultimately subservient to some manner of father' (2003: 214), suggesting that relations of domination and submission are also vital to an understanding of the genre.

These interpretations of the American Western evoke contradictory emphases, and to a certain extent each can be upheld or discounted depending on the corpus of films examined.[5] Notwithstanding the different accenting of the European variant (Schneider 1998: 147–52), critics agree that as a genre the Western is intimately concerned with maleness both as a physical attribute and as a social and mental structure. Thus however troubled and protean masculinity becomes latterly in the American and European Western, it remains the dominant focaliser in the Western's narrative universe, as a practice of mastery and also as a position based on that practice and process, enduring throughout a diverse range of films as the essential identity that saturates the imagery and structures the narrative. The genre anxiously rehearses the closing of the Frontier and the disappearance of the clear social boundaries, fearing that hierarchy might similarly dissolve into nothingness if not policed and enforced. In these worries that frontiers have evaporated, the genre concerns itself with land and law enforcement through the prism of the male body's on-screen presence; and even when martyred and debased, the male body emerges triumphant in the form of a very singular praxis, the mastery of practical strategies for success.

II. FRENCH COLONIALISM, MASCULINITY AND THE MALE BODY

The 'winning' of the American West from the indigenous inhabitants was itself a story of colonial domination, and the links between masculinity, femininity, land and racial Other played out in Western narratives have obvious echoes in European colonial discourse. Overall, the examination of masculinity in the Western springs essentially from the interest of feminist and psychoanalytic criticism in the representation of the body and its world on screen (Kitses 2004: 18–21; Lusted 2003: 28–32). This itself is allied with the interest shown by cultural critics in the body and gender as metaphors for social and epistemological practice. Edward Saïd's crucial work both in *Orientalism* (1978) and in *Culture and Imperialism* (1993) explained some of the epistemological processes by which other lands and peoples are gendered in the Western imagination, such that the non-Western is always exotic to the West, and this exoticism is always already feminised. Many others have explored discursive practices around gender in European narratives of pre-colonial exploration and of colonial administration and propaganda (see, for example, Spurr 1993; McClintock 1995; Thomas 1994 or Pratt 1992). Focusing down further, a number of cultural historians have argued that these notions were vital to representations of the imperial project specifically in French colonial discourse (Lorcin 1995; Clancy-Smith and Gouda 1998; Savarese 1998; Slavin 2001).

French colonial discourse was a major site of gender trouble. From the high colonial period onwards in France (roughly from the 1880s to the 1930s), questions of effeminacy and virility were embedded in French colonial discourse as part of a normative narrative of French national 'health' to which the colonies were vital. There was much anxiety, in particular concerning the loss of French territories felt as an 'emasculation' of France by the Prussians in 1870, over the idea that both the body of the nation and individual French male bodies were by the end of the nineteenth century suffering from feebleness and dissolution. Eugenics and proto-scientific discourses identifying the 'feeble-minded' and the enfeeblement caused by 'deviant' sexual practices were of course very much in the air in this period. Entropy was all around (Baguley 1990), and by their landmass, the acquisition of overseas colonies acted as a vital palliative by adding to the healthy growth of the 'body' of the nation. In *fin-de-siècle* France therefore, male settlership in the colonies was promoted as a means of re-masculating the body of the nation by increasing its size.

Further, settlership was idealised also as a way of re-masculating and returning to healthy balance the bodies of individual Frenchmen, through contact with rude nature and the domination of feminised Others and Other lands. The meaning and function of the bodies of male French *colons* ('colonials') in other lands were thus determined by multiple agencies: they were emissaries of *francité* (Frenchness) and the pinnacle of civilisation that this represented; at the same time, they were metonymic instances of the nation's body, which was marked discursively as weak and enfeebled; and they were bearers of individual and localised anxieties about the virility of the French man in a defeated (1870–1914; 1939–45) or martyred (1919–39; 1945–60) French nation, both of these latter understandings of French history figuring the nation as needing to consolidate and extend its wholeness and masculinity as it expanded outwards to become 'la plus grande France' (Bancel, Blanchard and Delabarre 1997: 20–5; Ageron 1984: 561–64). And yet in the French colonial context, masculinity was somehow never something that could be sustainably achieved; the masculinity inscribed in the location and practice of French male bodies overseas threatened constantly to melt into air, almost indeed by dint of the weight of national signification that the French male colonial body carried with it: a continual production of French colonial discourse across diverse cultural objects battled against the evaporative characteristics of virility in the colonies (Slavin 2001: 16–34, 55–56, 169–71).

On the other side of the colonial relationship, how was colonised masculinity presented? It is worth noting that although studies of the representation of colonised women are available (Dennis 1994; Coombes and Edwards 1989; Alloula 1981), little attention has been paid specifically to the way in which male bodies are represented in French colonial discourse. There is not space here to discuss in depth the representation of African male bodies in French colonial culture, but several common-places of representation can be discerned.[6] The first, contrasting starkly with the representation of women in the colonies, is that the colonised male body is not presented as passively sexualised, even when references are made to a man's circumcised or uncircumcised status. The second is that depictions of male bodies mark them predominantly according to ethnic and class categories. The third is that it is savagery that male bodies are seen particularly to instance in their 'natural' state, and infantilism or 'good pupil' status that they instance once Westernised, depending on the degree of assimilation to European norms of dress and domesticity. The final point to make is that when presented as savage, the naked or semi-naked African male body is depicted as challengingly wild and powerful, hunting, dancing or deeply entranced, while the Europeanised African male body is contained corporeally within clothing, and spatially within domestic, educational or work-place environments. There is an important paradox at the heart of these representations. The gaze of the male colonial photographer is drawn again and again to represent virile native masculinities from which his civilised status excludes him, but to depict these native masculinities as primitive and static or entropic. For the discourse of colonialism, while seeking to restore masculinity to the effeminate metropolitan Frenchman, and to the enfeebled France, seeks inevitably to contain the masculine quotient of its colonised others by Europeanisation, or by its presentation as on the verge of disappearance. It must never be suggested that savage masculinities can endure, ready to overwhelm the civilised but less virile Frenchman. To achieve virility abroad himself therefore, the French *colon* must deny or radically curtail the recognition of African masculinity. The boundaries of masculinity must be avidly policed on both sides of the colonial divide. The male body and its frontiers are as vital to Francophone colonial filmic culture as they are to the ideologies of the American Western.

III. INFLECTIONS OF THE WESTERN IN FRANCOPHONE AFRICAN FILM

In the preceding sections I have pointed up similarities linking the coordinates of masculinity in the American Western to the troubled nature of French colonial masculinities to sketch a context for the pervasive use of the Western genre by Francophone African filmmakers. The representation of masculinity in inflections of the Western genre by Francophone African filmic culture inevitably engages in transcultural and transhistorical dialogue with these other filmic discourses of unstable masculine identity, in which the inscription of the male body is key to the encoding of ideology – colonial, settler, liberal, revisionist – in film. The Francophone African films that will now be discussed have in common the use of tropes and motifs from the Western as analogies for the economic and cultural West. The Western's utopian escapism is highlighted, particularly the opportunity it affords both audience and characters to assume hegemonic identities linked to power and domination. But death stalks the Stetsoned African in all of these films, and the Western paradigm brings with it disruption and discord.

(i) Mustapha Alassane, *Le retour d'un aventurier* (1966)

Although not a contemporary film, a brief consideration of this remarkable film must be made. Not only is it one of the earliest films by an African director, it is also the first ever African Western, and as such sets up coordinates for African inflections of Western masculinity that are carried forward into contemporary filmmaking. The film interrogates the meaning of masculinity and the location of power, and was accompanied by a documentary made about the film, Serge Moati's *Les Cowboys sont noirs/The Cowboys are Black* (1966), which further examines the escapist power of the Western imaginary in an African context, at the same time as it extends *Le retour*'s questioning of gender, race and power.

Le retour opens with the typical Western narrative motor of the return of the stranger. In this case, Jimi (Harouna Diarra) brings with him a suitcase full of cowboy outfits for the friends he had for many years left behind in the village. Dressed as cowboys, the social roles of the members of the group change: their allegiance and respect for elders and fathers, and for traditional forms of knowledge and practice, is replaced by individualism and conflict over possessions, especially a new saddle. The role of the father is key to the film: it is the theft of this new saddle given by Jimi as a gift to his father, and later the suspected death of his father, which cause the cowboy gang members to turn on each other. Death and destruction ensues with three of the six friends dead by the end of the film. At this juncture, acceptance of the rule of the father or exile from the village are established as the only ways forward. 'Black Cooper' (Boubakar Souna) becomes again an obedient Moussa son, while 'Jimi and Queen Christine have set off again for adventure' (my translation). Thus while Western codes of masculinity are seen in the film to bring destruction, yet only one character returns willingly to the patriarchal and gerontocratic norms of the village. The end of the film therefore maintains a playful ambivalence concerning the worth of village values, with Black Cooper/Ibrahim informing the audience that the initiator of this Western drama, along with the only female protagonist, would rather be outlaws than return to village life.

As the sole female protagonist, la reine Christine (Zalika Souley) is a vital presence in the narrative, dressed similarly to the male cowboys throughout and with an on-screen presence indistinguishable largely from the men's. She emphatically does not occupy the classic Western woman's roles of cowgirl, whore or homesteader: she is deferential towards the leaders of the group, but not more so than the other gang members, and in all other ways – dress, weaponry, what she is mounted on – is an equal. It is striking that she is one of those who chooses exile from the village, as if the freedom garnered by borrowing the accoutrements of the Western male body, once experienced, cannot be renounced. For Black Cooper/Ibrahim, who chooses to submit once more to the rule of the father, power will come in time because he is male. For la reine Christine, power and freedom are located outside the existing community's gender roles, eventually as an outlaw runaway beyond society; however, this is not necessarily understood as empowering in the film. The film maintains a similar ambivalence as far as Jimi is concerned: he has been too long in the West to give up the destructive pleasures of individualism for the quietude of patriarchal village life by the end, but his initial return to the village has been the harbinger of death for his friends. Neither of the two models of male authority presented – individualist Western masculinity and communal rural African patriarchy – emerges as triumphant in Alassane's film, which also significantly interrogates both the coordinates of female gender roles and the unerring respect for the father that structure the American Western.

(ii) *Tilaï* (1990), *Samba Traoré* (1992), *Kini et Adams* (1997)

The problematics of male identity established in Alassane's influential and formative African Western track through into the work of contemporary Francophone African filmmakers. In *Tilaï* / *The Law* (1990), *Samba Traoré* (1992) and *Kini et Adams/Kini and Adams* (1997), all directed by the prolific Burkinabé director Idrissa Ouédraogo, the reference to the American Western is fundamental. Visually, there are strong echoes of iconic American Western sequences in all of these films. Thus the opening shots of the arrival of Saga on his donkey in *Tilaï* recall *Per un pugno di dollari/A Fistful of Dollars* (dir. Leone, 1964) as well as elements of *Shane* and *Pale Rider* (dir. Eastwood, 1985); in *Kini et Adams*, the evocation of images of mining and its depredations recall not only *Pale Rider* but also Enright's *The Spoilers* (1942) and Hathaway's *North to Alaska* (1960). The Western reference appears thematically in conflicts between law and justice mediated through outlaw figures who traverse established boundaries (*Tilaï*, *Samba Traoré*). Spatially, this emphasis on frontiers, liminal spaces and isolated rural environments which contrast with dissolute urban contexts indexes some of the prime narrative coordinates of the American Western.

Additionally, the problematisation of male identity via the narrative structure and the visual figuring of the male body is key to these films. The destabilising 'return of the male stranger' which opens Alassane's *Le retour d'un aventurier* provides the narrative motor for the atemporal screenplay of *Tilaï* and for the contemporary setting of *Samba Traoré*, while *Kini et Adams*'s narrative is concerned with the initial effort to escape from the original context, rather than the later return. Despite their very disparate settings, in all three of Ouédraogo's

African Westerns, powerful conflicts arise between the allegiances demanded by close male friendship or brotherhood, and the fulfilment of male heterosexual desire. Thematically, these tensions between heterosexual love and homosocial bonds present themselves in the films as a stark choice between emasculation (where the male protagonist accepts his expulsion from the homosocial, patriarchal order of power and takes up a male role defined by his individual function as provider within a nuclear family), or disappearance and death (exile and fratricide in *Tilaï*, a prison-sentence in *Samba Traoré*, suicide in *Kini et Adams*). *Kini et Adams* is particularly significant in this context, for it opens with a macho joke about men and the penis, a joke, however, where death lurks in the punch-line. Moreover, it is the unattached male Adams (David Mohloki) – whose name of course recalls that of the 'first man' in both Islam and Christianity – whose phallic attachment to the car and jealousy of Kini's (Vusi Kunene) love for his wife and daughter ends in his own body's annihilation.

The starkness of the choices available to the male characters in these films is echoed by the cinematography of the male body. It is striking that the fully naked male body is much hidden, unclothing taking place in night-time sequences in barely lit interiors, as if the tensions it creates marks it out for occlusion. The male protagonists of these films are often visually isolated, seen from afar and from without. When close focus is used, it is the male face and upper body that is in the frame, in line with established modes of representing dilemma and choice-making in a cinema where individual character psychology is not of prime concern (Ukadike 1994: 180–246). It could therefore be argued that the questioning of male identity and male power in these films, as in Alassane's, occurs in line with arguments about the preservation of male power through the keeping-hidden of the phallus (Lehman (1993: 5–9), Simpson (1994: 13–15)). Yet we must remember the extent to which the naked male African body is a site of colonial phantasm, and be additionally wary when discussing the figuring of both male and female genitalia in African film, since discussion of the significance of the figuring/hiding of the phallus is imbricated in issues of cultural specificity and cinema censorship regimes that are beyond the scope of this essay. However, within the overall context of the concealment of the male body in these films by Ouédraogo, two significant instances where the penis is shown on screen inevitably stand out.

In *Tilaï*, when Nogma (Ina Cissé) leaves Saga's hut after her first visit there, a full-length shot of Saga (Rasmane Ouédraogo) at twilight shows him bidding her farewell until the following day with his hand across his crotch, moving his penis inside his trousers in a full-frontal gesture which appears as a frank sign of beckoning, of self-satisfaction, of memory and of promise that is witnessed by both Nogma and Kouliga (Roukietou Barry), her much younger sister. In *Samba*

Traoré, Samba (Bakary Sangaré) is met at the river's edge by his wife Saratou's young son Ali (Moumouni Campaoré), who comes to tell him the sex of the new baby (a boy), for Saratou (Miriam Kaba) rejects Samba after her discovery that he has committed a robbery and murder in town. In scenes lit by firelight which recall a plethora of Westerns, Ali and Samba spend the night and morning together, sleeping by the campfire, then bathing naked at first light and washing their clothes in the river's pools and waterfalls. In these scenes, the young boy's penis is fully evident as part of the scene's realism, while Samba's genitalia remain submerged in the river along with the rest of his lower body.

The different emphases of these scenes in *Tilaï* and *Samba Traoré* are as instructive as the similarities. Where the Western American hero contains desire, and in particular is not commanded by the phallus but is in command because of it, Saga and Samba choose not to conform to the common values of a patriarchal community, and their challenges are based on the fulfilment of desire and not its containment, as in the American Western. Thus Saga and Nogma exchange comments on Saga's sexual strength, but Saga, by his hand movements, very clearly 'gives away' the site of his desire for Nogma, and thus cedes power. In the end, Saga is killed before his child is born, and the film shows the challenged patriarchal order ending in disarray, with village elders committing suicide and young men banished into exile. In *Samba Traoré*, it is the criminal act which makes Samba rich and in turn gives him the power to re-shape his community which challenges the phallic location of power. He hides the criminal origins of his money – his new power – from his community, a concealment paralleled in the ways that Samba's penis remains cloaked while he sleeps next to Saratou otherwise entirely naked, and later remains hidden in the water while Ali's is seen. A basis for distinguishing between the fates of Saga and Samba could then be the concealment or revelation of phallic desire, and their relative ability to command the phallus. For it seems instructive, that Samba's fate, once his desire for Saratou and his criminal act combine against him, is not death but imprisonment, while Saratou pledges to wait for him. Saga's tale in contrast is beset with death, even before he himself is shot dead by his younger brother who then departs in exile from the village.

(iii) *Bamako* (2006)

From Alassane's *Le retour d'un aventurier* to Ouédraogo's work, African filmic references to the Western portray male characters as troubled and challenged, and masculinity called into question. Male bodies are broken and destroyed, or mortally threatened; paternity and patriarchy are constantly interrogated. Sissako's

Bamako, the most recent African inflection of the Western film, selected for Cannes 2006, both extends and builds on this heritage.

Discursively, the film takes the form of a courtroom drama, with the West and the IMF accused of acts leading to death and destruction, as a series of witnesses attest. The West is defended by an elderly white lawyer, largely unequal to the task of defence when faced with the tide of prosecution witnesses. Parallel narratives run alongside the trial of the West, for instance a crime narrative of a stolen watch among the court spectators, and a dying man and a sick child hanging tenuously onto life in rooms giving onto the *cour* (meaning Court, courtroom and courtyard in French). Importantly as far as this essay is concerned, a Western interlude is included, announced diegetically as the television 'evening film' to the family members gathered in one of the rooms off the court. A group of multi-national cowboys (all actors and/or filmmakers appearing under their own names) is listed before 'Death in Timbuktu' (in English) appears in large play-bill script against a backdrop of West African adobe architecture.

This multi-nationalism is no coincidence, gesturing consciously to the cultural history of the Western as well as to the global economic oppressions being tried in the courtroom. In an important correction of, and allusion to, the elision of the Black experience in Frontier history, the African-American Danny Glover figures as the cowboy hero in the film, stalking the others who are on a mission selectively to murder Africans. African complicity with the havoc wreaked by the cowboy gang pursuing Glover is shown, with the cowboy group consisting of two Congolese and one Malian (Sissako himself as Dramane Bassaro), complemented by their French leader Jean-Henri Roger and the Palestinian-Israeli filmmaker Elia Suleiman. More or less indiscriminately, and with incompetence rather than classic Western mastery, the cowboys slaughter two school-teachers and a woman with a young child.

In this interlude of film-within-a-film, women and children are defenceless bystanders and victims, while the men rampage violently through the streets. Within the main courtyard drama, however, it is African men who are characterised as weak and powerless: male witnesses are unable to make themselves understood, come cowed to the stand with 'rien à déclarer' ('nothing to declare') despite their alleged education, or cannot gain entry to the court because they do not understand its rules of operation. In contrast, the African woman barrister and a 'well known Malian writer', Aminata Traouré, the former minister of culture in Mali, also a woman, fill the screen with their powerful physical presence and the potent articulacy of their indictment against the West. The first speech in the film is given by Traouré, and both women comment on the disastrous effects of high unemployment and allude directly to the loss of dominance of African men in such circumstances, arguing that, 'the father of the family, who possessed authority, who was influential, who had his dignity, all of this is taken away from him with an unfair sacking' (my translation).

The white male defence lawyer is no match for them, either in screen presence or rhetorically. Thus in Sissako's courtroom, African men have become the objects of the masterful rhetoric of authoritative African women, while the virile African male body lies broken and dying next door, homologous to the sick child's body, materially witnessing this state of affairs simultaneously as he is both audience to and object of the women's narrative. Moreover, there is no heroic masculinity to be found in 'Death in Timbuktu' either; the cowboy gang lacks competency and cunning, failing to master both environment and weaponry and acting with no particular rationale. Danny Glover's character seemingly takes up the position of mastery in this narrative, looking down on others from high buildings, largely silent and stealthy and depicted from the outset as at one with nature. However, Glover fails to prevent the slaughter of innocents, and the end of the sequence is the beginning of a shoot-out in the streets with more indiscriminate killing heralded.

This ambivalence around Glover's character – a saviour-hero from elsewhere who apparently subverts the more tainted of Western paradigms (racial exclusion), but whose classical Western *modus operandi* seems unequal to the almost post-modern incoherence of the multi-national cowboy gang's praxis – is a significant marker in the film, for the African audience depicted watching 'Death in Timbuktu' are not necessarily on his side. When Zeka Laplaine cries 'Hey, lads, lads! I fired at one and two of them fell down!' (my translation), Sissako cuts to the African television audience's profound amusement at these parodically double deaths of innocent African primary school teachers. This may be a visual illustration of the African woman barrister's identification of Western culture imported to Africa leading to 'the total degeneration in actuality of the foundations that the cardinal values in actuality of our society represented' (my translation); it certainly links back to the image of a small red bicycle emblazoned with 'Rocky' and 'Rambo' stickers that lies across the street in the opening shots of 'Death in Timbuktu'. This powerful image comments on the saturation of Africa with Western macho models of manhood, but also on the ineffectualness of such models, reduced to the dimensions of young boys' toys lying in a dusty street which is about to be the scene of unstoppable bloodshed.

Western masculinity is no answer for the Africans in Sissako's film any more than it was in Alassane's African Western forty years earlier. However, there is seemingly no model for African manhood that is marked with a potentially successful outcome in *Bamako*. Where *Le retour d'un aventurier* allowed for the possibility of a positive African masculinity in the form of Ibrahim's final exhausted acceptance of the father–son relationship as the best available solution, however patriarchal and gerontocratic, *Bamako*'s dejected masculinities appear, by the end of the film, irretrievable, and Glover's actions mere cowboy heroics in the most limited sense.

IV. CONCLUSION

The references to the American Western in Francophone African films make complex comment on the contemporary and historical coordinates of the relationship between Francophone Africa and the West, as well as parodying some of the conventions of this essentially escapist narrative form. In particular, through the prism of the emphasis on masculine identities and the male body which is inherent to the Western genre, Francophone African filmmakers have reworked elements of the Western as a way of negotiating and commenting on the problems of representing African identities in a narrative medium – the moving film – which is intimately linked to the history of France and to European colonialism, and latterly to continued dominance by the West more generally; and to a medium where a symbolic violence is rehearsed every time the camera rolls, through the allusively macho technical vocabulary of 'action', 'shoot', and 'cut'.[7]

NOTES

1 I am grateful to the British Academy for their award of a Research Grant supporting the research for this essay. I would also like to express my sincere thanks to Mme Jeannick Le Naour, director of the *Cinémathèque d'Afrique* at Cultures France, Paris, for sharing her expert knowledge of Francophone African film and in particular for her help in identifying lesser known instances of the Western genre in the work of Francophone African directors.

2 The reading of *Jerry Spring* and *Lucky Luke* adventures in the 1960s has been cited by the contemporary Congolese *Bande Dessinnée* artist Barly Baruti as a significant influence on his own understanding of French and Western American culture, as well as on his interest in becoming a practitioner of the graphic novel art form (Jacquemin 2001: 3).

3 Lucky Luke's adventures have latterly been translated 'back' into English and brought to the cinema screen in animated and in live-action format, thus providing an example of what Dan Harries sees as parody being absorbed into the generic norm, rather than sited as an external comment on it (2000: 121). There have been three animations of

the adventures created for cinema release (*Daisy Town*, dir. René Goscinny, 1971; *La Ballade des Dalton*, dir. René Goscinny and Henri Gruel, 1978; *Les Dalton en cavale/The Daltons on the Run*, dir. Hanna-Barbera, 1983). There have also been three animated *Lucky Luke* television series: from 1983–84, Hanna-Barbera studios released 26 episodes, and in 1990–91, Dargaud Productions released another 26. In 2001, Jean-Maire Olivier produced a series entitled *Les Nouvelles aventures de Lucky Luke/The New Adventures of Lucky Luke*. In the early 1990s, two live-actions films and a live-action television series, one directed by, and one also starring, Terence Hill were produced. Most recently, in 2004 a film entitled *Les Dalton/The Daltons* (dir. Philippe Haim) had Til Schweiger in the role of Lucky Luke.

4 Andy Warhol's *Lonesome Cowboys* (1968) must also be mentioned in this category. A far more provocative and sexually explicit take on the homosexual cowboy motif, Warhol's film rejects heterosexual models of monogamous romantic love. Desire is consummated by sexual practice, and the film as a whole marks the Western genre as fundamentally homoerotic, reworking the close framing of male faces that is associated with Leone's macho Spaghetti Western aesthetic into an overtly homosexual emphasis on the scopic.

5 Peak (2003) makes it clear that her interpretative framework fits best with post-1950s Westerns.

6 The photographs consulted are those in Bancel, Blanchard and Delabarre (1997) and Bergougniou, Clignet and David (2001).

7 It is important to note that moving film was born in France at the beginning of the colonial period, and that the Western narrative and European 'high' colonialism develop their characteristic features in the same historical period, roughly between 1875 and 1945.

6

The Square Circle: Problematising the National Masculine Body in Indian Cinema

Aparna Sharma

In recent years the Bollywood film industry has gained increasing attention within academic circles, film festivals and exhibition networks of Europe and North America.[1] However, much scholarly discussion, which occasionally and mistakenly tends to equate Bollywood with Indian cinema, sparsely contextualises the ideological implications of the Mumbai film industry on cinema practices and cultures within a wider framework relating either to the Indian subcontinent or more internationally. The problematic extends further – issues of subjectivity are overlooked and more specifically, the implications of the gendered body within them are sparsely addressed with sufficient critical rigour. Filmmaking practices in India, as elsewhere in the world, include disparate concerns, aesthetic and textual strategies; and more significantly, competing historico-ideological postures. It would be a rather vast undertaking to fully comprehend the complexities pertaining to gender and its representations within the cinema practices of India. However, one necessary attempt to broaden the scope of the discussion is by stepping, in a markedly divorced gesture, outside Bollywood. Here the territory is vast including regional cinemas of varying sizes and strengths, documentary practices, parallel cinema and the more formally radical, experimental cinema. In such a multifarious territory we encounter instances where the mainstream and conventional, necessarily heterosexual and patriarchal gender equations perpetuated by the mainstream cinema, i.e. Bollywood, get challenged.

It is not the intention here to institute a simplistic binarism between the dominant industry and every other form of cinematic practice as *other*, purely oppositional to mainstream cinema. In taking attention away from Bollywood the attempt is to introduce a consciousness that at once resuscitates genders and sexualities away from the reduced and pervasive mindset that equates any form of alternate sexuality as transgression or taboo; and further, evokes in these alternate forms a wider cultural claim linked to India's secular and esoteric philosophical and aesthetic traditions, be they the classicism of the high Sanskritic culture or the grassroots folkloric and mythic practices. In keeping with this, in this chapter I discuss the acclaimed film, *Daayara/The Square Circle* (dir. Amol Palekar, 1996) to unpack, as an example, the intricacies of how the male body is problematised critically and aesthetically through a non-mainstream modality.[2]

The male body within the dominant Bollywood cinema has been styled quite tightly in response to a popular imagination underpinned by an idealisation that is the outcome of the historical fashionings of Indian, particularly Hindu social and middle-class attitudes towards sex and sexuality. The ideal male is often posited as a 'hero' – the repository of physical prowess, heterosexuality, and rationalist, technological mobility alongside sensitivity towards a rather ahistoricised and archaic set of imagined 'traditional' Indian values. This fashioning coincides with the wider matrix linked to the ideological apparatus pertaining to an 'imagined' sense of community, in terms of the nation (Anderson 1994). While Bollywood stars have often performed an oppositional consciousness towards the dominant ideological apparatus, for example the working-class consciousness as in the 'angry young man' posture of Amitabh Bachchan in 1970s to mid-1980s, instances such as this have not been consistent or sustained so as to formulate as a determined intervention in problematising the national category, and more importantly, they have seldom interrogated pervasive sexual attitudes.

Daayara is a film that surrounds the marginal and socially ostracised figure of a transvestite (Nirmal Pandey). The film's narrative spans the transvestite's relationship with a young, sexually violated and abandoned village woman (Sonali Kulkarni).[3] This chapter will discuss how by focusing on the transvestite and through that the broader category of the transgendered body,[4] the film strikes at the core of pervasive middle-class and specifically Hindu attitudes towards sex and sexuality, alongside rendering unstable the image of the ideal hero in Indian cinema. Besides contextualising *Daayara*'s approach to the gendered body, I propose that by situating in the film's characters the prerogative for migration between genders this film complicates the binary nature of gender as an innate category or a constructed one. *Daayara* clearly posits gender as performative in the sense of Judith Butler's qualification of the performative as 'manufactured and sustained through corporeal signs and other discursive means' (Butler 1999b: 362).

In order to examine how the film suggests this aspect of gender as performative, this chapter focuses on the film's narrative and mise-en-scene. The film's narrative situates both political and spiritual imperatives in the transvestite figure. The chapter will locate and historicise these within the context of Indian art and philosophical thought, and then discuss how the film's strategies of mise-en-scene respond to this, particularly in terms of the construction of space and the transvestite body's relations to it. Spatial design of the film reveals the rural landscape, the backdrop for the narrative, as socio-historically constructed thus providing the film with an anthropologically precise edge that is usually unavailable in Bollywood cinema. The transvestite's spiritual predisposition, whereby he experiences a sense of unity with all forms of organic life, enables him in overcoming the limitations that his socio-cultural and historical definition include – as a low caste, dark complexioned subject from rural east India. Through these two aspects – the rural landscape as socially constructed and the transvestite as situated in it but not limited by it – the film becomes a critical intervention through which the limits of the masculine ideal in dominant cinema and, more widely, in the nationalist imagination, are problematised.

I. BACKGROUND AND CONTEXT

Daayara is a love story between the transvestite, Pandey and a young village woman, Kulkarni. The film commences by setting up how both characters, propelled by very specific social circumstances, undertake solitary journeys and eventually encounter one another. Pandey is introduced as a folk performer of the *gotipua* tradition from the east-Indian state of Orissa. The *gotipua* is one of three styles of classical Odissi dance. In the *gotipua* practice, pre-pubescent male performers are trained to cross-dress and play the roles of mythological women figures. It was through this that Pandey had first experienced transvestism and decided to integrate it more fully into his life. In the opening scene of the film, his *guru* (teacher) welcomes a woman performer into the troupe on the grounds that cross-dressing is being increasingly rejected by the conservative rural folk, the principal audiences of the *gotipua* style, who prefer only women to perform the roles of women. Feeling threatened by the inclusion of a woman performer and insecure about the social acceptability of cross-dressing generally, Pandey leaves his troupe and village including his wife with whom he bore an incompatible relationship having been forced through the conventional Hindu arranged marriage. The film presents Pandey as a nomad wandering through the countryside.

Kulkarni and Pandey meet on what appears as a small island where Kulkarni has landed after escaping a city-based pimp who was attempting to kidnap her to take her to a brothel. While Kulkarni is composing herself after a long and arduous chase her attention is drawn towards an ambiguous figure, Pandey, bathing in the water. As Pandey emerges from the water and dries himself, ties an *ikkat* sari and applies traditional Indian women's make-up including *bindi* (circular dot at the forehead) and *kaajal* (kohl), Kulkarni feels more fearful and scornful. She is unable to comprehend Pandey's sexual status. She speaks incoherently, attempting to probe his sexuality. Their conversation indexes their respective worldviews and logically extends into a dialogue over what constitutes the essence of womanhood. It is brief and inconclusive, and the two decide to part.

In the following sequence Kulkarni is gang-raped. Pandey learns about this, traces and composes her, and their journey together commences. It is dotted with situations that compel them to probe the volatility of their gender roles. They often argue because their worldviews and approaches collide, but eventually, a sense of affection and intimacy grows between the two. Kulkarni, is of a conservative mindset and bears a false romantic consciousness – she has never interrogated her sexuality and her kidnapping and eventual meeting with the transvestite appear to her as unwanted disturbances in the flow of her life wherein she was soon to enter an arranged marriage with a village youth.

For Pandey, his nomadic lifestyle is equivalent to the spiritual quest underpinning all organic life. In one of his conversations with Kulkarni he claims his body as not deprived or polluted, rather a 'miracle of nature'. In an ecological worldview such as Pandey's, socially sanctioned material and bodily pursuits such as institutionalised arranged marriage and property relations grounded in ahistoricised gender disparities perceived as originary, innate and essential – a posture that dominates the Hindu social worldview – are limiting of self-expression, simplistic in their materialism and, through that, impeding a deeper spiritual quest. As their journey continues Pandey and Kulkarni's conversations deepen and Pandey claims that unlike Kulkarni he does not hold herself as deprived or destitute by virtue of her gender – a view that, as he points out to Kulkarni, is itself conservative and socially conditioned. Pandey's cross-dressing amounts to transgression. His cross-dressing is not simply an alternative posture, but constitutes a deviation from and critique of normative gender and sexual practices in the Indian rural as well as urban middle-class contexts that reinforce the differences between 'man' and 'woman'. Pandey's cross-dressing is transgressive because it destabilises the binary oppositions at the heart of the restrictive Hindu worldview that appropriates transgender practices of any kind including cross-dressing as biological defects or errors. This transgressive gesture can be fully appreciated through Judith Butler's qualification of transgender as 'not exactly a third gender, but a mode of passage between genders, an interstitial and transitional figure of gender that is not reducible to the normative insistence on one or two'. She argues that the man/woman binary is the outcome of a 'restrictive discourse on gender' that utilises it as 'the exclusive way to understand the gender field' and to 'perform a regulatory operation of power that naturalises the hegemonic instance and forecloses the thinkability of its disruption' (Butler 2004: 43).

Cross-dressing in *Daayara* is not limited to Pandey only. Through the course of the journey both socially ostracised characters compel each other to assume opposing gender roles and functions and this surfaces as the only mechanism through which they can articulate their deviation from the gender norm. While the film opens introducing Pandey as a cross-dresser, Kulkarni too cross-dresses when she seeks revenge on her rapists. She is encouraged by Pandey who warns her against the social attitudes she will encounter being a woman (violence, subjugation, repression and exploitation). Cross-dressed as a man Kulkarni finds work in a highway mechanic's garage and on occasions performs with Pandey who composes folk songs for village audiences. By unpacking gender roles as assumed, either in terms of self-expression (through Pandey), or more circumstantially, through Kulkarni, the category of gender is rationalised and liberated – now understood as an acquired and performed attribute. This then subverts and renders unstable any socially sanctioned hierarchies that are perceived as determined by the interplay of non-immediate or intangible agents such as destiny. This subversion of conservative and irrational Hindu religious beliefs and practice coupled with Pandey's own ecological worldview situates in the film a crucial and necessary distinction between spiritualism and institutionalised religion. For Pandey the self is further than the definitions of gender and the physical body. He consistently alludes to the immaterial or transcendental dimension beyond the physical-social self. This is clearly articulated at one instance in the film, when in response to Kulkarni he states: 'This creation is so colourful and complex. And keeping this in view, I don't think the creator would have been satisfied with the binary compartments of man and woman' – alluding that there are further and more complex possibilities beyond compartmentalised gender in terms of the spiritual experience.

There are some specific historical reasons why Pandey's cross-dressing constitutes as transgression within the Indian context. Within Hindu society and worldview, issues of sexuality are clearly suppressed and it has been observed that there persists a hypocritical attitude towards sex generally. Alternate expressions of sexuality are outright scorned, ridiculed or formulated as topics of frivolous amusement such that outside the reductively designated categories of male and female, all else is taboo or transgression. Alka Pande observes that 'while most schools of Hindu philosophy acknowledge the existence of the female principle in men and the male principle in women, Hindu society per se does not take kindly to this in practical life and veritably disdains any public display of the "alternative" self' (2004: 40).

In his study of the Indian middle class, Pavan Varma has listed three attributes characterising the Indian middle class's approach to sex – hypocrisy, guilt and aggression. He observes:

> Hypocrisy because the appeal of sex cannot be openly admitted; guilt because even when pursued it is considered as something wrong; and aggression because the conservative milieu for the interaction between sexes allows limited scope for more normal relationships to develop, and the dominant media message is that women are 'available' for the assertive male to have. (1999: 163)

According to Pande, in the colonial milieu, it was confronting the 'aggressive Western concept of maleness, that any kind of gender equation outside the male-female binarism, in particular "femininity-in-masculinity" got perceived as a "negation of man's political identity"' (Pande 2004: 44). Pavan Varma further contextualises how sex and sexuality have been reduced and relegated as nearly forbidden subjects within Indian society. He identifies three historical factors for this. First, a new value system that arrived with the Muslims nearly a thousand years ago that 'frowned upon the importance given to physical desire in the [ancient] Hindu world-view'; namely through the traditions of kama (desire) whose prime exponent is the Kamasutra and sringara (the sensual aesthetic). Second, the transplantation of Victorian morality in the colonial era that strengthened the tendency to consider sex as 'something dirty'. Lastly, Mahatma Gandhi's propagation of celibacy on the grounds that sexuality was 'poisonous', the 'sex instinct an enemy to be resolutely exorcised from the human system' and his equation of passion with 'impurity and distortion' (Varma 1999: 159–61). Such a reduced mindset is pervasive in Indian society and consequently, in the Indian context transgender amounts primarily as transgression, a clear deviance from and resistance against socially normative behaviour and the worldviews that underpin it.

Though Pandey's cross-dressing amounts to transgression, he exceeds his oppositional equation with society through his spiritual commitments that lend to him an agency of another variety, beyond social or political subjectivity. The spiritual and political – the transcendental and physical-social self – are not antithetical in Pandey, rather the two are intertwined. He is challenging, at once rational and complex in his thought. For example, when Kulkarni moans her loss of virginity in the gang-rape, he retorts stating that the creator is not insane to concentrate all of a woman's honour and dignity in a tiny piece of flesh. The twin implication of the spiritual and political in Pandey is closely tied to sections of modern Indian thought in which the immaterial or spiritual is not abstracted from the material or socio-historical, most thoroughly argued by Rabindranath Tagore (Radhakrishnan 1918). Besides Tagore, numerous social and cultural historians have observed how cross-dressing and androgyny have both borne a spiritual imperative alongside political effects in modern India, specifically in the colonial era. Alka Pande (2004), discusses nineteenth-century social reformer, Ramakrishna Paramahansa's meditative cross-dressing as a means to experience the transcendental non-duality combined with a reformist consciousness challenging the irrationalities and unscientific attitudes of Bengali Hindus within the wider project of reformation to counter colonial oppression. Similarly, sociologist Ashish Nandy has proposed a reading of androgyny with reference to Mahatma Gandhi, whose political undertakings merit little discussion (Nandy cited in Pande 2004: 46). Within the context of India then, transvestism as indeed any form of alternate sexuality surfaces at once as a political gesture of self-expression against socially sanctioned norms, as well as a spiritual modality.

In the light of this it is important to note that when Kulkarni and Pandey cross-dress in the film, they adopt conventional dress codes linked to the cultural landscapes and performance practices particular to it. Pandey is situated clearly in a historically and culturally specific performance tradition that taps into Indian spiritual discourses. In her comprehensive study of the androgynous figure in Indian art, Alka Pande has asserted that in the Indological texts and context, the image of the *ardhanarishvara* (half-man/half-woman) and other forms of gender-bending including cross-dressing are more of a philosophical and spiritual construct, rather than principally forms of social or a cultural expression. In her view, 'the very harmony, resolution, and balance of the universe, in union' rests at the heart of androgyny and any form of gender-bending (2004: 41). Besides specific cultural coda pertaining to dress and make-up, Pandey's body is culturally defined further through a fine vocabulary of very sculpturesque postures, and graceful and curvaceous gestures and movements that resonate with the subtle and sophisticated codes closer to classical dance and folk performance, rather than the loud and exhibitionist, innuendoes encountered earlier in the film through the character of the city-based pimp who embodies her position not as an aesthetician trained in the art of sex, but as a trader in sex.

This situation in Pandey's body of historicised aesthetic imperatives serves more than the claim of cultural specificity. This identification of cross-dressing with classical and folk coda is not simply imitative for lack of alternatives, but it is a parodic instance that, for Butler, involves 'gender-subversion'. Butler has argued that the 'cultural practices of drag, cross-dressing and the sexual stylisation of butch/feminine identities' involve the parodic modality (1999b: 363). Such parodying, she says, is not 'an uncritical appropriation of sex-role stereotyping from within the practice of heterosexuality', but it is more complex:

> it is a production which, in effect – that is in its effect – postures an imitation. This perpetual displacement constitutes a fluidity of identities that suggests an openness to resignification and recontextualization; parodic proliferation deprives hegemonic culture and its critics of the claim to naturalized or essentialist gender identities. Although the gender meanings taken up in these parodic styles are clearly part of the hegemonic, misogynist culture, they are nevertheless denaturalized and mobilized through their parodic recontextualization. (Butler 1999b: 364)

Pandey and Kulkarni's switching of gender roles by using the hegemonic coda is both critical and interventionist in that it formulates as a gesture of resistance against the summarily reductionist appropriation of India's secular and esoteric aesthetic and cultural practices within the matrix of a restrictive discourse on the nation as a cultural category. There are further implications of cross-dressing within a wider socio-historical and cultural context. The film does not resolve cross-dressing as either innate or fully circumstantial or socially constructed. Pandey dresses as a woman, which in his words is because: 'One should be on the outside what one *feels* from the inside', alluding to cross-dressing as an expression linked to a felt condition – not as an innate or essential sense of gender, but in terms of a radical departure from social convention. Kulkarni, on the other hand, has been compelled by social circumstance to assume a male identity that she steadily comes to accept and perform with ease. Without presenting a determined take on either position, the film lends necessary complexity into the understanding of gender as exceeding genital identification. According to Stephen Whittle many transgendered subjects in confronting the dualisms of gender have been caught in:

> a process of self-apologia and attempted explanation which caused self-identified transsexuals to adopt the stance of being a 'woman trapped inside a man's body' (or vice a versa) [...] It was as if, without genital reconstruction, personal gender-roles could not be changed, and even with it, that reconstruction provided the point of change. (Whittle 1996: 204)

The film indicates how both genders co-mingle and interact in the subject such that gender-based identification surfaces as not biologically determined, total or foreclosed. This is useful in challenging established gender hierarchies particularly within the rural and feudal context wherein gender and other hierarchical categorisations such as caste are represented in terms of the convergence on the body of agents such as destiny and *karma*. Towards the end of the film, both subjects switch back to their conventional gender roles when they determine they are in love and Kulkarni insists on assuming the feminine position with Pandey performing as a man in the relationship. This fluidity and gender migration crucially prevents transgender from being understood as the biologically 'defective' condition that the nationalist imagination tends to posit it as.

II. ANTHROPOLOGICAL AND IDEOLOGICAL RELEVANCE

Aijaz Ahmad has observed that particularly in a third world and post-colonial context, when 'nationalism' is yoked together with the category of 'culture', a specific form of 'cultural nationalism' emerges that resonates with the problematic category of 'tradition'. In this equation the tradition/modernity binary of the modernisation theorists gets simply 'inverted in an indigenist direction' such that the category of 'tradition' is overemphasised as 'always better than modernity' (1992: 8). Ahmad argues that this risks opening up a space for defence of the most 'obscurantist positions' including ahistorical, essentialised and idealised practices and worldviews all in the name of 'cultural nationalism' – a risk numerous scholars and commentators across disciplines from the Indian subcontinent have raised (1992: 9 – see also Sen 2005). According to Ahmad, the risk is heightened because according to him culture generally and the literary/aesthetic realm in particular, are situated at great remove from the economy and therefore, among all the superstructures, they are most easily available for 'idealisation and theoretical slippage' (Ahmad 1992: 9). While *Daayara*'s value is that it has styled and embedded in the transvestite clearly historicised and culturally specific imperatives that in some measure evoke tradition through the aesthetic and spiritual idioms; it has at the same time confronted and contained any risk of perpetuating a summarily reductionist or idealised notion of indigenism.

The film mobilises a grassroots, folk consciousness in the transvestite. If we are to attend the film as a historical draft, there arise specific problems surrounding evocation of such a consciousness within the post-colonial context. Spivak (1997) has raised and articulated most clearly the problematic of historiography surrounding the subaltern (here the rural, low caste, folk and marginal subjects) in terms of the absence of subaltern agency and memory pertaining to the past, as well as the particular 'consciousness-effect' arising from the disciplinary training of the historian, who more often than not is an outsider of certain privilege. With respect to cinema, the historiographic prerogative is most squarely situated in the director, here Amol Palekar, and, more crucially, the scriptwriter (in this case the English author, Timeri N. Murari). Palekar has been an influential figure in Marathi, experimental and street theatre. He is a fine actor most remembered for his roles in middle-class comedies. He has directed critical films such as the Oscar nominated, *Paheli/The Riddle* (2005). Murari is an English writer whose works complicate the category of the nation. Together they have devised in *Daayara* a construction that commands an anthropological richness whereby the rural landscape in which the film is set is attended with precision as a historico-social and cultural construct responsive to wider movements linked to the nation. The rural is consequently not posited as a repository of *pure* indigenous traditions or knowledges – and thus it is not valorised. The rural is problematised. The principal level through which this occurs in *Daayara* is through the film's consistent references to technologies through which narrative transactions materialise. These include highways, railways, automobiles and communications technologies that within a post-independence and specifically developmental context are posited in assertive and progressivist terms. By showing these technologies as penetrating rural areas the film contemporises the Indian village landscape and here too the film is not too liberal setting up a primitivist nostalgia for the rural as past, unitarily sacrificed at the altar of modernity.

The film provides a critical reflection by revealing the complicity of rural masses in the exchange with modern influences such as technology, that is itself critiqued and inverted as 'progressive'. There are two key instances in the film when technology as implicated in a national, progressive discourse is rendered unstable. First, in the opening sequence when Kulkarni is kidnapped she is seen driven off in an Ambassador car. The Ambassador is produced by one of the early public-sector undertakings, Hindustan Motors, set up after India's independence. It is modelled on the Morris Oxford of the UK-based Morris Motor Company. It is implicitly linked to the nation's celebratory discourse of technology as progress with its nascent roots in Nehruvian politics. The kidnapping itself indexes the now widely established rural-to-urban sex-trafficking nexus proliferating across India including her borders thus registering the spiralling divide between rural and urban India that challenges the nation as a homogenous and unified entity. The implication of the Ambassador car in sex-related crime subverts any coherent sentiment in the ideal terms of the nation pertaining to law, coherence and unity.

The second instance is more disturbing. Towards the middle of the film, Pandey is seen performing a folk song amidst a rural crowd. As he finishes, the crowds demand him to perform to a lascivious Bollywood film song that had caused much controversy with the Indian Censor Board at the time of the film's release.[5] An audio cassette with the particular song is seen inserted into a portable tape recorder and without a sleight of resistance, Pandey breaks into pronounced movements and innuendos so linked to Bollywood's particular exhibitionist and consumerist idiom of song and dance. Besides referencing and critiquing Bollywood, this instance more importantly comments on the rural folk who surface as not 'infantile' or 'noble', unable to comprehend or in any way resist outside, urban influences. They are not presented as defending their little cultures; instead they emerge as absorbing quite selectively, 'modernising' and 'urban' influences in all their consumerist splendour. This contrasts with the cultural finesse that characterises Pandey's body as a folk performer and it ties in neatly with the film's opening when we see Pandey's teacher stating to the woman performer joining his troupe that the conservative village folk are no longer open to cross-dressing in *gotipua*. Conservatism surfaces as the corollary of modernisation. The context is clearly contemporary – the folk landscape is not being altered through a one-way flow of rampant or imposed modernisation that the globalisation critics would hold, but as the film reveals through the complicity of the rural folk in that process. This complicity is crucial as it contains the valorisation and romanticisation of the rural consciousness and landscape that do not surface as coherent, unified or stable. While Pandey does perform on popular demand to the Bollywood number, his gestures reveal he is more composed than to be disturbed or challenged by this demand on behalf of the rural audience. The complicity of the rural masses in the appropriations of technology in ways that contrast in sophistication to Pandey's holistic worldview, serves to remove him further from society, thus contextualising his social ostracisation and exclusion.

III. IMPLICATIONS OF VISUALISING THE TRANSVESTITE BODY THROUGH LONG SHOT

In *Daayara*, the transvestite's spiritual posture is grounded in an interrogation of all social conventions, norms and worldviews. Pandey is a fully marginalised body within the landscape that he is located in. While the film reflects the rural landscape in critical contemporary terms as discussed above, it nevertheless constructs a particular and contrasting equation for the transvestite body in terms of its relations with the landscape. Pandey exudes a close experience of nature and her elements. This is evident particularly when at one instance in the film while he and Kulkarni are meandering through the countryside and Kulkarni expresses as a 'need' her desire for a home Pandey retorts probing why the vast sky and the endless earth could not constitute as home. Pandey's spiritual agency informs his relation with the habitat that is grounded in a sense of ecological reverence. The film's mise-en-scene emulates and complements this.

Daayara is set in the lush and fertile backdrop of rural, coastal east India. This landscape has been the backdrop to some of the finest Indian cinema drawing masters such as Jean Renoir, Satyajit Ray, Ritwik Ghatak and Kumar Shahani. The region is home to two Indian states, West Bengal and Orissa (*Daayara* is set in the latter). In terms of mise-en-scene, two motivations underpin the film's treatment of the rural backdrop. In keeping with the contemporaneous take on the rural landscape, the key crises and tensions are positioned to unfold at sites linked to modernising and urban forces. At these instances, the framed space deploys the juxtaposition of modern technology and the lush green backdrop within the shot constituting a montage-effect based on 'critical juxtaposition' in which juxtaposition is culturally and historically specific and implies a wider social critique within the stated context.[6]

When Pandey is alone, however, he is usually seen in a densely forested, predominantly green background. These shots are framed such that they deploy distance from his body. They are either long or extreme long shots. In the extreme long shots his body is accommodated fully. These shots are wide-angle and they serve in integrating Pandey's body with the landscape. This complements his holistic and ecological approach towards nature. Such use of the long shot reverses conventional theoretical discussion surrounding its usage in third cinema. Within film studies the long shot has often been posited as a characteristic of third cinema, in terms of accommodating the communal collective, which is held as a necessary feature in the social experience of peoples outside Europe and North America (Wayne 2001). In *Daayara*, the long shot is deployed for Pandey who is an ostracised and marginalised subject, fully excluded and positioned outside any communal collective. Further, unlike the conventional usage of the long shot within mainstream fiction and documentary for contextualising action and characters in space, in *Daayara*, the long shot in fact extracts and abstracts Pandey's body from the wider context of the village as a social backdrop and his body surfaces as melding with the green backdrop. This fractures and effects a disparity in the rural landscape. A distinction, of the kind Deleuze and Guattari propose with respect to 'smooth' and 'striated' spaces, surfaces (1987: 474–500). The village, a site of social gathering emerges as striated, a space that is 'heavily coded with normative boundaries' wherein movement produces a tightly defined identity, while the lush and untamed forest backdrops in which Pandey is filmed alone, make for a smooth space, one that is nomadic, and that has 'no normative significance' (Shapiro 1999: 162).

When seen in long shot, Pandey is usually wandering, singing his folk compositions. These images link and make references to the works of many masters who filmed in this region. The extreme long shot where his body is seen from a distance reminds of Renoir's impressionist colour compositions in terms of the mise-en-scene for *Le Fleuve/The River* (1951). Pandey's wandering and singing itself remind of Bangladeshi filmmaker, Tanvir Mokammel's documentary, *Achin Paki/The Unknown Bard* (1996), about the Baul singer. Most strikingly *Daayara*'s mise-en-scene is reminiscent of Kumar Shahani's acclaimed documentary surrounding the Odissi maestro, Guru Kelucharan Mohapatra, *Bhavantaran* (1996). In *Bhavantaran*, Shahani consistently filmed Guru Kelucharan's body while in performance from a distance, in exterior locations. The long shot fully accommodated the dancer's body such that intricate movements in all parts of his body could be experienced at once. Guru Kelucharan's body emerges as tightly linked with the landscape as some of his gestures are experientially co-extensive with the landscape. Besides melding the body with the landscape, in both *Bhavataran* and *Daayara*, the long shot by virtue of its distance complements the performer's sexual ambiguity. Both Pandey's, and Guru Kelucharan's bodies appear as bearing an elegant and scuplturesque androgynous edge whose pleasure exceeds vision.

This is a subtle approach that effects our relationship as viewers to the film and the performer's body particularly. The long shot frames our relationship resisting voyeuristic probing or objectification of the body. Pandey conducts his body firmly, standing erect and walking tall. Through the long shot and its resultant ambiguity his body appears as dangerously beautiful and spectacular. The distancing effect of the long shot attributes a disparity and dignity to the audience's eliciting relation with the performer's body and in this measure it amounts to an intervention in approaching the transvestite body not as taboo but as an aesthetic category in its own right.

IV. CONCLUSION

Daayara is a complex work. Within the cinema context of India, it does not fit into a purely oppositional category such as conventional Indian documentary espousing socially relevant causes in a rather ventriloquist and non-self-reflexive gesture; or the formally experimental cinema that critiques dominant ideology through a complex aesthetic. The film is however, clearly, anti-nationalist, critiquing nationalist hegemony by bringing to the centre the marginalised and socially ostracised figure of the transvestite. It problematises gender disparity and the accompanying stereotypes that percolate the dominant nationalist imagination and mainstream cinema that implicitly emphasise heterosexuality and imbibe, in rather simplistic and superficial terms, archaic and feudal social hierarchies between the genders.

By privileging the male body as the primary site for cross-dressing and thus transgression of socially normative behaviour, the film subverts dominant imaginations surrounding the male body and subjectivity. Within a nationalist imagination the male body has been conventionally projected with the desire of technological and industrial mobility coloured with a rationalist and progressivist take, while the female subject is summarily and in opposing terms considered as eco-friendly, irrational and infantile, and in that way easily on hand for transgressive slippage. *Daayara* completely reverses both projections and in doing so it disassembles gender stereotypes and more broadly, renders unstable the notion of gender as a determined and foreclosed biological category as emphasised through an institutionalised national ideology. The film problematises the naturalisation effect underpinning the construction of gender, sexuality, love and desire within the dominant national imagination and through that it muddies the conventional mechanisms for the institution and performance of desire. There is a process of denaturalisation in effect here.

Denaturalisation is the key modality in the context of cross-dressing wherein the characters of the film assume very conventional and heterosexual codes of dress. The film's mise-en-scene deploying the juxtaposition between rural and urban imperatives alongside the framing of the transvestite body through the long shot serve in fully contextualising the body socio-historically and at the same time lend to it necessary ambiguity that resists objectification of the body. The framing of the body through the long shot complements the denaturalisation effect underpinning cross-dressing and unpacks the performance of desire. The projection of desire on the body in *Daayara* is not in terms of an innate or essential tendency. Rather the gender fluidity in *Daayara* liberates desire from an essential or fetish link with body parts. This process can be better understood through Butler's conception of *performance* and the construction of desire:

> 'becoming' a gender is a laborious process of becoming naturalized, which requires a differentiation of bodily pleasures and parts on the basis of gendered meanings. Pleasures are said to reside in the penis, the vagina, and the breasts or to emanate from them, but such descriptions correspond to a body which has already been constructed or naturalized as gender-specific. In other words, some parts of the body become conceivable foci of pleasure precisely because they correspond to a normative ideal of a gender-specific body. (1999a: 89–90)

Daayara's muddying of the conventions and norms surrounding desire within the national context is not so much a modality of confusion per se, as it is a radical process of confronting the policing framework through which desire and its performance through body parts is legitimated ideologically, and then re-performed and affirmed through institutionalised cinema practices such as those of Bollywood.

Towards the close of the film Kulkarni faces ostracisation and ridicule when she returns to her village where her fidelity is questioned by her father and fiancé. This compels her to leave the village and reunite with Pandey. As they decide to head to a new destination to start life afresh, Kulkarni's rapists once again attack her and in the process Pandey gets stabbed. What is most crucial in the last exchange between Pandey and Kulkarni is Pandey's insistence to die dressed as a woman. In a sense this closing is dystopic for the transvestite eventually succumbs. His death ratifies the force and predominance of patriarchal and social conservatism that manifests variously through the exclusion and social ostracisation of non-male subjects (women and third gender subjects such as transvestites, androgyns and homosexuals), all of whom face very specific social exclusionary attitudes. Though dystopic, the union that is indicated through Kulkarni's acceptance of Pandey irrespective of gender is crucial, for it stands in for the unity of the socially and historically marginalised, despite the disparities of their individual subject positions and the exclusionary and divisive treatments linked to them. This resists divisiveness and hierarchisation of the variously marginal and ostracised social bodies.

Lastly, *Daayara* usefully complicates the polarities of whether gender is a constructed category or a biologically determined, essential one. The film does not have a clear take on either position but sets forth both possibilities. Pandey cross-dresses as a mode of self-expression, while Kulkarni has been compelled by her particular circumstances to cross-dress as a man. This lends necessary complexity to the essentialist/constructionist dialectic and, more importantly, gender surfaces as not a foreclosed and ahistoricised category. In this way, the conventions for its social and cinematic representation are subverted.

NOTES

1 The interest in Bollywood, and 'third' cinemas generally is a response towards the cultural opacities in film scholarship and exhibition networks (Stam 2002: 662–63). It also overlaps with rising academic interest and research into diasporic viewing practices and their impacts on Bollywood aesthetically and in terms of distribution.

2 By modality I refer to the nexus of history, ideology and aesthetic with respect to cultural practice generally.

3 The characters are not given a name in the film. For the purposes of this chapter I will refer to each character by the relevant actor's surname: Pandey as the transvestite and Kulkarni as the village woman.

4 Though the chapter focuses on the transvestite figure, it is more broadly concerned with the transgendered body – including, as Janice Raymond defines them, 'pre-operative and post-operative transsexuals, transvestites, drag queens, cross-dressers, gays and lesbians interpreted as "transgressing" gender-roles' (Raymond 1996: 215).

5 I am referring to the Bollywood film *Khalnayak/The Villain* (dir. Subhash Ghai, 1993).

6 The term 'critical juxtaposition' was first proposed in anthropology by George Marcus. He argued that critical juxtapositions of multiple spatialities, temporalities, voices, narratives and foci constitute a 'modernist ethnography' that is not descriptive of culture as 'other', but critical and analytical (see Naficy 2001: 28). Marcus's discussion of critical juxtaposition was derived from cinema particularly Sergei Eisenstein's montage theories.

Part 2

Feeling the Body: Dissections, Textures and Close-ups

7

Tran Anh Hung's Body Poetry

Robert Davis and Tim Maloney

Vietnamese director Tran Anh Hung's three films to date – *Mùi dud u xanh/The Scent of Green Papaya* (1993), *Xich Lo/Cyclo* (1995), and *À la verticale de l'été/ Vertical Ray of the Sun* (2000) – are unusually fixated on the male body.[1] Tran's films emphasise the male body as a physical object, with its attendant material properties. The buoyancy of bodies suspended in *À la verticale de l'été*'s lake and The Poet's bloody nose, 'leaking' throughout *Xich Lo*, direct attention to the bio-physical properties of Tran's actors' bodies. Bodies in *Xich Lo* are regularly treated as canvases: The Madam's retarded teenage son paints his arms, chest and head yellow; and in the film's penultimate sequence, the protagonist, high on some unidentified volatile liquid, transforms himself into a modern art mixed-media masterpiece using acrylics, a plastic bag, flickering light and a goldfish.

Tran's camera selects curious angles, focus points and aperture settings on his male subjects: a three-stop overexposure of a naturalist as he steps towards a Jurassic era lake; a foreground focus point, on the sole of the protagonist's shoe, while he naps; a startling angle, exactly perpendicular to the musculature of a young man's exercising back; another dorsal view, of a boy fishing off a boat; a mobile, extreme high angle, relentless tracking shot as a pimp murders one of his clients; an overhead shot of the cyclo driver and his grandfather that conveys no plot information, but rather, the tops of their heads, the boy's bare shoulders, and the sweeping movement of their hands; to mention but a few examples. But unlike most narrative filmmakers, for whom the body is either a vehicle for characterisation or a component of lurid pleasures – dismemberment in the horror film, display in the pornographic – Tran seems interested both in the texture of the body and its subtle movements and in its capacity to function as a component in an overall filmic *poesis*. That Tran's poetry, like Brakhage's and Bresson's, for example, is often rhythmic is evidenced by his actors' short, metrical, monotone whispers, his films' dreamlike dissolves and abrupt jolts, and their sudden overexposures. But it is Tran's dissection on the male body and his manipulation of it as a rhythmic device that seems *sui generis* and subtly effective.

I. TRAN'S MALE BODIES AND THEORY

Tran's fixation on the structure and texture of bodies is one that current critical theory will find difficult to accommodate, since this emphasis rarely has to do with his characters' sexuality or desire. Indeed, the psychoanalytical approach that has dominated film studies seems often less interested in what is actually on screen – including characters, their bodies, and their bodies' disposition in the overall mise-en-scene – than in (unverifiable speculation about) the subjective experience of the spectator. Typical of this Lacanian method is what Steven Shaviro calls 'The Metz/Mulvey Model'. Responding to Mulvey's 'Visual Pleasure and Narrative Cinema' in his *The Cinematic Body*, Shaviro rejects what he sees as that model's 'phobic construct' (1993: 14–15), according to which visual pleasure is the bearer of unhealthy ideologies and must be girded against. Though Shaviro systematically dismantles this psychoanalytical approach to film criticism and seeks, in its place, to 'articulate a subversive micro-politics of postmodern cinema' (1993: 24), he retools Bataille, Foucault and Deleuze but, in the end, continues to regard cinematic spectatorship as his primary focus. Borrowing from Studlar (1984), Shaviro seeks to establish spectatorship as a masochistic relationship in which the viewer succumbs to the aggressive mastery of the cinematic presentation. But this is merely switching one set of references (Mulvey's Freud and Lacan) for another (Shaviro's Bataille et al.). Shaviro still positions a metaphysics – rather than a scientific analysis of seeing based on visual perception, anthropology or evolutionary biology – as the key component of film spectatorship. Above all he sets spectatorship as the cornerstone of film studies. Nowhere in this approach is there a method appropriate to the analysis of bodies as elements in a poetic system, as objects the texture and character of which are used for expressive effect.

Peter Lehman (1993) argues that Mulvey's model can accommodate a wider range of male sexualities. Unlike Shaviro, Lehman accepts Mulvey's ideas about the male glance and the female presentation for the glance, but sees in this heterosexualised process a clear definition of the woman (as object, as lover, as desired) but no clear definition of the man. He is the desiring one, the one who acts and who glances, a stand-in for the spectator, but there is, according to Lehman, no representation of his sexuality. Men have 'kept themselves out of the glare' (1993: 6), he writes in his introduction, 'escaping from the relentless activity of sexual definitions'. In dominant narrative cinema, for example, we rarely see men exhibiting themselves for other men, and when they do, Lehman argues, it is considered intolerable. Thus, politically, for Lehman, all (and especially alternative) representations of male sexuality are 'radical'. In an effort to bring some of these depictions to light, his book is replete with chapters devoted to specific and detailed depictions of male sexualities across media. Though Lehman's work is more attentive to the on-screen construction of images of male bodies – his analysis of Mulvey's essay considers the 'system of glances' that is key to her work – his approach to such images is marked by his specific political aims and, as such, is difficult to apply to Tran's films. Tran's male bodies are neither sexual nor sexualised, but sensual. Their representations are not overtly constructed for desire, and yet corporeality, the physicality of the body is the primary emphasis.

In 'Against Interpretation' Susan Sontag suggests a different starting point for film criticism. She first claims that 'the earliest *experience* of art must have been that it was incantatory, magical' (1966a: 3) and then reviews the history of art criticism in the West: Aristotle counters Plato's attack on art as mere *mimesis* by asserting art has a therapeutic value, a usefulness; and subsequent defences imagine art as statements of intent which require translation or interpretation ('What artwork X is really saying is'). For Sontag, these justifications are tantamount to the subsuming of art under thought, the transformation of art into intellectual property, the voiding of art's energy and sensuality, what she calls 'the revenge of the intellect upon art' (1966a: 7). Rejecting both the Marxist-psychoanalytical and the literary critical reduction of art to secret meanings and didactic lessons, Sontag instead advocates a senses-based *erotics* of art, a criticism focused on a work's *surface* and designed to teach us 'to *see* more, *hear* more, to *feel* more' and 'to make works of art – and by analogy, our own experience – more, rather than less real for us' (1966a: 14, emphasis in original). According to Sontag, proponents of this approach might work to 'supply a really accurate, sharp, loving description of the appearance of a work of art' (1966a: 13) or to 'dissolve considerations of content into those of form' (1966a: 12). They would work to 'show *how* (a work of art) *is what it is*, even *that it is what it is*, rather than to show *what it means*' (1966a: 14, emphasis original).

This kind of analysis seems particularly well-suited to the films of Resnais, Godard or Tran Anh Hung, whose surface is *prima facie* sensual.[2] Since Tran himself has asserted his intention in making films is 'to put pure emotion on the screen' (Sklar 2001: 69), to attempt a Sontagian erotics might be a methodologically secure starting point from which further discussion may be fruitful. To consider the male body as a poetic component of visual art, then, is first of all to see it outside the semiotic confines of signifier and signified, to disregard, at least at first, whether or how it has been constructed for the viewer's consumption, and to table the social implications it and its *being seen* may have on viewers. For to concentrate on these matters is too often to ignore the primary experience of the body in some films.

If a Tran Anh Hung film is a particularly sensory experience, the poetic modes and physical manifestations of this sensory experience – both the specificity and aesthetics of each body shown and the precise way in which it is shown, in other words, its erotic qualities – should shape our initial approach to his films. Therefore, rather than weigh the psycho-social meaning of Tran's fixation with the male body, we will emphasise, in a descriptive analysis of four scenes, how he uses it as part of an erotic poetic system. Our aim, then, is to isolate the Sontagian *what* and *how* of the male body in Tran's films, the results of which may then serve as a prolegomenon to further analysis.

II. THE PLASTIC BODY

Already in Tran's first film, *Mùi dud u xanh*, there were signs of the director's interest in the potential plasticity of male bodies. There, in an early scene in the pre-teen brothers' bedroom, Tran frames the boys' static, oddly arranged bodies for maximum aesthetic effect. The younger brother, on his back, is draped over his bed, his bare feet pinned, somewhat absurdly, above his torso to the wall in the background, one bare arm flopped towards the camera and the ground. The older brother is precariously balanced on the window sill, knees to his chest, buttocks at his heels. Tran places the camera perfectly perpendicular to the older boy's back, an angle which makes him look like a mere torso-and-head, perched on a ledge. In Tran's second film, *Xich Lo*, the poetry of corporal pliability becomes more pronounced. One narrative hinge-point concerns The Madam's mentally-impaired teenage son, who is prone to squat half-naked, his head twisted ninety degrees and tilted up, neck stretched, fledgling-like, to the sky. In this awkward position, the boy mechanically opens and closes his mouth, valve-like, in imitation of a fish. Tran emphasises the sculptural qualities of the boy's unusually disposed body and the motoric quality of his mouth by shooting him, often, from an extreme high angle. Tran's third film, *À la verticale de l'été*, opens with a shot of young Hai, an aspiring actor, asleep on his bedsheets. He rolls over to silence his alarm clock, and, a perfectly placed shaft of morning light spilling across his exposed *pectoralis major* and underarm, stretches himself awake. A series of squats, chin-ups and crunches follows. Tran's camera positions (both frontal and dorsal on the young man's muscular body) and his cuts between maximally contrasting callisthenic positions (the actor's elbows crunched towards his knees in shot A, then, suddenly, arms outstretched in shot B) encourage audiences to focus on the precise positioning and movement of Hai's limbs, to feel the elasticity of the exercising male body.

The body's role in Tran's visual poetry is particularly evident in the first of the examples that we are about to discuss. Midway through *À la verticale de l'été*, Kiên (Tran Manh Cuong), a writer who cannot seem to finish his first novel, has an opportunity to cheat on his wife during a research retreat to Ho Chi Min City. A beautiful young woman he meets on the plane has slipped him her hotel's card on the back of which she has handwritten, in lipstick, '23:30 324'. In the hotel corridor outside the door to room 324, Kiên cautiously inspects the hallway for any witnesses to his impending infidelity, checks his watch and then gently knocks three times. When he gets no response, he knocks again. This time, on the third tap, the door gives way an inch or so, clearly unlocked. Kiên looks left, then slowly pushes the door open. When he hears the sound of an elevator door open down the corridor, Kiên quickly disappears into the room.

Tran, his production designer Benoît Barouh, cinematographer Li Pin-bing and editor Mario Battistel have carefully constructed this pivotal scene in which Kiên decides to meet the mysterious woman. The hotel hallway's warm monochrome – its deep red-orange wood panelling and matching patterned carpeting, its high tone orange lampshades, and the peculiar vibrant orange of the three numerals on the plot-crucial door – conspicuously contrasts with the cool, bluish interiors, of the women's bedrooms which precede and follow this scene. The urgency of Kiên's decision-making as the elevator arrives is reflected in some quick-cutting for the scene's last narrative beat. And the camera's rendition of space suggests a mathematically precise dissection of the location. There are four mechanically symmetrical, one-point perspective deep space shots down the length of the hallway and a fifth in which that deep space is thrown out of focus in the background, the foreground of which features Kiên's stark flat profile.[3]

The scene's surface distinctiveness, however, derives especially from the director's idiosyncratic disposition and framing of Tran Manh Cuong. Indeed, the scene opens on the unnatural, gravity-defying curve of the actor's bent body (see Figure 9), completely motionless for two long seconds. This stance is particularly curious from a narrative point-of-view in that it puts the writer in no better position to spot unwanted witnesses down that deep space hallway than had he

Figure 9: Tran Manh Cuong in *À la verticale de l'été*. Les Productions Lazennec. Paris.

stood upright. Rather, the ludicrously arced body draws attention to itself as *ludicrously arced*, as plastic. And the actor's bowed body is further emphasised, graphically, in contrast to the visual rhythm of the series of straight vertical lines regularly disposed left to right across the frame. Both *what* it is (a plastic body) and *how* it is what it is (an arced body encased in a straight, vertical framework), its Sontagian erotics, contribute to the scene's affective impact.

Furthermore, this scene begins, unusually, *in medias res*, the actor's body *already* bent. Typically, an editor would cut right *before* – and therefore show the entirety of – a character-enhancing action like Kiên's paranoid checking whether someone is watching him as he contemplates knocking on the hotel room door of a woman not his wife. This conventional editorial strategy, called 'cutting on action', is meant to facilitate the flow of the drama, to smooth the transition between scenes. Tran and Battistel's decision to start the scene on the actor's static, bowed body instead *freezes* the film for a moment and further emphasises the actor's fixed, sculpted body. The human body is momentarily transfigured; it becomes an object of visual attention, an anomaly in the film's visual rhythm, a poetic element, suspended, temporally as well as spatially, in the composition.

But the scene's longest and most emotionally intense shot – in which Kiên stands in front of the door, knocks three times, waits, and then knocks again – evidences even more powerfully Tran's drawing attention away from narrative concerns and onto surface erotics, concerns associated especially with his actor's body. This shot's crucial plot point, its narrative 'reveal', is the room number: 324. But that number is in neither the brightest nor the sharpest region of the frame (see

Figure 10: Tran Manh Cuong in *À la verticale de l'été.* Les Productions Lazennec. Paris.

Figure 10). The most strongly lit is a carefully circumscribed area, significantly below the underexposed orange '324', where Tran Manh Cuong delicately knocks on the door, underhanded, with his right knuckles, palm towards camera, and later pushes open the door with the three central fingertips of his right hand. Li's 'soft' fluorescent lighting matches the gentleness the actor's hand gestures conveys. But the intensity of the light (a snooted 'spot') causes the hand to overexpose two stops each time it penetrates the small lighted area.[4]

Even more surprising, Tran and Li focus their camera's lens not on the plot-central information of the room number but, significantly and idiosyncratically, on the back of Tran Manh Cuong's neck! Directing attention to that surface detail at a moment when the viewer might expect to be shown, for instance, the actor's facial expression, his reaction to his current narrative dilemma, only increases suspense and creates a dynamic tension among the story, the lighting and the lens' focus-point. And because the composition's visual weight (the hand's overexposure, the neck's sharpness) favours the actor's body, Tran has made this corporal locus the site of these various tensions.[5]

III. THE RHYTHMIC BODY

Tran's visual poetry, like many other auteurs', is principally rhythmic, but what sets Tran's work apart is his use of the human body as a primary rhythmic device. Talking about his first feature, *Mùi dud u xanh*, Tran claims what was important for him was

> to create a specific rhythm, to find the very movement of the Vietnamese soul. [...] What I think I have understood about the Vietnamese people is that they don't have to talk to one another in a rational way in order to communicate. Rather there is this notion that they kind of mentally impregnate or penetrate one another. They understand things without being precise, without using words. (Cross 1993: 36)[6]

Tran explicitly cites Bresson (whose emphasis on the body's physicality has been discussed in detail elsewhere), and Bresson's direction of actors as an influence.[7] For Tran, the difference between Bresson's work and his own is inherent in their tones, their erotics: his precursor's films were 'monochromatic'; his own, 'enormously sensual' (Cross 1993: 35).

Tran's fixation on and manipulation of the body as a sensual rhythmic device is evidenced in the second of our examples: the hypnotic scene, fifteen minutes into *À la verticale de l'été*, in which each of seven family members pays his or her respects before the family altar. Everything seen and heard in this scene suggests that visceral and poetic rather than intellectual or psychoanalytic aims, Tran's desire to project 'pure emotion' onto the screen, lie behind his application of music, editing, composition and performance.[8] In the first shot, for example, incense wafts up through the frame. The shot is front focused, drawing attention not to the inscription in the middle ground but to a foreground plane of strands of ephemeral blue-gray smoke snaking up the frame's height. In the next shot, cinematographer Li Pin-bing lights not the deceased mother's photograph but the lily buds and the candle positioned in front of it. Composer Tôn-Thât Tiêt's halting, atonal harp over these and the next six shots unifies them and evokes a drifting daydream. Another, visual, music results from the series of dissolves between the seven shots of supplicants at the altar. And each of these dissolves has its own rhythm. The score and dissolves, however, function here as a foundation against which the rhythmic particularities of each performer's idiosyncratic gestures can, by contrast, be felt. Tran's fixation with these actor's bodies and their rhythms is indicated by the way he shoots them engaged in the ritualised movement which constitutes the bulk of the scene. Shots three through nine are all taken from a single static camera position. This set-up captures the exact same medium-wide shot of each family member's moment at the shrine. Dissolves from shot to shot cause the actors to appear and disappear frame left in front of a slightly overexposed top-lit table, centred, laid out with food and drink offerings. Each actor's peculiar rhythm, a rhythm determined by the speed, scale and duration of three ritualised hand movements, contributes to a body-based visual poetry. Suong stands perfectly still before the altar for three long seconds then bows; Quôc, by contrast, bows as soon as he appears. Quôc, Khan and Kiên lower only their heads; Hai, his head and shoulders. Hai's hand gestures are slowest;

Liên's, very quick. Suong's are broad, large-scale hand gestures; Khan's, minimalist; and each of Hai's three gestures is distinct in depth. Khan holds her hands farther from her body than her older siblings do, and her three movements vary in tempo. Unlike the others, Kiên clenches his clasped fists.

Taking seriously a scene in which physical poetry dominates the *what* and the *how* means resisting the temptation to assign meaning to the individuation of the characters' performances. It is not that Suong's initial immobility and then her hurried gesticulations suggest 'a troubled relationship with her mother' or 'a reluctant reconciliation'. For while, to be sure, in the post-Stanislavskian world, the multiplicity of role preparation strategies is so vast that it is likely some actors and directors do develop psychological profiles which may be reflected in the details of physical actions, the hypothetical relevance of such things here palls before the scene's obvious Sontagian *surface* concern with the interplay of rhythmic components, including each actor's body.[9]

IV. THE BODY IN A TRANCE

Our third example, perhaps the most strikingly designed scene in *Xich Lo*, comes forty-five minutes into the film. In an abandoned loft on a busy street, the young cyclo driver (Le Van Loc) expresses qualms about carrying out another assignment for the gang whose leader, The Poet (Tony Leung), is a pimp for whom the cyclo driver's sister (Tran Nu Yên-Khê) has fallen. After The Poet's subordinates force-feed the boy a gasoline-laced cocktail, he vomits his noodles onto the floor. The Poet squats down next to the young protagonist and caresses the back of his head. A quiet male voice begins to recite a poem in short, chopped phrases.

Nameless river,
I was born sobbing.
Blue sky, vast earth,
Black stream water,
I grow with the months, the years,
With no one to watch over me.

Nameless is man.
Nameless is the river.
Colorless the flower.
Perfume without a voice.

O, River! O, Passerby!
In the cycle of the months, the years,

I cannot forget my debt to my roots.
And I wander through worlds
Towards my land.

Over the recitation, Tran and his cinematographer Benoit Delhomme offer bizarre 'living portraits' of first The Poet and The Sister and then nine Vietnamese children, all posed on a rocky rooftop overlooking some shanties. The first of these shots startles in contrast to what preceded. Delhomme's hand-held camera, which had been free-floating through the abandoned loft's desaturated blue-gray concrete, finding soft close-ups of Leung's hands and face, Le's jet black hair, and wisps of smoke from the cigarette in Leung's quivering hand, is unexpectedly replaced by the high-contrast, warm-hued roof's fixed camera, slightly high angle. Each of the eleven shots of the exterior scene is then taken from this single static position.

The first two portraits show Leung and Tran, first in a medium shot, then in a medium close-up. Both are frontal, and so, clearly 'composed' rather than self-effacing, unobtrusive, organic. To juxtapose two frontal shots of slightly different image size of the same subject matter at the same location at ostensibly the same time will inevitably cause a 'jump' or 'pop', a spatial discontinuity between shots. But the filmmakers actually stress that discontinuity by cutting between two clearly distinct postures of their cast. In the first shot, Tran relaxes her head on Leung's shoulder after which he looks left, at her. In the second, both sit bolt upright, shoulder-to-shoulder, their eyes now closed, as if hypnotised. The effect is the visual equivalent of a 'skip' in a recording and draws attention to the awkward stiffness of the actors' bodies.[10]

The nine shots that follow are even more enigmatic. Each shows a five- to twelve-year-old child standing where, in shots one and two, Leung and Tran had been sitting. As in the two examples considered above, the filmmakers have used their actors' bodies to indicate temporal and spatial suspensions, but here those suspensions are bio-physically more extreme. Every child has his or her eyes closed and is posed in an odd, sometimes difficult to sustain position. One boy, his head shaved except for three tufts of thin brown hair, leans forward a bit, his left thumb suspended between his teeth, his lips involuntarily sucking it. Another faces right, eyes clenched, his left arm awkwardly extended exactly parallel to the ground, away from his face (see Figure 11). His eyelids flutter, and he rocks slightly, as if unstable. Another holds his left arm by his side and his right askew at a 30-degree angle. He wobbles back and forth. Another tilts his head back. His nostrils flare uncontrollably. Each of these children seems to be in a trance.[11]

As in *À la verticale de l'été*'s family-altar scene, the sameness of the background from shot to shot allows the viewer to focus on what is peculiar to each portrait, the children's anomalous poses and the minutiae of their bodily

Figure 11: Unidentified boy in *Xich Lo*. Les Productions Lazennec. Paris.

instability. By juxtaposing a series of images of this type, Tran has also effectively used the children's bodies as poetic units, each of which, to be sure, has its own affective and associative qualities, but the juxtaposition of which creates an undeniable visual rhythm determined by contrasts in stance, hairstyle, physical type, colour of clothing, if any, and position within the frame.[12] Of course, for a viewer steeped in the methods of traditional art criticism, these images may elicit conventional questions of cause-and-effect, plot and theme. Who are these kids? (We haven't seen them before and will not see them again.) Are Leung and Tran dreaming them? (A reasonable Kuleshovian inference from the cut from the adult couple, eyes closed, to the series of incongruously posed children.) What is the relation of these images to the text of the spoken poetry? (Are the first two children depicted, a boy and a girl, eyes closed like Leung and Tran, meant to somehow 'be' their predecessors and to 'symbolise', if vaguely, the 'cycle of months and years' and the 'debt to my roots'?) All perhaps legitimate questions, but each of which sidesteps the primary affective power of the combination of image and sound, the scene's erotic focus on hypnotic aural, visual and bodily poetics.

V. THE BODY AND DREAM-SPACE

Another aspect of Tran's poetry involves spatial disorientation, especially in regard to the male physique. In addition to focusing on infrequently featured body parts – the back, the neck, the ear – Tran's camera defamiliarises faces, treats them as some kind of foreign territory. Unmotivated high-angle, three-quarter-face close-ups fetishising Vu Long Le's dark hair and eyelashes in *À la verticale de l'été* are typical of Tran's erotics. An overhead shot of a panting Loc Le Van in *Xich Lo* pinned against a door is so disorienting it is all but unreadable. And the frame's subsequent dissection (extreme close-ups) of his mud-encrusted face renders his nose and lips a topography which tiny insects explore. But moments of spatial disorientation in Tran's films are not always matters of eccentric camera positions. In *À la verticale de l'été* Tran twice marshals his idiosyncratic and poetic manipulation of the body's plastic and rhythmic potential to create scenes in which spatial disorientation effects a dream-like world.

The first of these scenes, our fourth and final example, takes place on a fishing boat.[13] Though the viewer does not know it yet, Quôc (Hung Chu) is grappling with his unusual domestic situation: he maintains two families, one in Hanoi, another on the lake. As the fisherman (Nguyen Huy Cong) rows him out to the houseboat where his second wife and son live, Quôc asks him how he manages his loneliness. The fisherman's response is poignant and ironic – he has no family and no spouse while Quôc has abundance. Tran imbues the scene with visual ambiguity simply by frustrating any desire to know where the two men are positioned relative to one another. In a standard dramatic Hollywood narrative, a scene often begins with an establishing shot that orients the viewer to the spatial arrangement of characters. During the course of a dialogue scene, then, the viewer will be able to read a character's reactions and specific body language based on this previously established spatial orientation. In this scene, however, Tran keeps the position of his actors to himself and his crew. When Hung begins to speak in shot one – a centred profile medium close-up, Hung looking frame left – the filmmakers have not yet shown to whom he is speaking. According to traditional editing conventions, shot two – a centred profile medium close-up, Nguyen looking right – reveals that the two men are either back-to-back (Hung on the left, Nguyen on the right) or facing each other (Hung right, Nguyen left) in conversation. Here, it is impossible to determine which of the two configurations is meant, and even the ropes on the edge of the frame, suggesting the rigging of the boat, do not privilege one over the other.

If the first two shots are ambiguous, the subsequent ten – which, according to convention should clarify, either by camera position or interactions of the characters, the actors' relative positions – only complicate matters. Tran offers only two camera set-ups (the two aforementioned medium close-ups) and so no new information about the men's spatial relation is divulged. Worse yet, the interaction of his actors not only does not clarify spatial relationships but in fact confounds them. As the scene progresses, Hung and Nguyen adjust their eye lines several times, each new axis indicating what *might now be* the actual spatial relation of the actors. The general direction of the eye line shift is from the edge of the frame and towards the lens. The progression, however, is not regular nor is there a strict coordination of the two actors' movements. The overall effect is a scene that deliberately eschews conventions of classical construction and dislocates its subjects. Hung and Nguyen do not inhabit a narrative space but, rather, a kind of dream-space. That dream-space further manifests the actors' stylised performance. Hung and Nguyen methodically pause and slowly reposition their inexpressive faces before and after speaking. They deliver their lines in a measured monotone. Oddly, they never blink. Their fields of attention seem unnaturally distant, eyes focused towards the horizon. The effect is that the actors appear dissociated not only from each other and from the physical world around them but also from the audience. Though these men speak and though each responds in turn, it does not seem to matter whether they are speaking to each other. Their statements are, like the poetry recitations in *Xich Lo*, enunciations in their own right, washed of any narrative context. Their rhythmic, plastic bodies contribute to the scene's dream-like Sontagian surface. Time and space are curiously stylised. And by avoiding the norms of mimetic filmmaking and substituting his own body-based erotics, Tran seems to want to induce in his audience a similar trance-like state.

In sum, as the Sontagian description and analysis of these four examples has shown, Tran's films' deployment of the male body does not lend itself easily to the kind of treatment typical of post-Lacanian spectatorship studies. The male bodies in these examples do not suggest axes of desire, hetero or homosexual, nor do they point to specific male sexualities. Bodies in Tran's films have been used overtly as part of an aesthetic, poetic system rather than as indicators of the psycho-sexual states of either characters or audiences. We are not, of course, arguing that application of Sontag's method is some kind of cure-all for the ills of film studies or a new Grand Critical Theory, but we do believe it makes a good starting point for films, like Tran's, whose concerns with the body are so obviously surface.

NOTES

1 Despite his including his own wife as a lead actress, and despite the considerable screen time he devotes to her characters, Tran trains his camera more often on the male figure *qua* figure and offers an unusual visual meditation on the plastics of male bodies.

2 Sontag herself (1966b, 1966c) wrote extended analyses on Resnais's and Godard's films before publishing 'Against Interpretation'.

3 Block (2001) provides a basic introduction to the vocabulary of space, movement, line, tone and other visual components in film, as well as a physiology-based account of the perceptual dynamics of these components. His mapping out of the 'dynamism' of a series of images is a step towards the development of a temporal vocabulary of film form Sontag calls for (1966a: 12).

4 Davis (2001) presents a more full account of Tran and Li's poetic use of exposure and lighting in *À la verticale de l'été*.

5 Imagine, for comparison's sake, Danny (Danny Lloyd) scooting along the halls of The Overlook Hotel and passing the dreaded room 237 in *The Shining* (dir. Kubrick, 1980). It is unthinkable, in Kubrick's visual system, that such a striking low angle shot from behind Danny's head, aiming up at the room number on the door, would be focused anywhere but the number. Kubrick's shot design is pure drama; Tran's, physical poetry.

6 Tran's place in Vietnamese national cinema is an unusual one. On the one hand, though his three films so far have all been set in his native country, Tran has lived most of his adult life in Paris and even recreated the Vietnamese village in which *Mùi dud u xanh* takes place on a French soundstage. On the other hand, Tran seems to be one of the few young Vietnamese filmmakers who are not simply imitating Hollywood and Hong Kong patterns in local settings but are grappling with national identity. Panivong Norindr (2006: 45) cites three others – Le Hoang, Vu Ngoc Dang and Phi Tien Son – but they, unlike Tran, seem particularly concerned to create a commercial, as opposed to auteurist, Vietnamese cinema. Though Tran's principal audience is certainly an international one – *Mùi dud u xanh* won the *Caméra d'Or* at the Cannes Film Festival, *Xich Lo* won the top prize at Venice, and *À la verticale de l'été* grossed over $1 million in its release in France and the US alone – according to the director, the single print of *À la verticale de l'été* exhibited in Vietnam was projected 'until it wore out' (Sklar 2001: 70). The fact that only one print of the film was in distribution in Vietnam needs to be considered in context. According to a French Embassy survey of cinema in Vietnam, in the late 1990s only twenty (of eighty total) movie theatres nation-wide were equipped with 35mm projectors, between 1998 and 2001 only twenty-five films were shot in Vietnam, and the average budget of Vietnamese films shot in 1999 was about $71,000 (Norindr 2006: 51, 214).

7 Amiel, for example, contends that 'the primacy of body over consciousness' is 'the material of [Bresson's] entire work' (1998: 55). And Bresson himself suggests he works to eliminate the psychological elements of performance from his actors, to reduce them to automatic bodies he called 'models'. According to Bresson (1986: 4), traditional actors start with the interior (character psychology) and move to the exterior (willed physical movement), while he uses his models' exterior (their physical bodies) as windows to their souls.

8 Tran's control of the visual components of his films is rigorous. Tran claims that for *Mùi dud u xanh*, for example, '[e]verything on the set was, in fact, directed by me – I determined every detail of the set, every colour, and every nuance of light' (Cross 1993: 35). Tran's obsession with visual design extends to his physiognomy-based casting. The actress who played *Mùi dud u xanh*'s Old Thi was chosen, according to Tran for 'her face and her size [...] She has a kind of simian face. I like that' (Tran cited in Cross 1993: 36).

9 It may be worth noting that after shot eight Tôn-Thât's score is replaced by Nguyen's quiet instruction to 'Little Mouse'. Her whispering continues the scene's aural rhythm, but also brings it to an end. Shot ten, a 'repetition' of shot two from a wider point-of-view, begins completely silent. Filmmaker Paul Schrader, who has considered some specific formal qualities of film and their 'spiritual' effect (1972), might have seen in Tran's repetition here an Ozu-like transformative *stasis*. What is striking, however, is that Tran brutally interrupts the *stasis* he has achieved with a loud and cranky off-screen, non-diegetic, voice-over announcement – 'Let's eat!' – and an abrupt cut to the decapitation of a skinned chicken, an orange rose sticking out its beak. This kind of scene-ending rhythmic jolt is typical of Tran's films.

10 *Xich Lo*'s cinematographer further contributes to the poetry of the moment by slowly opening his lens's aperture over the course of the second shot, causing the brightness levels throughout the frame to edge towards white and draining the colours a bit.

11 François Waledisch and Marie-France Ghilbert's arresting sound design is perhaps the first indication of this sequence's trance-like quality. During the final shot of the loft scene the roar of unmuffled street-bikes that had been competing with Tôn-Thât's dissonant strings suddenly, non-diegetically, drops out of the sound mix, leaving only the suspended high-register violins and, after a beat, the poetry recitation. The strings dissipate, but the poetry reading, accompanied by a single Asian flute and some wind-chimes, continues throughout the rooftop scene.

12 Because children of various heights have been placed in front of a locked-down camera the position of each child's face in the composition differs. Some are higher in the frame than others; some, more frame left or right. As a result, each cut introduces another 'pop' and further develops the aforementioned visual counterpoint to the soundtrack's fluid rhythm.

13 The second, a scene involving Quôc, his extra wife and their son, takes place on their houseboat three-quarters through the film. Since the strategies Tran uses in the two scenes are the same, we will consider only the first.

8

Closer than Ever: Contemporary French Cinema and the Male Body in Close-up

Gary Needham

The past fifteen or so years have seen a new engagement with the male body in French cinema suggestive of an intense fascination and over-investment in its cinematisation. This obsessive concern with the rendering of the male body as cinematic object is often through the close-up shot, revealing the body's shapes, contours and textures with unprecedented detail and proximity. This new visibility of the male body would also seem to run in tandem with the ascendancy of several French gay filmmakers and women filmmakers among them François Ozon, Sébastain Lifshitz, Gaël Morel, Olivier Ducastel and Jacques Martineau, Claire Denis and Catherine Breillat. These filmmakers have offered spectators new ways of seeing the male body, in close-up, with particular emphasis on nakedness and the penis (Figure 12). This chapter attempts to map some of those new visibilities of the male body in French cinema asking what is at stake in the work of those particular filmmakers as well as some ways of thinking about the male body and the penis in cinema as it is brought into proximity through the close-up shot.

I. EXPOSING FRENCH CINEMA

Unlike many other cinemas French cinema since the 1970s has exhibited a *laissez-faire* approach to the nakedness of the male body, rarely shying away from its display when it works to render the veracity of a particular scene and the body within it credible. Male nudity in French cinema has been a very casual affair

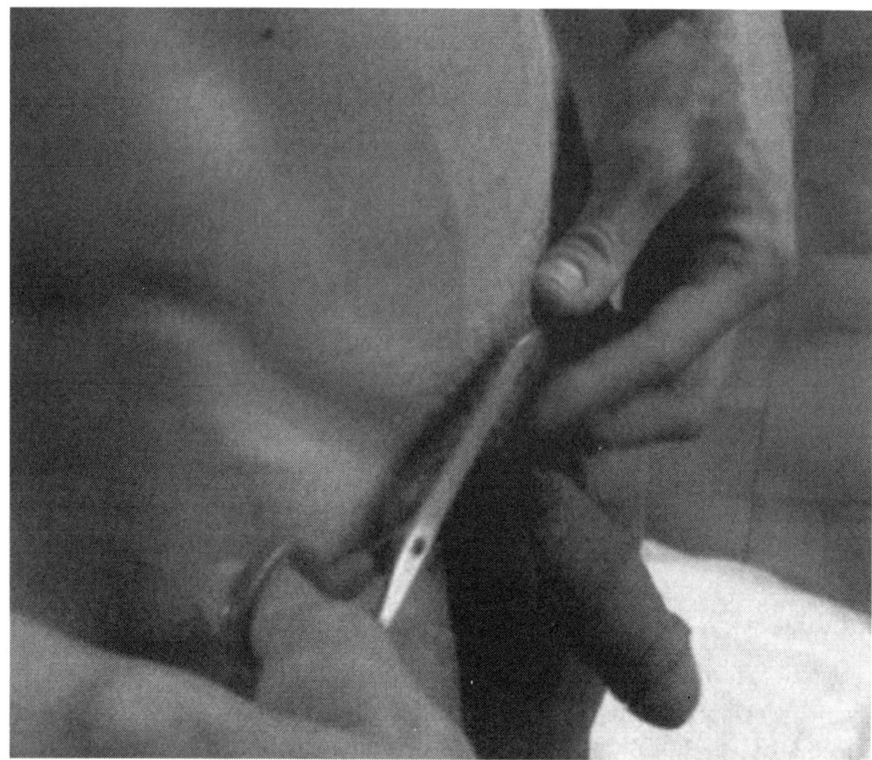

Figure 12: Nicolas Cazalé in *Le clan*. Sépia Productions. Montreuil.

neither deliberately revealing nor hiding the nakedness of the male body in both sexual and non-sexual contexts. Instead the naked male body in French cinema is allowed to move within the context of the scene as it would, one might assume, in real life whether it is the bedroom, the hospital or the gym showers. Therefore, a glimpse of full-frontal nudity and the penis is not necessarily by design or intention although the frontal male nude is generally on display when such scenes call for it to be logically present. I am thinking here of a few examples like *Les valseuses/Going Places* (dir. Bertrand Blier, 1974) with the casual male nudity of Gerard Depardieu and Patrick Dewaere, *L'homme blessé/The Wounded Man* (dir. Patrice Chéreau, 1983) with Jean-Hugues Anglade or more recently Vincent Cassell in *Irréversible/Irreversible* (dir. Gaspar Noé, 2002). In many ways nudity is almost expected from a French film; an indication of both its maturity constructed through concepts of art cinema (Bordwell 1979; Neale 1981) and the notion of Frenchness as libertinage, as something clandestine, licentious and sexy. Both of these discourses, art cinema and Frenchness, were cemented in the 1950s with *E Dieu…créa la femme/And God Created Woman* (dir. Roger Vadim, 1956) and the film's star Brigitte Bardot and continue on through *Emmanuelle* (dir. Just Jaeckin,

1974) up to *Romance* (dir. Catherine Breillat, 1999). The number of ways in which the word French qualifies the sexual, the saucy and the erotic in English (for example, a French letter (a condom), a French kiss, a French polish (fellatio)) is testament to the Victorian legacy as sexual mores are displaced onto France and continental Europe.

What concerns me in this chapter is a number of shifts taking place in the representation of the male body and male nudity predominantly in gay, queer and feminist filmmaking contexts in France. These shifts are from casual and contextual nakedness, both sexual and non-sexual, to the intentional and the staged representations that register shifts from the natural body to the erotic body of sexuality, from a relationship of distance to one of closeness. These shifts are strongly marked in a number of ways: the first being the proximity of the spectator to the body through close-up shots which brings the details of the male body into extremely close view and renders the body as texture and abstraction, what might be thought of as a landscaping of the body; the second shift is the way in which the male body is invested with intense erotic fascination through the mise-en-scene and the casting of the especially beautiful photogenic male bodies; lastly, the foregrounding of the body's penis itself both in its magnified presence through the close-up and its ideological insecurity transformed by the conspicuous presence of the prosthetic strap-on. These multiple shifts will allow me to consider some of the ways in which we can think about how the male body comes to be represented in distinct ways as a French cinematic object, principally through queerly inflected authorships of the close-up, as well as the cultural context of French cinema's ongoing investment in the male body as a site of aesthetic indulgence. Even the everydayness of the naked male body in those casual cinematic encounters in a film like *Le clan/The Clan* (dir. Gäel Morel, 2004) are becoming increasingly stylised in ways that stress how male nudity is also linked to sexuality, class and race: a form of expression that is more comfortable located within queer, post-colonial and feminist expressions of French cinema that have no need to hide and mystify the male body and instead locate sexuality, power and class in erotic displays of masculinity and homosociality.

It is tempting to group the several queer directors *a priori* under the banner of an emergent 'French Queer Cinema' but it is worth offering a note of caution before it coalesces around an umbrella term in some critical form or another. As a titular analogy with the Anglo-American 'New Queer Cinema', the recent crop of French films under discussion emerge within a different context of national and cultural politics suggesting any kind of consistent and coherent response to a similar kind of identity politics misguided. This also works against including the heterosexual women directors like Claire Denis and Catherine Breillat within a group of films that clearly share similar approaches in rendering the male body as a cinematic object of fascination. In proposing a number of ways in which this group of films is very different from 'New Queer Cinema' it gives a sense of definition to a particular group of films linked through their occupation with the male body rather than a shared, a very public, identity politics rooted in activism and collective thought. Rather than through the queer politics like the one that gave shape to 'New Queer Cinema', the body of French films under discussion here are often personal visions, intimate and subjective, which do often result in rather out-dated narrative occupations *vis-à-vis* the more radical queer films outside France which transgress the boundaries of gender, age and sexuality like *Boys Don't Cry* (dir. Kimberly Pierce, 1999), *Mysterious Skin* (dir. Greg Araki, 2005) and *Wild Tigers I Have Known* (dir. Cam Archer, 2006). Locked into coming-out stories and tales of first love, *Douches froids/Cold Showers* (dir. Antony Cordier, 2005), *Juste une question d'amour/Just a Question of Love* (dir. Christian Faure, 2000), *Ma vraie vie à Rouen/My Life on Ice* (dirs Olivier Ducastel and Jacques Martinez, 2002) and *Presque rien/Come Undone* (dir. Sébastien Lifshitz, 2002), are restricted by the narrative banality of the teenage milieu and its homosexual angst. However, despite these well-worn stories of queer youth from yesteryear the French films' organisation of the image and what they can authorise visually through an erotics of the male body is often far more compelling than their sassy American post-closet counterparts. One thing that is very striking about 'New Queer Cinema' and the films that come after is the ongoing reluctance to really invest in the male body as an aesthetic object, to show male nudity or even be close to the male body, seeing it in detail. 'Courtesy covering' is still the mainstay of many films and the flash of penis in recent queer films *Eating Out* (dir. Q. Allan Brocka, 2004) and *Testosterone* (dir. David Moreton, 2003) is often a brief split-second and thoroughly token gesture to get the mainstream gay audience hooked through clandestine images that circulate in the blogosphere. In recent US queer films, bodies are filmed at a modest distance offering an indication of something that the film cannot deliver with any intellectual or aesthetic commitment beyond the glimpse.

The emphasis on the personal, the private and the intimate which informs the narratives of French films with queer themes point towards a final point in cautioning against these films as some kind of 'French Queer Cinema' equivalent. These films never exhibit a collective, political or public face, they respond to private, personal and introspective feelings contained with the family and the formation of families, queer as they may be, as the core reference point from which to anchor the politics, in other words, the political is literally personal. This is most evident in a film like *Wild Side* (dir. Sébastian Lifshitz, 2004) with its ménage-a-trois relationship of disaffected outsiders who come together forming a queer family through their gender, racial and ethnic marginalisation in contemporary France. In *Wild Side* there is no bringing together of a culturally expressed dissidence in the formation of an identity politics or concern that responds to institutional and national homophobias and racisms, there is only the traffic in people, sex and bodies. In his analysis of the film, Nick Rees-Roberts also notes 'the relative limitations of the film's political scope' and the ways in which the *Wild Side*'s politics are reduced to the level of an 'experimental relationship' (2007: 148). This sort of political engagement in the film is conducive of modern France being built on the Republican model of nationhood. Republicanism does not acknowledge or identify individuals as group identities and collectives such as the Russian, Arab and transgender characters who inhabit *Wild Side*. The debate is more visible in France's post-colonial context where the republican ideal is marked by controversy and debate in racial and ethnic politics often resulting in violent social conflict and civil unrest. The effect on citizens in a nation that conceives of itself through a model of Republicanism means that difference and marginality, sexual, racial or otherwise is never accountable in national policy, legislation and citizenship. Every citizen is conceived of as being in direct relation with the state thus negating the importance of identity-based politics which has even resulted in considerable homophobic sentiment coming from the unlikeliest of places such as the public intellectual culture of France (Eribon 2004). The malcontent of difference is dealt with in the private rather than the public sphere with no anti-discrimination laws put in place to protect those who most need it. It is no surprise that many of the films under discussion make no attempt to mobilise a broader politics of the tension between concepts of the straight nation and the queer nation in France and instead focus on the minutiae of daily existence, the problems raised by the narratives and character psychologies become personal agendas and are contained to the individual (*La confusion des genres/Confusion of Genders* (dir. Illan Duran Cohen, 2000)), the experimental relationship (*Wild Side*), and the family (*Crustacés et coquillages/Cockles and Muscles* (dirs Olivier Ducastel and Jacques Martinez, 2005)). However, such conventional introspection only works to magnify the role occupied by the body, in close-up, as the location for the unveiling of micro-political discourses.

In thinking through the cinematic body, what defines the approach to the male body and masculinity in this particular group of French films is the very specific deployment of the close-up shot often of bodily surfaces, fragments, skin textures and the penis. The use of the close-up shot brings the body into a different kind of perspective begging for its meaning to be properly made sense of as its own textual unit especially when the shot takes the penis as its object and then contextualises its representation through queer sexuality. The most sustained analysis of the close-up shot in film analysis comes from an article by Mary Ann Doane (2003) whose work I will be drawing on in this chapter to suggest how we can understand the meaning and purpose of such a close mapping and intimate style of camera-work in relation to the male body and the construction of masculinity. The rendering of the male body through its surfaces and parts in the close-up shot also incorporates the work of Laura U. Marks (2000) and the concept of haptic visuality. I shall in due course explain how the close-up shot and haptic visuality offer ways of thinking through the male body as cinematic, brought in to unprecedented proximity for the spectator's view: the body in these films is so close to the screen that our experience of looking as spectators becomes one which suggests touching. A particular kind of cinematic culture of looking emerges around the male body which moves from merely invoking the visual to suggest cinematic experiences of touch and tactility, this is the haptic, or at least the feeling of wanting to touch and feel our way through the film and purview the male body as landscape. These films offer moments which actually work against the logic of voyeurism central to 1970s film theory (Metz 1977; Mulvey 1975), that is, cinematic and erotic displays of the body construct an obvious spectatorial structure between the powerful viewing subject and the passive object being viewed unknown to itself. The closeness achieved through cinematic technique in these films, that emphasis in the close-up shot, is one where the gulf, both formal and ideological, between the all-perceiving subject of voyeuristic spectatorship is denied through a logic of extreme closeness. Therefore, what is still a distance from the body and a glimpse of the penis in film outside France and increasingly European cinema as a whole, becomes a concrete invitation to come closer and touch with the eyes, not just to look but also to feel.

II. THE CLOSE-UP

In conventional cinemas, meaning most popular and commercial cinemas in Hollywood, Asia and Europe, the close-up shot is a motivated device in that it usually serves and is subordinate to a narrative function. The close-up shot indicates a closer look at something usually following a cutaway, like the finger that gestures towards a point of interest, 'look here' the camera says, the close-up draws attention to a specific element of the mise-en-scene and flags it up for closer inspection because there is nothing else to look at. The close-up is usually part of a larger visual unit, the face of the body that just entered the scene, the ornament in a room, the gun in the drawer, the hand turning the doorknob. As Doane's (2003: 92) analysis points out and what should be obvious to most of us, the face is the most common subject of the close-up, suggesting 'proximity, intimacy, knowledge of interiority' (Doane 2003: 107). As the Norma Desmond character in *Sunset Boulevard* (dir. Billy Wilder, 1950) once famously remarked 'I'm ready for my close-up'. One of the points of interest in this particular context is that the French term for the close-up shot differs from the English term. The close-up in English terminology refers to proximity and distance, in other words, how close the spectator is to the object on screen. However, in French the term is *gros plan* and refers to the size and scale of the image represented and suggests magnification rather than closeness. Conceptually the close-up is both of these definitions in that the proximity and closeness of the shot renders the image as 'a spectacle of scale' (Doane 2003: 93). In rendering an image in close-up and extreme close-up, the shot 'transforms whatever it films into a quasi-tangible thing, producing an intense phenomenological experience of presence, and yet simultaneously, that deeply experienced entity becomes a sign, a text, a surface that demands to be read' (2003: 94). When the close-up becomes its own autonomous shot it threatens the coherence and the unity of the film's invisible construction, it separates itself from the chain of meaning inherent in classical editing structures as a series of spatio-temporal rules and challenges; remember narrative realism is the chief organising principle. Doane goes on to suggest that the close-up is marked through 'separability and isolation' (2003: 91) and 'resistance to narrative linearity' (2003: 97), although it is difficult to see this being fully achieved with such antagonistic relish or aesthetic investment in the classical Hollywood cinema that forms most of her discussion. However, the close-ups in art cinemas and non-Hollywood cinemas, for example the extreme close-ups of Agnès Godard's cinematography for *Trouble Every Day* (dir. Claire Denis, 2001) and *Wild Side* (2004) or the close-ups in the Japanese films of Ozu Yasujiro and Hiroshi Teshigahara, are frequently unmotivated by cutaways and narrative realism allowing them to become all the more potent as their own powerful units of meaning and aesthetic design. There are two types of close-up of the male body that I want to consider; the first is the close-up of the penis and part of this discussion will also account for the conspicuous and ever-increasing presence of the penis substitute, usually a large strap-on dildo, and always filmed from medium shot to long shot rather than close-up with deliberate low-level lighting. The second type of close-up is of skin, close-ups of body texture resulting in landscapes and cartographies of the male body.

III. CLOSE-UP ONE: THE PENIS

The most common representations of the penis in cinema, when it is visible, have always been from a distance usually in a long shot, at the very most a medium shot and only then for a fleeting moment often obscured with low-level lighting or the body in motion. Peter Lehman's groundbreaking work on the representation of the cinematic penis has thrown up countless examples of how the penis comes to be represented in this mode through a range of American and European films (1993; 2001b). The penis in cinema is the subject of intense regulation and management at the level of cinematography, mise en scene and editing. There is also a resistance in offering up the image of the penis as the object of someone's point-of-view, it's just there, only briefly, so that we know it exists, but no one is looking. Lehman (2001b) also investigates what is at stake in representing the penis and the scope of his work accounts for films which merely refer to the penis in film dialogue as well as those films like *The Crying Game* (dir. Neil Jordan, 1992) where the penis's exposure is a melodramatic shock. The penis is seen most often at a distance and flaccid, literally in the choice of film shot and the context of its representation, the visibility of the penis is an act of careful management and controlled exposure. There will always be several counter-examples that problematise attempts to define its representation in such general terms, *Young Adam* (dir. David Mackenzie, 2003) or *Sebastian* (dir. Derek Jarman, 1976) spring to mind, but by and large Lehman's account covers most of the popular and mainstream cinemas' ways of representing the penis.

As I have already discussed, French cinema since the 1970s has adopted a rather casual approach to male nudity, not marked by the kind of insecurities, taboos and anxieties that govern other cinemas' treatment of the male body and the penis. However, it is only recently that the penis has come to be the subject of its own shot in the close-up and almost in French cinema alone. This does not even include the shift in French cinema towards real sex pioneered by Catherine Breillat. There is a smattering of early examples of the penis as a close-up shot in French cinema, mostly for purposes of shock, although the intention and rarity of these particular instances does not mark any sort of trend in representation like the one presently under discussion. *Maîtresse/Mistress* (dir. Barbet Schroeder, 1976) is probably the most shocking as it infamously depicts the real sadomasochistic abuse of a man's genitals; small nails are hammered through the skin of the scrotum. In *Tout va bien/All is well* (dir. Jean-Luc Godard, 1972) Godard includes a close-up of the penis through montage. The final, and most impressionable close-up is the opening scene of *Ridicule* (dir. Patrice Leconte, 1996) which places the penis right in the centre of heritage cinema and makes full use of the close-up as a spectacle of scale. This particular penis is all the more outré because the period and heritage genre with such heavy emphasis on costume and dialogue, is the last place one would expect to find a close-up shot of the penis like the one that opens *Ridicule*. In order to return a verbal humiliation the Marquis de Malavoy (Charles Berling) walks up to an older man, paralysed in a chair, he then takes out his penis (the close-up shot), and begins urinating on him. In 1996 this was an eye-opening shot to experience in the cinema unexpected as both a close-up shot, the penis magnified by the cinema screen as 'spectacle of scale', and in the context of the heritage genre only recovering from the sex and violence of *La Reine Margot/ Queen Margot* (dir. Patrice Chéreau, 1994) a few years earlier. The image itself is striking because of the scale afforded to it on the cinema screen and the shot's context in heritage cinema which seems to further emphasise the penis as a spectacle of proportion; the penis is unsheathed from the period costume, hanging alongside the authenticity of historical detail possessed by the clothing that takes up the rest of the space in the shot, it is out of place. *Ridicule* is not an isolated incident.

The 1990s seems to be the decade in which the penis and its prosthetic substitute become conspicuous in French cinema with several directors, including Leconte, offering up examples of the penis as a close-up shot as a means to shock. Unlike these examples there are several queer films that present the audience with the close-up of the penis, not in order to shock, but instead to suggest the kind of intimacy and affect that the facial close-up invokes. Through the close-up images of the penis in *Presque rien*, *Le clan*, *Wild Side* and *Garçon stupide/Stupid Boy* (dir. Lionel Baier, 2004) we are invited to engage with the character's self-discovery often as a queer subject through an intimate relationship with the body that draws attention to touching and feeling. The penis is often touched, investigated, intrinsically linked to the sexuality of the character and his body, never presented as our voyeuristic fascination as much as the character's own fascination with a new-found relationship to their body. *Presque rien* offers the most fully realised version of this scenario of self-discovery and intimate knowledge of the body as our look is filtered through that of the main character Mathieu (Jérémie Elkaïm) as he touches his penis in the bathroom. This close-up framed as the character's point-of-view looking down at his penis recalls Doane's suggestion that the close-up transforms the image in extreme proximity 'producing an intense phenomenological experience' (2003: 94) which is reinforced through the foregrounding of the point-of-view shot as close-up. The act of touching his body, specifically the penis, importantly follows on from an earlier scene on the beach when Mathieu first makes visual contact with his soon to be first love Cedric (Stéphane Rideau). Subsequently they both return to the beach in order to have sex which Lifshitz shows us involves a sensual touching of the skin traced by the finger, all filmed in extreme close-up. The image of the penis in *Presque rien*, like the facial close-ups of Hollywood cinema, is to allow us access to character interiority, to forge a relationship marked by formal and psychological closeness, but here in *Presque rien* the penis comes to represent the emergence of queer subjectivity and the desire the penis stands in for represents in the very image of itself the desiring homosexuality that mainstream cinema disavows through the regulation of the male body as a site of heteronormative representation. Therefore, in *Presque rien* the penis comes to represent a potential queering of the close-up, a challenge to the normativity of film form and its constant circumventing of the male body's potential to be represented in many ways but especially those that invite us to share a queer moment of proximity.

IV. CLOSE-UP TWO: THE PHALLACY

The new visibility of the penis in French cinema is not yet a cause for celebration as there are a conspicuous number of fakes in circulation. The freeing up of the male body from the conventions of heteronormative visual regulation through nudity and the representation of the penis is a slow process and several films often show us more than what we actually see. What I am referring to here is the size and number of phallic representations, in the literal sense as prosthetics, rather than actual penises. There is a difference between the close-ups of the penis as a register of queer subjectivity, desire and intimacy and the prosthetic erections on display in *La chatte à deux têtes/Porn Theatre* (dir. Jacques Nolot, 2002), *Sitcom* (dir. François Ozon, 1998), *Le temps qui reste/Time to Leave* (dir. François Ozon, 2005) and the earlier mentioned *Crustacés et coquillages. Crustacés et coquillages* is very telling in terms of the logic involved in the representation of the phallus in the absence of actual penises. The film gives over an entire DVD extra to the filming of 'the shower scene'. In the film one of the main protagonists Martin (Edouard Collin) takes a shower and begins masturbating. We share the point-of-view shot of another character Marc (Gilbert Melki) and watch with him as he observes the masturbation. In the point-of-view shot, it is obvious that a penis is present yet obscured by the frosted glass of the shower screen. On-screen masturbation might seem to be conducive to an ethical reading, that the erect penis represents the fact of sexual arousal and 'acting' doesn't cover this particular use of the body outside pornography. However, there is another story here that the DVD extra makes very clear; the actor in the scene does not think it is an ethical issue, rather it is a size issue. We are told by one of the directors that the actor requested the largest prosthetic penis be available to be used in the scene. The prosthetic is also not a custom-made film prop, but rather a strap-on dildo routinely available in any sex shop. The making-of of this particular scene in *Crustacés et coquillages* (Figure 13) certainly recalls the central debate about the differences between the penis, the dildo and the phallus in feminist and queer thinking. The prosthetic penis in *Crustacés et coquillages* reveals the arbitrary nature of phallic power as a performative act that can be literally strapped on (Reich 1992). The presence of the dildo as both the penis substitute and signifier of the phallus in *Crustacés et coquillages* merely foregrounds the insecurity or lack of power the penis has in representation recalling a key argument made by Richard Dyer: 'this leads to the greatest instability of all for the male image. For the fact is that the penis isn't a patch on the phallus. The penis can never live up to the mystique implied by the phallus' (1982: 71).

In *Crustacés et coquillages* we are not meant to know about the prosthetic and instead believe that a large penis is teasing us from behind the shower screen that the literal phallus is in fact the penis. It is no surprise that all the films mentioned above that feature prosthetic penises have opted for the upper end of the size scale as a sort of phallic compensation for the vulnerability of the male nude and the

Figure 13: Edouard Collin in the 'making of' *Crustacés et coquillages*. Agat Films et Cie. Paris.

penis from which the notion of the phallus has been fashioned. However, there is a potential for the plastic phallus to transcend the ontological experience of having a penis much like the dynamics of prosthetic sex in *Crash* (dir. David Cronenberg, 1996) discussed by Vivian Sobchack (2004: 176–77). The prosthetic erection always appears in scenes of low-level lighting, often at night-time and usually from a medium long-shot as it does in *La temps qui reste*, *La chatte à deux têtes* and *A ma soeur/Fat Girl* (dir. Catherine Breillat, 2001). The composition and style of these dimly lit scenes masks the solid rigidity of the prosthetic form and the plasticity of its appearance but a discerning eye can see that it is obviously too erect, too stiff, motionless, positioned either too low or high on the body in order to conceal the actor's real genitals masking their insecurity and vulnerability. In these scenes we only ever see the prosthetic penis once in each film and often as a quick glimpse and it doesn't serve a function unlike the close-ups of the real penis in *Presque rien*, *Garçon stupide* and *Le clan*. One must assume that the presence of the large prosthetic penis is an attempt to provide sexual scenes with verisimilitude albeit through something fake, but whether this is in the absence of an actor's willingness to allow us to see this aspect of his body, the difficulty of filming unsimulated sex scenes, or whether it is simply the logic of the phallus all lead to different avenues of interpretation. *Sex is Comedy* (dir. Catherine Breillat, 2002) stages a similar dynamic of the phallus through a female director's difficulty in filming the performance of male heterosexuality through the body. Here, a female auteur Jeanne (Anne Parillaud) is filming a difficult sex scene, the centrepiece of Breillat's previous film *A ma soeur*. Both films include the use of a prosthetic penis as a substitute for the male actors which, for Vincendeau, dramatises the power relations between the female director and her predominantly male cast and crew (2003: 22) finally going on to suggest that 'the character's fooling around with his prosthesis for the benefit of the male crew is a childish attempt to undermine Jeanne's authority' (2003: 22).

V. CLOSE-UP THREE: HOMOEROTIC TACTILITY

Gäel Morel's *Le clan* is one of the most homoerotically obsessed films about masculinity and the male body, and the most illustrative of the issues raised by the close-up. *Le clan* is a visual roster of homoerotic tropes and something of an authorial signature of its director whose approach to filming the male body is intensely arousing and fascinating. As with the films previously discussed, the investment in visualising the body connects the main protagonists in *Le clan*, three brothers, to their class and sexual identities. The film literally channels its politics through the body's various encounters with violence and sexuality, and the close-up shot often becomes a device through which this happens. One of the most interesting aspects of Morel's films is the emphasis he also places on touching and feeling, often including scenes where touch becomes a central aspect of connection between men and their bodies.

The opening scene of Morels's debut *A toute vitesse/Full Speed* (1996) is a tender scene in which the blood from a cut finger is licked off by the other partner. This scene was used as the poster image drawing attention to the shared moment of intimacy through the finger is a symbol of touch as much as the scenario confronts the phobia around blood and contamination since AIDS. This small gesture through the finger signals the centrality of tactile perception, of feeling and touching as both an emotional process and a physical act, as something that impacts on the cultural identity, connection and meaning between people and bodies. The development in Morel's films around touch and tactility which begins with this moment from *A toute vitesse* leads onto further scenes involving touch and tactility which culminate in *Le clan*'s invitation for the spectator to touch the bodies through close-ups and homoerotic images of the body and surface textures of the skin which here can be interpreted as haptic images (Figure 14). Laura U. Marks proposes the concept of haptic visuality as an alternative to optic visuality in her book *The Skin of the Film* (2000). She suggests that 'haptic looking tends to move over the surface of its object rather than to plunge into illusionistic depth, not to distinguish form so much as to discern texture' (2000: 162). Haptic visualities are like acts of touching through visual perception, drawing the spectator into an intimate relationship with the body on screen, rendering the

Figure 14: Nicolas Cazalé in *Le clan*. Sépia Productions. Montreuil.

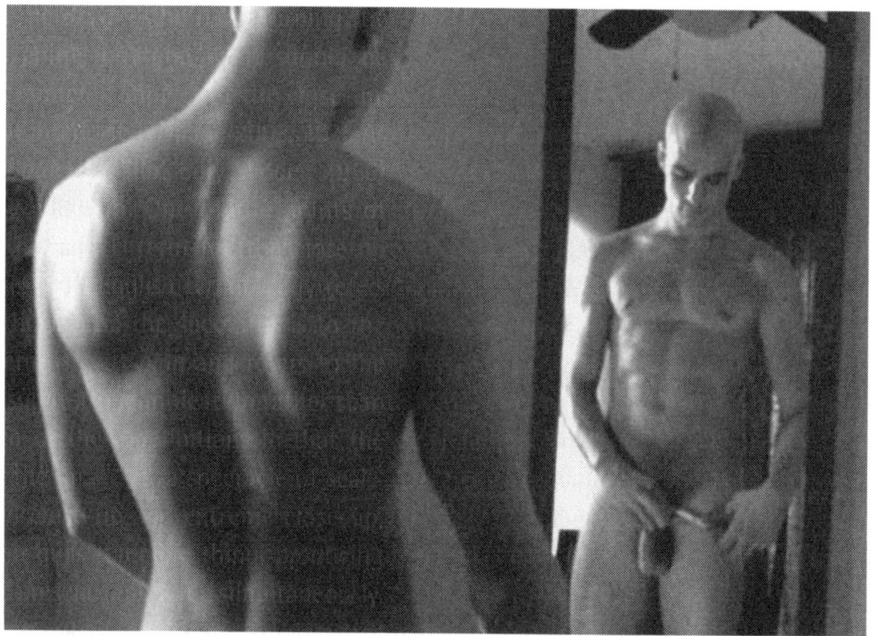

Figure 15: Nicolas Cazalé in *Le clan*. Sépia Productions. Montreuil.

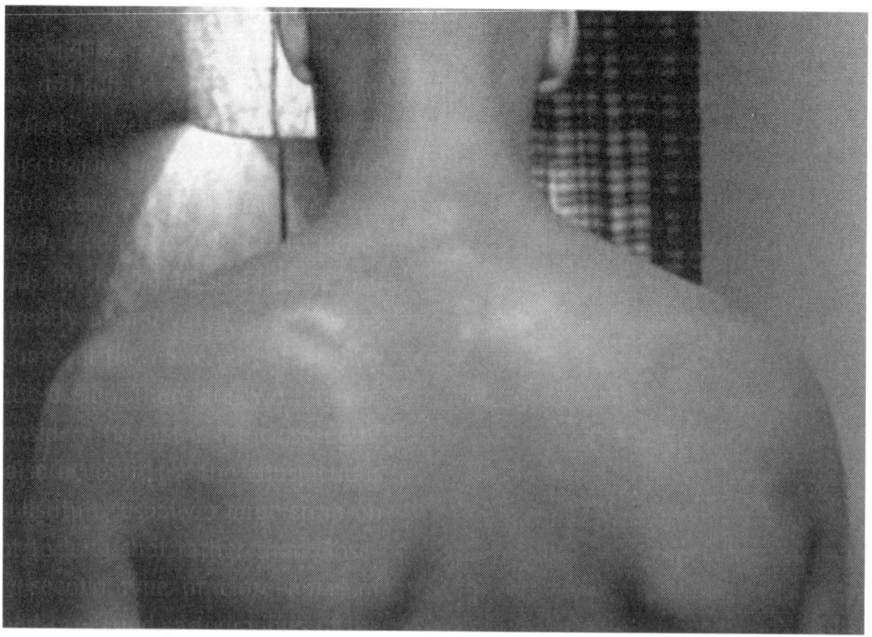

Figure 16: Nicolas Cazalé in *Le clan*. Sépia Productions. Montreuil.

body as materially present through close-up shots of skin. The skin is mapped through the camera's proximity to the body and becomes a texture both as an aesthetic and sensual experience. *Presque rien* also involves a scene of touching in which the close-up of a finger traces the intimate contours of the body, moving the sand and salt water from the sea over the skin. *Wild Side* opens with fragments of a body, including the penis, the camera mapping shapes, textures and surfaces in a coding of the skin that, for Claudia Benthien, defines Western thinking of the organ through a 'plural sense of closeness, intimacy and eroticism' (2002: 221). The relationship between the three brothers and their male friends in *Le clan* often involves touching as an index of their intimate connections and through the film's intensely homoerotic logic configures all homosociality as underpinned by an erotic tension of physical contact and touch. The film also finds other ways for men's bodies to be in contact with one another through exercise and violence as well as unclothed as they bathe, change and exhibit narcissistic obsession in front of the mirror (Figure 15). The camera is often fixed on the male body as the men are often fixed on their own bodies and the bodies of others. Morel frequently films the male body from behind and our point-of-view is often fixed on the muscular backs and shaven heads (Figure 16), the light refracting from the sweaty musculature of the shoulder and neck, in what Ellis Hanson has referred to in relation to Gus Van Sant's *Elephant* (2003) as cinema *a tergo*, a sort of queer looking from behind (Hanson 2007).

VI. CLOSER THAN EVER

What I have been suggesting in this chapter is a newly emerging mode of representing the male body in French cinema defined by images and experiences of close-ness in films predominantly directly by queer auteurs. This proximity to the body in the films discussed is often marked by an investment in representing the penis through the close-up shot. This view of the penis in numerous films is often filtered through the look of a queer character which conveys an intimate and subjective point-of-view and I argue that this offers a formal queering of the close-up shot. Our proximity to the male body as spectators is now closer than ever as the aesthetic close-ness to male bodies collapses into an experiential closeness – we are both seeing and feeling close to the image of the male body. This close-ness to the male body is further confounded by extreme close-ups of skin, its surface, musculature and texture, facilitating in a haptic perception where a queer paradigm of spectatorship now gestures for us to imagine touching what we see.

9

Caresses: The Male Body in the Films of Ventura Pons

Santiago Fouz-Hernández

I. AN INTERMITTENT PORTRAIT: THE MALE NUDE IN PONS'S FILMOGRAPHY

Ventura Pons is a prolific Catalan director who has produced some twenty feature films in his thirty-year career in cinema to date (in the latter half of this period at the rate of one film per year).[1] His first feature-length film, a documentary on Andalusian painter and famous Barcelona-based drag artist Ocaña (1947–83) (*Ocaña, retrat intermitent/Ocaña, an Intermittent Portrait* (1978) – *Ocaña* hereafter) was heralded upon its release as 'the first Spanish film with a clear post-Franco atmosphere' (Guarner [1978] cited in Campo Vidal 2004: 223) and has since been consistently regarded by film critics and historians in Spain and abroad as a key text of the Spanish political transition (see Smith 2003: 125, Fernández 2004: 88, Mira 2004: 454).[2] In the documentary, the artist openly discusses his homosexual encounters with other boys during his childhood in his native Andalusian village, Cantillana, and his then more recent experiences with men in 1970s Barcelona. Scenes from the interview are combined with footage of his gender-defying provocative public performances, famously in and around the iconic *Ramblas* in Barcelona's *Gòtic* quarter.

Ocaña featured one of the first male full frontals in the history of Spanish cinema (Fouz-Hernández and Martínez-Expósito 2007: 190). Released less than a year after the abolition of censorship and only three years into the transitional period, it was a milestone in the cinema of the newly democratic Spain. The artist's account of homosexual life in Barcelona, his passionate description of sexual contacts with other men and the verbal and visual scrutiny of the male body throughout the documentary, would be perceived as a liberating experience for the still repressed Spanish gay spectator.[3] As seen in some of the street drag performances filmed for the documentary and in his account during the interview, Ocaña was a self-confessed exhibitionist. Walking down the *Ramblas* in drag and heavy makeup, arm in arm with a camp male companion dressed like Ocaña's pimp in a white male suit, Ocaña lifts the skirt now and then to reveal his male genitalia. He later playfully hides the penis between his legs in a provocative fort/da game that heightens the significance of his biological sex even as it attempts to destabilise it. The prominence of nudity as an issue in the documentary is clear by its 'bookend' positioning in both the interview and the performance segments. Nudity comes up in the very first question of the interview and is reinforced in the performance segment that closes the film. Ocaña's first words are: 'You ask why I undress in the street... well, I would like to know why people are dressed' [...] 'why can't we walk around naked? It is like breaking something and I love breaking things [taboos].' Nudity, then, as noted by critics at the time of the film's release, was politically charged. The interview reveals Ocaña's fascination with provocation, a way perhaps to get his own back after the abuse he suffered during his childhood. As a child he may have unwillingly provoked others just for being different; yet it is now his choice to engage in public provocations in the big city. Childhood memories, though, are not only painful: Ocaña vividly recalls his apparently frequent sexual encounters with other kids in such a detailed way as to make such memories and those bodies visible for the audiences:

> sex was and still is very important for me [...] accumulated sperm is very bad for the body. It should be released and I did that night and day. It was wonderful for me to leave mass in the morning [...] and go with my friends to do 'things'. In the vineyards, when we'd feel our little things. Some would have more hair or it was bigger. Oh! That was wonderful. No women, just guys. Mmmm!

As Mira has argued, the artist's detailed accounts of various erotic episodes of his teenage years recreate 'an intensely homoerotic atmosphere sometimes deformed by memory: the remembrance of sex scenes in barns are reminiscent of a porn film' (2004: 456, my translation). Indeed, memories of clandestine sex in a pigsty or involving a smouldering log would recall S&M fantasies and/or memories of gay porn films for the knowing gay spectator nowadays, although this was surely not the case for the average gay spectator in 1970s Spain. What interests me here is that, as much as his memories may have been embellished by a more adult and (un)conscious gay fantasy filter (the questions, direction and editing of the film should not be underestimated either), Ocaña's re-living of such memories with detailed accounts of these highly erotic episodes opens up the possibility of a queer pleasure that had been largely unavailable to previous generations of Spaniards. The detailed descriptions of the male bodies, his physical pleasure in recalling them, facilitate their visualisation. While the film does not include any flashback or any kind of fictional re-enactment of the events and we only hear about them, the detailed and passionate description invites audiences to see them and even 'feel' them. Take this account of his sexual experience with a boy in a pigsty: 'What an orgasm. He had a tremendous penis, real thick lips, big hands.' This is reinforced in the last interview segment, which, to a certain extent, goes back to the beginning. The confessional character of the documentary (emphasised, as Fernández (2004: 88–89) notes, through the use of medium shots and close-ups) seemingly peaks in the final interview segment with the following revelation: 'I am fascinated with public toilets, as well as public gardens and staircases… [they are good] for sucking penises. I love it. It was hard to accept it, but it fascinates me…and most people, I think.' This is followed by the last illustrative segment, in which we see Ocaña in drag again, dancing on a stage in full flamenco dress. As he rips the dress apart and takes it off he shouts his last words in the film: 'I want to be naked […] what good are clothes to me if I was born naked? Why did repression give me these dirty rags? I don't want my clothes. I offer them to my audience. Here I am. I am naked.' Nudity is here portrayed in opposition to the repression of the dictatorship. To a certain extent, Ocaña's own male body and his memories of other male bodies dominate the film, becoming its one durable memory.

Pons's first fiction film, the comedy *Vicari d'Olot/The Vicar of Olot* (1981) also places sexuality and the male body at its centre. While the focus of the narrative is the changing sexual and moral costumes at a small Catalan village (the main event is the organisation of a conference on 'Catholic sexuality' to coincide with the visit of religious authorities), the film's critique of the Church and old-fashioned Catholic morality (associated with Francoism) is centred on discourses of the body. In the opening scenes, a young priest's self-flagellation morning routine is contrasted with the harmlessly lascivious comments about the priest's good looks (and his butt) made by members of the female congregation later during his mass. The changing role of women in the newly established democracy is further emphasised in two other instances: in the midst of a wedding ceremony, the bride refuses to commit to her new husband 'till death do us part', because she likes to have fun with another, younger man, on the side. Meanwhile, the priest's live-in servant's niece has loud sex with a young man in the priest's house. Although there is no room to discuss the film in detail here, it is relevant to mention that the intervention of the village's prostitute and a pre-op transsexual are crucial to the film's happy and liberal ending. The presence of a middle-aged closeted gay man (the village's pharmacist) and his young bisexual lover are also worth noting. Such a relationship, between a middle-aged man and an often bisexual or yet undefined attractive and much younger boy will become a frequent pairing in Pons's portrayals of homosexuality, as we will see in the last section of this chapter. Interestingly, the young and athletic bisexual man, Bernardo, is often seen topless in the film. Despite being a secondary character, he is in fact the object of desire of the three 'dissident' characters mentioned: the bride, the servant's niece and the pharmacist.

The presence of an athletic and handsome object of desire shared by various characters in the film is a recurrent element in Pons's filmography, as seen in virtually all the comedies that followed in the 1980s and, as we shall see later, in his more up-market productions of the last two decades. *La Rossa del Bar/The Blonde at the Bar* (1986), based on a comic strip by Raúl Núñez that appeared in the iconic 1980s fanzine *La luna de Madrid*,[4] features another bisexual character (played by the then successful rock star and heartthrob Ramoncín) who is a pimp but also consumer of male prostitutes and who is specially obsessed with North-African rent boys. The racial undertones of the story are humorously played out in a tongue-in-cheek sequence in which some of the characters have to pose for an erotic photo novella. The story will recreate an interracial marriage between a Western lady and a muscular black man with a big penis in an exotic location. The overweight girl's parents, dressed up as explorers, come to visit. The mother is fascinated with the black man's muscular body and touches his muscles in admiration. The flabby bodies of the Westerners are contrasted with the muscular body of the black man. His inability to get a hard-on due to the tension on the set, however, cleverly dismantles the prejudiced racial discourse.[5]

In *Què t'hi jugues Mari Pili?/What's Your Bet, Mari Pili?* (1990), a father and his son end up being completely naked (at separate moments) in the middle of the kitchen of an all-female shared flat after spending the night with one of the three flatmates. The well-defined body of this young, athletic man appropriately named Ángel (Marc Martínez) is admired by the two jealous flatmates who are having breakfast in the kitchen. In a reversal of the typical '*destape*' films of the transition (in which women were often undressed while men remained fully dressed), here it is the man's body which is completely exposed (in long shot from the back and medium shot when facing the camera) while the desiring women remain fully dressed. The two jealous flatmates scrutinise and visually devour Ángel, admiring his entire body and staring at his penis while dipping their fingers on a tub of margarine and demonstratively licking them.

Figure 17: Joan Cossas and Anna Azcona in *El perquè de tot plegat*. Els Films de La Rambla. Photograph by Pere Salva.

The idea of the penis as something to be devoured (already anticipated in Ocaña's vivid confession of his interest in fellatio) is another recurring motif in Pons's cinema. Two memorable examples include the story 'Gelosia' ('Jealousy') in *El perquè de tot plegat/What's It All About* (1995) and the opening sequence of *Amor idiota/Idiot Love* (2004). In 'Gelosia' a man (Joan Cossas) becomes jealous of his own penis due to his female lover's (Anna Azcona) obsession with it (to the point that she needs to have it in her mouth before she goes to sleep – see Figure 17). 'I also exist' protests the man. In the first few minutes of *Amor idiota*, a drunk Pere-Lluc (played by media celebrity Santi Millán) unexpectedly unbuttons his jeans at the start of his 35th birthday party and drops his penis on a plate, next to the meat and vegetables, threatening to stick a fork in it as a way to ensure that he will have no children. The scene not only grabs the attention of every spectator from the very start by provoking either desire or a fear of castration, but also serves the purpose of justifying the character's seductive power and sexual potency (further illustrated by his numerous and acrobatic sexual acts throughout the film – some sixteen edited in one single sequence), selling the film with the promise of having Millán, the actor's manhood literally served up on a plate and in close-up within the first five minutes of the film (see Fouz-Hernández and Martínez-Expósito 2007: 196).

II. MEN AND THE CITY: HAPTIC SPACE, HAPTIC BODIES

Space, and in particular the city, is one of the aspects of Ventura Pons's work that has attracted most attention of journalists and academics alike and one that is hard to ignore. From the very first images of the iconic Plaza Real in *Ocaña*, to the overview of the city from the Montjuïc vantage point in *La rossa del bar* or to the prominent role of the Liceu Theatre in his recent *Barcelona, un mapa/Barcelona, a Map* (2007), virtually every Ventura Pons film includes Barcelona exteriors easily recognisable for the locals and, in some cases, such as *Food of Love* (2001), explicitly seen from and for the eyes of the tourist.[6] Pons himself often talks about his love for his city and his interest in filming it. In his prologue to the published script of *Amor idiota* he writes: 'I feel immensely attracted to Barcelona's urban landscape. It is obvious in *Amor idiota* that the deep relationship between my city and my work is still developing' (Pons 2005: 11). In line with the director's desire to film in Catalan, adapting literary works by prominent Catalan writers and with a by now familiar cast of Catalan actors (thus, as Fernández notes, 'contributing to the establishment of a Catalan "star system," and creating recognisable images and motifs' (2004: 98)), the Catalan capital is his main setting of choice. Barcelona is to the cinema of Pons what Madrid is to the cinema of Almodóvar.[7]

The successful *Carícies/Caresses* (1997) presents a less idealised vision of the city than one might have come to expect from a Ventura Pons film. As highlighted in the press book, the vastness and fast pace of city life 'at the end of the millennium' creates a sense of coldness and isolation among its citizens, who are described as 'loveless' and 'rootless'.[8] The sense of anonymity is symbolically underscored by the fact that the characters are nameless, simply described as 'man', 'old man', 'boy', 'girl', 'woman' and so on. The pairings between them are also quite simple and easily identifiable: partners; friends; lovers; mother/daughter; brother/sister; father/daughter; prostitute/client and so on. There is also a disquieting sense of confinement in the cramped interiors in which most of the eleven semi-autonomous and yet related stories develop: a kitchen, a bathroom, a dining room or a studio flat. The relative autonomy of the stories, as well as their narrative, also stresses the lack of communication in modern-day large cities.

Based on a famous Catalan play by prominent playwright Sergi Belbel, the structure allowed Pons a new return to his theatre origins after the success of his adaptation of the Benet i Jornet's play *Actrius/Actresses* a year earlier. Yet, whereas in the earlier film the sense of theatrical space was largely respected, in *Carícies* the possibilities of cinema are exploited in the fast-moving bridging segments of the city (three images per second) used to link the stories.[9] The concept, according to Pons, was that 'the camera would look for the characters throughout the city [...] stopping when it finds them' (cited in Arenas 1998: 94). Although alienating, the city is the common denominator that 'unifies' the various stories and, as such, as Pons has argued (cited in Smith 2003: 133), the main character of the film. Appropriately, the usually recognisable Catalan capital is less so in this case, also defaced (by the speed with which the images of the cityscape are reproduced when 'travelling' between stories) and dispossessed of most of its iconic architecture (with some exceptions, such as the recurring long shot of the Plaça Catalunya and long and close-up shots of its unmistakable clock).

In her detailed reading of space in *Carícies*, Sally Faulkner notes how the 'denial of the body in the fast-forward sequences frames the abuse of the body in the narrative vignettes' (2003: 145). Indeed, the fleshiness of the film is evident from the very first vignette, in which a heterosexual couple have an extremely violent (bloody) fight upon the realisation that they no longer have anything to say to each other. The fight escalates as they move from moments of polite conversation ('what do you fancy for dinner?') and a sudden exchange of kicks and punches over the salad ingredients. Thus, the opening story opens up the themes of lack of communication and violence (physical and psychological) that will dominate the film until the circle is closed at the very end in the last story, when two of the characters come into closer and warmer physical contact. The man of the first story (played by David Selvas), whose face is now visibly bruised and full of cuts as a result of the fight with his partner, asks the downstairs neighbour (Rosa María Sardà) if he can borrow some of the missing salad ingredients. She notices his wounds and caresses him, perhaps as a way to compensate for her own estrangement from her son, demonstrated in the preceding story. He caresses her back.

In her study of embodiment and moving image culture, Vivian Sobchack draws on Shaviro (1993); Williams (1999) and Marks (2000) among others to develop the concept of cinematic tactility. As she notes, 'carnal responses to the cinema have been regarded as too crude to invite extensive elaboration' (2004: 57), often associated with sensationalist journalism and 'rhetorical or poetic excess' (58) and yet 'critical discussions often also suggest that films that appeal to our sensorium are the *quintessence* of cinema' (57, emphasis original). She proposes that the viewer's lived body is posited as 'a carnal "third term" that grounds and mediates experience and language, subjective vision and objective image' (60). In other words, our bodies become an essential filter through which we experience and understand cinematic conventions. We have already seen how Pons's films bring their audiences into an intense physical connection with the visual narrative: what is striking in these films is precisely the extent to which this is true. Whether the viewer identifies with or desires the male bodies on display, the 'carnal third term' intensifies the identification/desire dialectic. The fork-in-penis episode of *Amor idiota*, for example, displays both the vulnerability and the materiality of the penis and invites a complex physical response in the male audience which is key to the meaning of the scene. The 'fleshiness' of *Carícies* is heightened in the contrasting opening and closing sequences: the opening forces us to confront the physical violence by means of a shocking contrast between the (largely civilised) dialogue between the couple and their violent fight; while the final sequence nourishes the by now physically alert body of the spectator with an unexpected caress which affects our perception of the city. The camera, which had been moving frantically around the city for most of the film searching for a moment of tenderness, finally finds it and slows down. The view of the now romantically lit city seen from the neighbour's window replaces the sense of alienation and hurriedness that dominated the previous shots of the city seen from the fast-moving car. For Faulkner, these final scenes (the caress and the view of the street in slow motion) signal a move from 'the "abstract" space of the city, conveyed cinematically by "visuality"' to 'an "absolute" space, represented by "hapticality"' (2003: 146). Now the previously unseen pedestrians dominate the street in a peaceful harmony largely undisturbed by a passing car. The haptic body, then, felt here in close-up shots of the man's bruised face from his neighbour's POV, has an important impact on the way in which the city is perceived by the characters and by the camera.

There is one scene, earlier in the film, which further exemplifies the tactile potential in the cinematic experience. A father (Sergi López) and a son (Naïm Thomas) have a long conversation in the bathroom about each other's dick sizes and pubic hair:

> Father (on seeing his son submerge in the bath) – 'Big, huh?'
> Son – 'Not as big as yours'
> Father – 'Almost'
> Son – 'Yeah, I wish'
> Father – 'Lots of hair'
> Son – 'Not as curly as yours'
> Father – 'You'll get there'
> [...]
> Son – 'Why are you looking at me?'
> Father – 'And you?'
> Son – 'Do you want to take a bath?'
> Father – 'No'
> Son – 'Where is mum?'

> Father – 'Sleeping'
> Son – 'Hot!' [...] 'The water, I mean'

Beyond drawing attention to their genitals (barely shown on long shot) through dialogue and glances (and thus inviting the audience to take an interest in their bodies), the scene is full of sensorial enticements that draw the viewer closer to the characters' flesh. Although the father refuses two further invitations to have a bath (but accepts a final one when the son suggests that they should share a bath together like in the old days), he offers to do his son's back with a sponge and there are constant references to the water temperature. The narrative investment in the 'lived' body, enhances the audience's sensorial experience when viewing this scene.

Interestingly, before joining his son in the bath, the father reveals that he has a big surprise in store for the family: tomorrow they will get a new car. By insisting on the fact that the son will like the surprise much more than his wife and that the surprise is a secret between them, the father is temporarily excluding the mother from the scene and (unconsciously) increasing the son's physical excitement indirectly by talking about the car. The introduction of the car into the conversation has multiple functions. Firstly, as we have seen, 'the secret surprise' draws father and son closer together and further apart from the sleeping mother. When the father finally joins his son in the bath (see Figure 18), the son immediately gets a hard-on after commenting once more on how much bigger and hairier his dad's penis is. The son's words: 'Feel it [...] Look how big it is now' [...] 'Mum is snoring' emphasise the obvious need to exclude the mother from the act that the whole scene had been building up to. But the car also provides both a convenient distraction from the tense physicality of the scene (and the 'taboo' subjects of homosexuality and incest) and a necessary reaffirmation of the men's masculinity and heterosexuality. They may get excited talking about each other's genitals, but only as some sort of 'masculine' competitive ritual. Like 'proper' men, it is cars that they are really interested in. Yet, conversely, the car attracts even more attention to the men's bodies, as the discussion about its different parts (air conditioning, hi-fi system, electronic sunroof) and performance (power steering, catalyst converter) works a symbolic displacement of what is becoming an unbearably tense situation in the constant comparison of their own body parts and qualities. In the next vignette, we see the father break up with his (female) lover (Mercè Pons) partly due to her intense vaginal odour. The uncomfortably humorous scene is practically a monologue that, in its extraordinarily detailed description of the woman's odour, heightens the spectator's sense of smell:

Figure 18: Sergi López and Naïm Thomas in *Carícies*. Els Films de La Rambla. Photograph by Pere Silva.

> It stinks terribly [...] It's not that smell of rotten fish or a dirty pussy during your period [...] Yours is more sour than sweet, like a mixture of ammonia and rotten meat [...] The first time I almost felt sick. What a stench! I looked at your crotch, held my breath and expected to see a thick vapour come out. It really stunk.

While the film is not at all misogynistic in its narrative, the viewer's sense of smell is nonetheless heightened here and these two related episodes encourage an association of the female body with unpleasant experiences and the male body with cosiness, as revealed in the man's words: 'When I was a kid I used to like the smell of my balls in my shorts. But now, I don't get it.'

III. FOOD OF LOVE: MEN OLD AND YOUNG

Beyond aspects of homosexuality and incest in the *Carícies* bath scene discussed in the previous section, the physical comparison between father and son also introduced the element of age, which is later developed in another story of the film, in which a middle-aged, closeted 'family man' (Jordi Dauder) visits his rent boy in his apartment. The man's initial confrontational, demanding demeanour with the boy is reminiscent in part of some of the tense moments in the father/ son bath scene, except here the sexual element is much more evident. The man asks for a drink of water and quickly asks the boy to give him a blowjob. Interestingly, the man demands that the boy removes all his clothes, while keeping his on (the shirt is unbuttoned and the trousers pulled down). POV shots from the perspective of the man linger on various body parts of the boy while he unwraps a large mirror that the man bought as a present for the occasion. He asks the boy to place the mirror next to them during the sexual act but does not let the boy look at the mirror images. Faulkner reads the scene as emphasising the 'simulacrum' of bodily experience in the phallic solitude of abstract space (2003: 145): after reaching climax, he addresses the boy and the two mirror images and says 'you three... the only ones who love me', seemingly denying his own sexual subjectivity. Yet, there is room for an alternative reading. Prior to the climax, during the stimulation, the man explicitly says 'we are four'. The mirror reflects his gay alter-ego, lived out 'for real' during the sexual experience, but withdrawn after the climax ('you three') when he will presumably return to his closeted self. On the other hand, far from self-destructing desire, the doubling up of the images visually heightens the experience for the man and for the audience. This is further suggested by the man's insistence that the boy squeezes his nipples (shown in medium close-up) and even further when the man touches the boy's smooth back, affectionately shot from the man's POV and then from behind, and says: 'Your skin. I'm alive.' Despite the fact that this act is part of a financial transaction that benefits the boy, it is suggested that the boy enjoys it, visibly devouring the man's penis even after he has ejaculated. Yet, the issue of age is far from obviated. Visually, the boy is stark naked in contrast with the old man who remains partially dressed for the entire scene, despite the boy's request that he should undress too. This follows the pattern of gay subjectivity in cinema as described by Waugh (1993): 'The third body [the gay subject] puts on costumes as readily as the objects of his desire take them off' (145). The focus in the scene is unmistakably on the young boy's nude body. While the old man merely unbuttons his trousers to prepare for the blowjob, he asks that the boy undresses fully before asking him to move to another side of the room to unwrap a present (the mirror). This provides further opportunities for soft-lit POV frontal shots of the boy, alternated with medium close-up shots of his muscular back and pert buttocks in flattering medium and low angles. The age issue also comes up in the dialogue. Before sex, the man and the boy discuss the man's age:

> Man – 'Do you know how old I am?'
> Boy – 'I don't want to know'
> Man – 'Why?'
> Boy – 'It would trouble me'

Man – 'Fifty'
Boy – 'That troubles me'
Man – 'Who could tell?'
Boy – 'Nobody'

The visual narrative and the dialogue, then, bring attention to the issue of ageing in gay relationships, which would become a central aspect of Pons's next film, *Amic/Amat/Beloved/Friend* (1998), about the relationship between an ageing man – a semi-retired university professor played by Josep María Pou – and his favourite student (David Selvas), who turns out to be a part-time rent boy. As discussed in more detail elsewhere (Fouz-Hernández and Martínez-Expósito 2007: 129–33), this type of relationship between an ageing man and a rent boy was also widely explored in the films of Eloy de la Iglesia during the 1980s and it follows the Greek model involving a process of mentoring beyond the physical. In *Amic/Amat* the professor's wish is to encourage his talented student to take up writing and to father a child, thus securing a heritage. He will support the boy's studies and his child by means of a double inheritance: financial and intellectual. The discourse of the body and the contrast between the old, decaying, sick body of the old man and the fit, muscular body of the cocky student/rent boy is also emphasised by their different states of undress during their surprising encounter. This is further heightened by the physical and verbal violence that the young man aims at his professor. Sexual contact is avoided and replaced with kicks and punches at the old man and cruel words: 'you will have to pay for sex' [...] 'the day that [...] I find my body half as repulsive as I find yours now [...] I will kill myself' (see Fouz-Hernández and Martínez-Expósito 2007: 132). Ageing has been seen traditionally as a process that affects women more negatively than men (see, for example, Sobchack 2004: 36–52). Indeed, it would seem that, while women become 'invisible' in their old age – partly to the biological inability to naturally conceive after a certain age, men would seem to acquire more respect and even sex appeal. In her study of the 'ageing Clint [Eastwood]', Holmlund has noted that, in films like *Pink Cadillac* (dir. Van Horn, 1989), 'visually the film underlines Eastwood's age [...] narratively [...] the film insists that [...] Clint is the toughest, smartest, nicest and funniest guy around' (2002: 152). Similarly, Aguilar has argued that the high number of relationships between ageing men and beautiful young women in Spanish cinema is at odds with the proportion of such relationships in Spanish society (1998: 60). Zecchi's study of the ageing male body in Spanish cinema directed by women also reveals a surprisingly conservative approach to nudity of older women who have sex with young men (2006: 193). This seems to mirror the pattern in gay relationships of this type. Yet, as she notes, female directors compensate the usual conception of biological inferiority of older women with regards conception with superiority when it comes to sexual potency and the man's need to get an erection. In some films directed by women, ageing male bodies are disregarded 'as male directors do with the older female body' (Zecchi 2006: 194). This seems to be an issue in many cinematic representations of gay male sex, where procreation is not an issue but where the young, fit male body is usually revered. As Holmlund also notes, however, ageing is no longer a worry for women only, as suggested by the boom of anti-ageing cosmetic ranges for men and the fact that ageing men are the fastest growing market for plastic surgery in North America (2002: 145).

Pons would revisit the issue of age-difference in gay relationships in his next gay-themed film, *Food of Love* (2001). Here, the object of desire is Paul (Kevin Bishop), and his older mentor is not an academic but a world-famous pianist, Richard Kennington (Paul Rhys). Although the age difference is not so great in this case (Richard is a well turned-out middle-aged man), the pattern is similar. The boy is a failed pianist who instead becomes a professional page-turner (that is how he meets Kennington). Enamoured with the older man's talent, he visits him in his hotel while on holiday in Barcelona. Yet, it is the older man (in a committed relationship with his male manager) who will lead the inexperienced boy into having sex with him. The contrast between the two bodies is not as pronounced in this case: Richard is almost twice Paul's age, although he is also in very good shape. Yet, the opposition is stressed in other ways. The scene of the sexual encounters between Richard and Paul in Barcelona is followed by a scene in which Richard's partner contracts the services of a rent boy in their shared apartment in New York (it is suggested that both encounters happen almost simultaneously). Paul's relationship with Richard arguably provokes a pattern in his future relationships with older men, including a one-off sexual encounter with Richard's own (older) partner Joseph (Allan Corduner) and his own new regular partner, who happens to be Richard and Joseph's neighbour. On the other hand, the fact that Paul's recently separated mother (Juliet Stevenson) – who is travelling with him but is unaware of the situation – makes a move on Richard suggests that he is more apt as a father figure for the boy. The inexorable passing of time is also emphasised with his birthday party towards the end of the film. Richard's age is also visually evident not so much from his body but on the frequent medium close-up shots of his face and of Paul's (either together or in reverse shots – see Figure 19). Finally, their professions are also metaphorically significant: as Richard's page-turner, Paul is just another page in the more experienced man's life: the pianist will use his trained fingers to massage the boy and will explore his body with similar passion. Indeed, as one reviewer noted, the Shakespeare reference of the title does not go amiss: 'music may be the food of

Figure 19: Kevin Bishop and Paul Rhys in *Food of Love*. Els Films de La Rambla.

love, but in the movie, it's the kid who finds himself getting devoured' (LaSalle 2002).

Elsewhere, comparisons between sightseeing and the exploration of the boy's body are also evident. Once again, affectionate shots of Barcelona's architectural wonders abound, ever so alluringly consumed by the tourist's eyes (and, through them, by the international audience of Pons's only English-language film to date). While Paul's mother explores Barcelona and takes pictures of Gaudí's *Sagrada Familia* from a sight-seeing bus, Richard explores Paul's body, melting an ice-cube all over his back. The camera takes as much pleasure tilting down Gaudí's famous building as it does travelling across Paul's body. This visual comparison had been established earlier in the dialogue preceding a previous sex scene. In the hotel lobby Richard asks Paul: 'so, what do you want to do this afternoon? You know, we could go and see the Gaudí or we could go to my room.' Clearly, the film invites the audience to compare interest in Paul's body with the tourist's gaze at Gaudí's masterpieces.

Such comparisons exemplify one of the ways in which Pons shortcircuits the gaze, the carnal body and visceral knowledge. It is the male body in particular that is charged with the task of stitching together visual and physical pleasures, and of managing the effective narrative motor. As I have tried to show in this chapter, the male body is not just an important element in the films of Ventura Pons, but serves as a key structural linchpin of his aesthetic. His films often draw attention to a central attractive male figure, often nude, and often contrasted with older males, in order to bring a visceral charge to the visual. The camera celebrates the male figure by proximity, drawing us closer to it and making the audience 'feel' the male body, as it were. This sense of hapticality is enhanced by establishing a visual comparison between the pleasure experienced in the haptic space of the city (Barcelona) and in the desirable male body which share protagonism in his films.

NOTES

1 I would like to thank Margarita Lobo and Trinidad del Río at the archives of the Filmoteca Española for their assistance with film viewings during November 2007 and to the library staff for providing access to numerous relevant books and press cuttings during the same period. Jaume Cuspinera at Els Films de la Rambla provided the stills used in this chapter and Ventura Pons generously granted copyright permissions.

2 A striking still from the documentary, depicting Ocaña in full drag adopting a classic Spanish look with black shawl, comb, flamenco earrings and white carnations, illustrates the cover of the first English-language monograph on Spanish Cultural Studies (Graham and Labanyi 1995).

3 While I agree with Mira's critique of Ocaña's rejection of (sexual) identity 'labels' and the apparent fact that he cannot escape such labels even as he strives to avoid them, the open discussion of such topics and its visualisation was a novelty in 1970s Spain – as Mira also acknowledges (2004: 458–60).

4 *La luna de Madrid* was a Madrid-based fanzine widely acknowledged as the unofficial mouthpiece of the underground artistic movement that followed the end of the dictatorship known as the *movida*.

5 A similar critique of the eroticisation of the foreign male body is apparent in *Què t'hi jugues Mari Pili?* (1990). Here, a middle-aged, overweight lady (played by Pons's regular Amparo Moreno) is crazy about a much younger and supposedly Moroccan man (Àngel Burgos) – stereotypically called Mohammed – who turns out to be a Spaniard from the neighbouring region of Valencia.

6 Even *¡Puta Miseria!/Bloody Pittance* (1989), set in Valencia, is filmed in Barcelona. Notably, the Italian setting of *Food of Love* in Levitt's novella is changed to Barcelona in the film script.

7 Smith (2003) discusses aspects of Catalan identity and Catalan cinema in Pons's oeuvre.

8 References to the press book are based on the Spanish-language electronic version available at Ventura Pons's official website: <http://www.venturapons.com/filmografia/cariciasp.html> Last consulted January 2008.

9 These bridging segments can be likened to those showing bits of a map of New York City and serving a similar purpose in the later film *Shortbus* (dir. John Cameron Mitchell, 2006).

10

Destroying the Male Body in British Horror Cinema

Alison Peirse

Rather than attempting to provide a wide-ranging overview of British horror cinema, this chapter explores the textual dimensions of *Dog Soldiers*, made in 2002 by Neil Marshall and shot in the UK and Luxembourg. Examining the bodies of the terrified and attacked British Army soldiers, known as 'squaddies', this chapter situates *Dog Soldiers* in relation to other examples of the werewolf film genre and British horror films in general. In opposition to the traditional generic conventions of the horror film, *Dog Soldiers* concentrates exclusively on the destruction of the male body. Horror is evoked through the constant bodily trauma and/or annihilation of the squaddies – Cooper, Campbell, Spoon, Kirkley and Milburn, led by Sgt Wells – by a lycanthropic family, led by the beautiful young female werewolf Megan. Until the final moments of the film, when the denouement offers the redemption of the male body through Cooper's salvation, the squaddies' guns, machismo and the performance of masculinity are ineffective against the murderous and primal predilections of the female werewolf and her lycanthropic family. As such, the film offers a particular interesting moment for analysis in the horror genre.

Dog Soldiers creates an interesting dichotomy between conceptions of masculinity and the male body, and moves against the traditional patriarchal and hegemonic conception of the male body as a singular unified construct. Elizabeth Stephens and Jørgen Lorentzen point out,

> traditionally, male bodies – especially white, heterosexual male bodies – have been subjected to an act of double erasure: first, its norms are projected onto a

> generalised category of "the body", which is assumed to be a stable construct; then, this corporeality is displaced onto the bodies of cultural "others", leaving masculinity to occupy the place of reason, rationality, and the disembodied mind (2007b: 5).

The all-male white, heterosexual group of British soldiers fulfil this typically stable construct. Their lexicon of swearing, gun-toting and group camaraderie firmly places them within the dominant masculine norm. However, the stable male body is undermined by the horror of the female werewolf and her family. Recently, Judith Halberstam has analysed *Bride of Chucky* (dir. Ronny Yu, 1998) to 'comment on the representation of embodiment in horror as a form of gender flexibility', and draws upon Judith Butler (1993 and 1999a) to ask 'whether bodies that splatter produce gender stability or whether they dismantle the very conventions upon which that stability depends' (2007: 30–1). Engaging with Halberstam's essay, this chapter will suggest that through the dissolution of the phallic white male body, *Dog Soldiers* questions the fixity of gendered, sexual and corporeal categories. It is argued that the contemporary werewolf film highlights the performed nature of masculinity and femininity in contemporary culture.

I. HORROR FILM, GENDER AND MASOCHISM

Masochism can be understood as an important mode of spectatorship in horror film. This chapter suggests that the masochistic spectatorial experience in *Dog Soldiers* is envisioned through the destruction of the male body. Masochism has been addressed in a wide variety of ways by theorists as divergent as Freud (1979 [1919]; 1991 [1924]), Theodor Reik (1941) and Gilles Deleuze (1991). Freud radically revised his theory of masochism between his 1919 study 'A Child is Being Beaten', and 'The Economic Problem of Masochism' in 1924, while Deleuze and Reik both offered up their own major revisions of Freud's ideas. This extensive and complex set of ideas has been usefully theorised by Kaja Silverman (1988). Rejecting Laura Mulvey's (2000 [1975]) stance which prioritises sadistic active gazing, Gaylyn Studlar's (1992) study of Marlene Dietrich's films emphasises masochistic looking, while Barbara Creed (1993a) and Carol Clover (1992) have both investigated masochism in relation to the contemporary horror film viewing experience. Described by Jean Laplanche and Jean-Bertrand Pontalis as a 'sexual perversion in which satisfaction is tied to the suffering or humiliation undergone by the subject' (2004: 244), masochistic spectatorship can be interpreted as a passive mode of looking available to both male and female viewers that emphasises viewing moments of shock, fear and horror.

In her study of gender and the horror film, Clover explores the adolescent male viewer's stake in horror spectatorship and his relationship to the female victim-hero. She argues that the male viewer betrays his biological sex to identify with the screen female, a form of displacement which means that 'the boy can simultaneously experience forbidden desires and disavow them on grounds that the visible actor is, after all, a girl' (1992: 18). Clover employs Freud's writings on feminine masochism to explain this object-choice on the part of the male viewer. In her reworking of spectatorship for the modern horror film, Clover presents feminine masochism as an explanation for young male spectators' identification with the on-screen female body of the victim in order to experience fear and pain. This masochistic identification offers the space to play out forbidden desires located in the unconscious.

Peter Hutchings has argued that it is the masochistic and passive elements of the spectator's response which are most important for understanding the address of the horror film. While Hutchings's argument is based on 1970s horror film and is focused on the experience of the male spectator, some of his ideas can be related to the masochistic textual organisation of contemporary British horror film. He summarises the now frequently contested position that horror is a misogynistic genre; that the male spectator identifies with the active and powerful psychopathic monster and, in order to compensate for feelings of inadequacy, sadistically revels in killing passive female characters. Hutchings argues that this position is inadequate and that as a result of Clover's pioneering work on male spectatorship further attention must be paid to the analysis of the masochistic subject. Hutchings claims that the male spectator is capable, at an emotional and psychical level, of 'shifting back and forth between victim (conventionally feminine) and victimiser (conventionally male)' (1993b: 86). Through this oscillation between positions, a masochistic or passive dimension opens up a space for the patriarchal male to empathise with the victim's trauma and disempowerment.

Although Hutchings provides a useful theorisation of the spectator's masochistic pleasures, he continues to offer the well-trodden binary oppositions of female/victim versus male/monster as central to his analysis, arguing that when the male spectator identifies with the victim he is taking up a feminine position, even while Hutchings acknowledges this presentation of femininity is a social construction. Like Hutchings, Clover limits herself to binary gender positions by analysing only the adolescent male spectator and his identification with the female victim-heroine. This reinforces gender-specific viewing positions, rather than opening out the field to a variety of multiple and divergent identifications. This chapter makes no gender distinctions in its framework of masochistic spectatorship, suggesting the masochistic will to submission is available to all. Utilising the idea of a masochistic look, this chapter explores how *Dog Soldiers* moves beyond binary gender positioning and disrupts not only the performance of masculinity and femininity, but the fixity and stability of the male body itself.

II. THE FINAL BOY

The film begins with a prologue, as an anonymous couple go camping in the Scottish highlands. The woman gives her boyfriend a present, a small and polished silver knife. That evening, the couple are inside their tent and about to have sex. Their copulation is rudely interrupted as the woman is pulled out of the tent by her legs and dismembered by a werewolf, offering an aside to the slasher film trope, lovingly parodied in *Scream* (dir. Wes Craven, 1996) that to have sex results in death. The nameless woman (played by Tina Landini) screams and blood gushes across every surface, while the man cowers at the back of the tent. It is important to acknowledge that the woman is not the conduit of fear in this scene. Her death is outside the tent and beyond the limits of the frame, occurring off-screen. The camera focuses on the man's reaction as his girlfriend's blood splatters his face. In *Dog Soldiers*, fear and death are predominantly located upon the male body. The man's face is displayed in tortured medium close-up as he looks into off-screen space to see his lover dismembered. His eyes widen as the werewolf re-enters the tent – again the monster stays *off-screen* – and then he is attacked. His final moments are shown directly from the werewolf point-of-view, suggesting a sadistic and aggressive look that focuses not on the monster, but the reactions of the terrified man who is about to be brutally murdered. This sadistic gaze by the monster can still be understood in terms of masochistic spectatorship, for an essential part of the passivity evoked in masochistic looking relates to the destruction of the male body on screen.

The following scene introduces the male protagonist, Private Cooper (Kevin McKidd). By attending to certain generic conventions of gender in horror film, it can be argued that Cooper embodies the traditional 'Final Girl' role of slasher films, as theorised by Clover. Writing on Sally in *The Texas Chain Saw Massacre* (dir. Tobe Hooper, 1974), Alice in *Friday the Thirteenth* (dir. Sean S. Cunningham, 1980) and Laurie in *Halloween* (dir. John Carpenter, 1978), Clover describes several key traits that mark out the Final Girl of the slasher movie: 'she is the one who encounters the mutilated bodies of her friends and perceives the full extent of the preceding horror, and of her own peril; who is chased, cornered, wounded; whom we see scream, stagger, fall, rise and scream again', and that 'she alone looks death in the face, but she alone also finds the strength to either stay the killer long enough to be rescued (ending A) or to kill him herself (ending B)' (1992: 35). Cooper is introduced at the beginning of the film prior to the rest of the squadron. This emphasises the character's importance, for as Clover argues 'the Final Girl of the Slasher film is presented from the outset as the main character' (1992: 39). He is shown in North Wales, four weeks prior to the main story on the Scottish highlands. Trying out for the Special Air Service Regiment (SAS), the elite Special Forces unit in the British Army, Cooper is successful in a series of gruelling tasks but is denied entry at the last moment. When Cooper refuses to shoot a dog at the culmination of the trial, Special Operations Captain Ryan (Liam Cunningham) kills the dog himself and Cooper fails the initiation. This sets up a clear antagonism between the two men which resurfaces later in the film, while also displaying Cooper as a fair, level-headed and compassionate protagonist for the viewer to identify with.

The narrative then moves forward four weeks to Scotland, where Cooper's band of squaddies are dropped on the highlands for a training exercise. It is later revealed that the men are pitted against the Special Ops squadron, led by Cooper's nemesis, Ryan. Upon landing, Cooper is immediately assigned map reading and analysis duties by Sergeant Wells (Sean Pertwee). Allocating Cooper the most important and intellectually demanding tasks further aligns him with the Final Girl of horror film, for Clover claims that 'she is the Girl Scout, the bookworm, the mechanic [...] above all, she is intelligent and resourceful in a pinch' (1992: 39). Thus, Cooper is shown to be highly skilled, reasonably intellectual and motivated, physically strong and able to look after himself, while embodying conscience and humanity, essential traits for a horror film survivor. As the sole survivor of the film, Cooper proves himself to be a true Final Girl. This suggests that *Dog Soldiers*' writer and director Neil Marshall understands the language of the horror genre, and wilfully manipulates generic expectation, gender and convention. While Clover argues that the smart Final Girl contains masculine traits, *Dog Soldiers* both acknowledges and subverts this generic convention, playing with notions of transgender by offering up a Final Girl within a biologically male body.

The squadron set out on their routine training exercise. Masculinity is reaffirmed through group discussions of football and women, punctuated by excessive banter. They soon discover the Special Ops campsite, which has been decimated by unknown aggressors, leaving Ryan as the sole survivor. Ryan is rescued by the squaddies and the group move on with much trepidation. Shortly after, Corporal Bruce Campbell (Thomas Lockyer) is put on rearguard duty. Campbell's ocular point of view, displayed as he scans the dense woods around him, is constantly contrasted with his head framed in close-up. Suspense

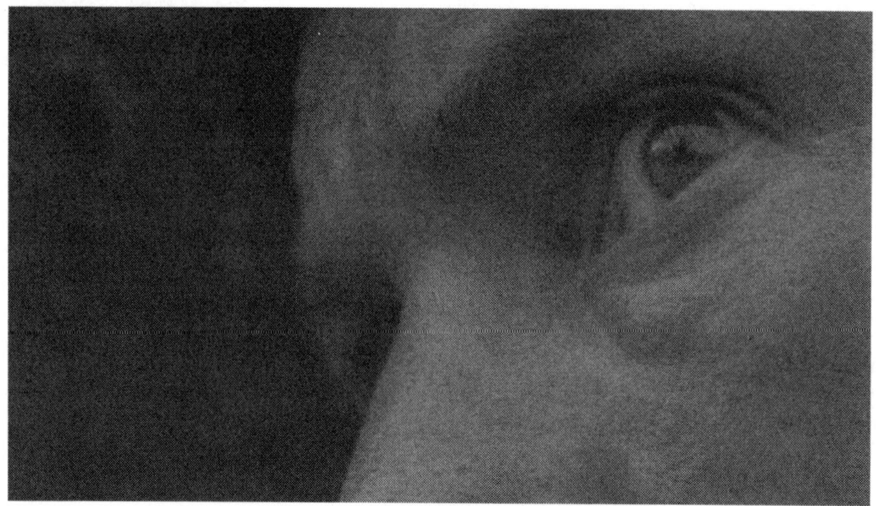

Figure 20: Thomas Lockyer in *Dog Soldiers*. Carousel Pictures Production Company, The Noel Gay Motion Picture Company and Kismet Entertainment Group.

is created in the juxtaposition of the first person point-of-view and the framing of the male victim. A werewolf approaches off-screen, and as Campbell sees it, he attempts to fire his gun. However his phallic weapon repeatedly fails to fire. His inability to save himself or his squadron is highlighted, and he turns and runs. Campbell suddenly stops mid-flight, looking surprised. In extreme close-up, blood oozes from his mouth. Campbell has impaled himself through the stomach on a jutting out tree branch.

III. BLIND SPACE

In extreme close-up, the camera focuses on Campbell's eye, signalling that the werewolf lurks in off-screen space (Figure 20). A paw cuts through the edges of the frame, without warning, and swipes off Campbell's face. Campbell's body is destroyed by the werewolf's paw that physically attacks him, and by the violence of the camera itself, its own technical cropping and manipulation of off-screen space signalling his imminent death. It could conversely be argued that the werewolf is also subject to the fragmentation of its body, as only a paw appears through the line of frame. However, I would like to consider the realm of off-screen space in terms of horror film conventions. Writing on the film *Jaws* (dir. Spielberg, 1975), Pascal Bonitzer offers some pertinent points regarding off-screen space:

> Technically speaking, filmic space is divided between two fields: on-screen space and off-screen space; we could say, between specular space and blind space. Specular space is on-screen space; it is everything we see on the screen. Off-screen space, blind space, is everything that moves (or wiggles) outside or under the surface of things, like the shark in *Jaws*. If such films 'work', it is because we are more or less held in the sway of these two spaces [...]. The point of horror resides in the blind space. (1981: 58)

Bonitzer's ideas on blind space are at the heart of the formal construction of the monster in horror cinema. In the 1930s British horror film *The Ghoul* (dir. T. Hayes Hunter, 1933) one of the central moments of horror is Professor Morlant's (Boris Karloff) resurrection, taking place predominantly off-screen behind the closed door of the crypt, only for it to swing open at the last moment and Morlant to stagger out into the night. Similarly, another British horror classic is the story of 'The Ventriloquist's Dummy', contained within the portmanteau film *Dead of Night* (dirs Alberto Cavalcanti, Robert Hamer, Charles Crichton, Basil Dearden, 1945), where the true horror comes from the uncanny movement of the dummy in the blind space. It is the suggestion of animism, of the wooden doll scurrying around in places that we cannot see that creates menace and disquiet. Indeed, it is when the sanctity of the blind space is not respected that horror can misfire. The problematic juxtaposition of specular and blind space in horror is nowhere more apparent than in *Night of the Demon* (dir. Jacques Tourneur, 1957). Writing on British occult films, Leon Hunt acknowledges that while *Night of the Demon* is only seen as 'nominally British' due to its 'American star, producer, director and narrator, and British émigré writer (Charles Bennett)', in fact 'there's certainly much pleasure to be had from fire demons materialising on the 8.45 to Southampton' (2002: 83). Filmed in such illustrious locations as the Reading Room at the British Museum and Stonehenge, the narrative expertly creates suspense as the sceptical psychologist Dr John Holden (Dana Andrews) is pitted against occult leader Julian Karswell (Niall MacGinnis). Horror is created initially through suggestion and unease – are Karswell and his followers mad, or do demons truly exist? However, fairly early in the film, the fire demon is fully revealed on camera, destroying all feelings of uncertainty and creating an unpleasant tension between the horror of the blind space and the disappointing revelation of the demon in specular space.[1]

Dog Soldiers offers a faithful acknowledgement to the importance of blind space in horror film. The werewolves are only truly revealed in their full glory in the last twenty minutes of the film, and at that point their horrific effect is somewhat deadened, despite the excellent puppetry and mechanical masks. The werewolves are only truly scary when residing in the off-screen space, when a paw

Figure 21: Emma Cleasby and Kevin McKidd in *Dog Soldiers*. Carousel Pictures Production Company, The Noel Gay Motion Picture Company and Kismet Entertainment.

flashes across the screen and fragments Campbell's face. The squadron see the monsters directly, but we are rarely granted with their point-of-view. As such, it can be argued that the confinement of the werewolves to the blind space turns the attention onto the bodies of the squaddies. *Dog Soldiers* does not create horror through the visualisation of the monstrous body. Rather, the werewolves are the conduit for the trauma of the male body. This is reiterated later when the remaining squaddies have retreated to a deserted farmhouse and are defending it from attack. When the werewolves break through the doors and windows the camera never lingers upon them; instead the image is focused upon the reactions of the men – yelling, firing and dying.

IV. THE BITCH WITHIN

After Campbell's death the squaddies continue to be overwhelmed by the werewolf attacks and Wells is almost killed. He begs to be left for dead but Cooper (the ever resourceful and loyal Final Girl) drags him onwards to temporary safety. The only female character (aside from the nameless woman murdered in the prologue) Megan (Emma Cleasby) is then introduced into the narrative. Appearing in her Landrover, she rescues the squaddies from the werewolves and takes them to a deserted farmhouse. The werewolves repeatedly attack the farmhouse, and in a brief lull between attacks, Megan and Cooper have a 'moment' (Figure 21). The scene is coded for romance: it is lit in warm, red tones, and Megan and Cooper are framed in a medium two-shot. Their eyelines match as they look closely at each other, almost kissing. However, instead of succumbing to Cooper, Megan apologises. She reveals that the farmhouse is her home and that she knows who the werewolves are. They are all from the same family, and, in fact, Megan is one of them. The revelation that Megan is a werewolf offers a play on gender roles in the horror genre, reinforcing the location of the male body as the site of violence and death, and refuting the usual critiques that, in horror, women function as victims. Similarly, writing on British horror films of the 1960s, Hutchings points out that when feminist critics argue horror is a misogynist genre where females function only to be victimised they 'fail to grasp that particular horror films might – depending on the context in which they are produced and received – challenge or problematise certain patriarchal attitudes and definitions' (1993a: 18). Hutchings's suggestion that gender roles can be problematised in horror as a form of patriarchal critique is self-evident in *Dog Soldiers*, where the power of nature, woman and the female is shown to overthrow masculinity, the training of the Army, and ultimately, the sanctity of the male body.

As Megan prepares to transform, she sneers that it is 'that time of the month', explicitly linking menstruation and sexuality with lycanthropy. This triad is also explored in the 1980s British horror film *The Company of Wolves* (dir. Neil Jordan, 1984) , a re-telling of the fairytale *Little Red Riding Hood*, and adapted from two short stories from Angela Carter's collection *The Bloody Chamber* (1979). In this film, the protagonist Rosaleen (Sarah Patterson) succumbs to the handsome but dangerous young huntsman (Micha Bergese) who is 'hairy on the inside'. Frightened but curious, Rosaleen chooses to break away from her family, kiss the huntsman and transform into a wolf, leaving her family behind to run wild. In her recent book on the werewolf in literature and popular culture Chantal Bourgault Du Coudray suggests that there are distinct gendered differences between male and female werewolves: 'for male werewolves lycanthropy finds expression primarily in the murderous hunger for flesh and blood, while for female werewolves, the opposite is true: lycanthropy is essentially a release for sexual hunger' (2006: 114). In his analysis of *The Company of Wolves* Hutchings argues that it is an impressive film, but it does not attempt 'to engage in any meaningful sense with a specifically British reality' (1993a: 187). *Dog Soldiers* is an interesting text for analysis, not only because of its attempts to overturn conventional depictions of gender, sexuality and the body, but because of its particularly British qualities. The colloquial language, the pop culture comments, Army references and windswept and bleak Scottish locations all contrive to produce a distinct British atmosphere.[2]

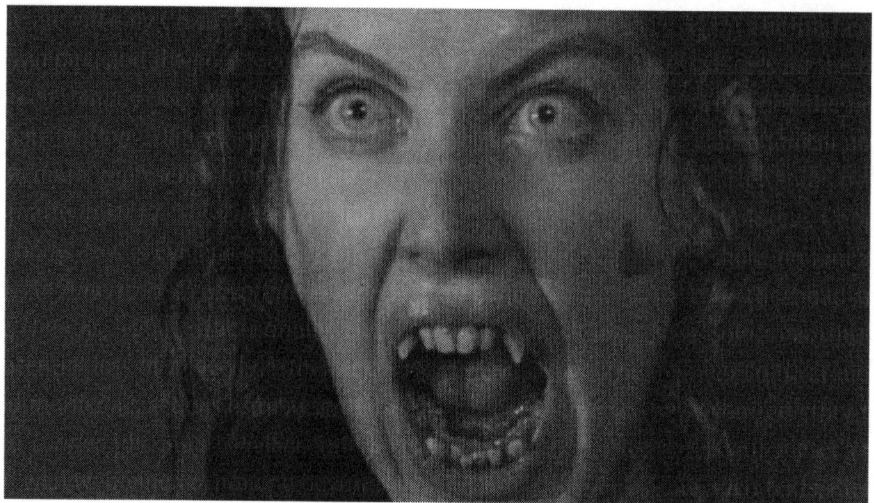

Figure 22: Emma Cleasby in *Dog Soldiers*. Carousel Pictures Production Company, The Noel Gay Motion Picture Company and Kismet Entertainment Group.

Heightened sexuality, menstruation and the female lycanthropic body are also at the heart of the Canadian horror film *Ginger Snaps* (dir. John Fawcett, 2000). Like *Dog Soldiers*, Fawcett's film takes the central precepts of the werewolf myth – the lunar month, increased body hair, excessive blood and amplified sexual desire – and relates them specifically to the horror of the 'Othered' female body. This distinction between screen accounts of male and female werewolves has also been noted by Du Coudray who argues that 'if variants on the struggle against the "beast within" have dramatised the experience of male lycanthropy, the pervasive cultural association of femininity with nature, embodiment and biology has animated most accounts of female lycanthropy' (2006: 112). After admitting her bestial ontology, Megan becomes distinctly canine, yellow eyed and teeth bared (Figure 22). Her lycanthropic family appear from inside the kitchen and loom up behind her, ready to attack the few remaining soldiers. Megan states that 'You may think that they are all bitches, but I'm the real thing.' However, she is unhappy about her fate, shouting 'Do you think I like being part of this fucked up family?' Consequently, the female werewolf Megan contradicts other contemporary depictions of female lycanthropy such as Ellie in *Cursed* (dir. Wes Craven, 2005), Rosaleen in *The Company of Wolves* and high school teenager Ginger Fitzgerald in *Ginger Snaps* where 'the change' and all of its menstrual and abject connotations results in a pleasurable and emergent (if temporary) female sexuality.

In her book *The Monstrous-Feminine: Film, Feminism, Psychoanalysis*, Barbara Creed argues that woman is represented as monstrous in a significant number of horror films. Figures of the monstrous feminine are cited by Creed as: 'the archaic mother; the monstrous womb; the witch; the vampire; and the possessed woman' (1993b: 7). However, she makes no mention of female werewolves. As such, the female werewolf, emblematised by Megan in *Dog Soldiers*, offers a new opportunity to problematise ideas around cinematic representations of gender, sexuality and the body. Throughout cinematic history, the werewolf has traditionally been figured through the male body. This is evident in such films as *The Wolf Man* (dir. George Waggner, 1941), *An American Werewolf in London* (dir. John Landis, 1981) and *Wolf* (dir. Mike Nichols, 1994). Traditionally, the werewolf film concentrates on the loss, or potential loss of a loved partner as a result of the male werewolf's bestial urges and murderous actions as represented by Dr Glendon and his wife Lisa in *Werewolf of London* (dir. Stuart Walker, 1935).

There has been a distinct paradigm shift in werewolf cinema, moving beyond the fascination of the bestial male transformation (evidenced by iconic scenes of body alteration in *The Wolf Man* and *An American Werewolf in London*) to the masochistic vision of dismembered male victim at the hands of the female werewolf. Megan and her werewolf family reveal that guns and machismo will not work and the sanctity of the male body is transgressed. Following on from depictions of emerging and powerful female sexuality in *The Company of Wolves* and *The Howling* (dir. John Dante, 1981) and more recent cinematic configurations of the female werewolf in *Blood and Chocolate* (dir. Katja von Garnier, 2007), it can be argued that the female werewolf is aggressively sexualised and the male body is now the focus of violence and death.

After her transformation, Megan is swiftly shot in the head by Wells, who is recovering rapidly from his werewolf attack. Megan is never shown on screen again and it is assumed she has been killed. This raises certain questions around the limitations of the female werewolf and destruction of the male body, and will be addressed later in the chapter. After Megan is destroyed, the werewolf family move in on the remaining three men: Spoon, Wells and Cooper. Spoon (Darren Morfitt) fires his machine gun, only for it to run out of ammunition. The phallic weapon, traditionally associated with masculine dominance, has failed Spoon, just as technology continues to thwart and fail the squaddies throughout the film. Retreating to the kitchen, Spoon hits the werewolf over the head with a frying pan (Figure 23) and stabs the beast with a kitchen knife, screaming as blood splatters across his face and drenches the kitchen units around them. Just as Spoon appears to be winning, a second werewolf enters the fray. The second werewolf grabs him by his neck and pins him to the wall. Spoon's head encompasses the entire left hand side of the frame, his body literally cut out of shot. In the right hand side and centre of the frame the drooling mouth of the werewolf is revealed,

Figure 23: Darren Morfitt in *Dog Soldiers*. Carousel Pictures Production Company, The Noel Gay Motion Picture Company and Kismet Entertainment Group.

sharp canines jutting out. The majority of its body continues to reside in the horror of the blind space, a place that only Spoon can see and the spectator can only imagine.

However, seconds before his death Spoon does something that represents a turn in the narrative for the destruction of the male body, offering a brief moment of redemption. Spoon spits on the werewolf's muzzle and snarls 'I hope I give you the shits you fucking wimp.' He is then dismembered. This one moment of defiance, of masculinity's last stance symbolised by swearing and bodily functions, creates the final narrative propulsion that allows Cooper to survive. Spoon's refusal to be a victim signals to the audience a change in the male victim and female/familial monster mode that has dominated the film up until this point. Immediately after this event, Wells and Cooper take control of the upstairs space of the house, barricading doors, tunnelling through walls and dropping through ceilings in order to evade their canine pursuers. This active reformation of the spaces surrounding them results in 'Final Girl' Cooper evading the werewolves and surviving the night. After showing Wells and Cooper, the camera briefly returns to the kitchen. It zooms in on the remains of Spoon, a pile of blood and gizzards on the kitchen floor. The werewolves are fighting each other to devour his insides. Only lingering on the tearing for a few moments, it emphasises carnality as the canine teeth intimately tear at the cadaverous remains. Isabel Pinedo has argued that 'body horror can be accomplished with only a part of the body standing in for the mutilated whole' (1997: 19).

In *Dog Soldiers*, the intestines of Spoon demonstrate his capture, mutilation and murder effectively.

V. DESTROYING THE MALE BODY

Dog Soldiers explicitly disrupts the penetrated/penetrating dominant binary of hegemonic culture by presenting wounded, screaming and dying male bodies. Horror is inherent in the dissolution of male bodily boundaries. Halberstam's work on postfeminism, gender and horror, can usefully be considered here:

> maleness and masculinity, and femaleness and femininity, are bound to one another, not through the body, but through the way in which bodies are made intelligible. The masculinity of the male is secured through an understanding of his body as impenetrable and as capable of penetrating. Femininity, then, becomes that which can be and must be penetrated but which cannot penetrate in return. (2007: 32)

Masculinity is revealed as a cultural performance through bonding, weapons and football, and is swiftly undermined by the female werewolf and her family. The film chooses to focus on the dissolution of the male body, reiterating that Army training and powerful phallic weapons are almost useless against the archaic and abject might of her family. Aside from Megan's swift and rather unconvincing death, weaponry and Army training is shown to be inferior to the cunning and power of the werewolves. Male bodies are penetrated and destroyed regularly, with the camera lingering greedily on the red overspill of their insides.

The on-screen dissolution of Spoon's bodily boundaries is inextricably bound up with abjection, as the boundaries of the body, those 'boundaries, designed to keep the abject at bay, threaten to disintegrate, collapse' (Creed, 2004: 52). Spoon's dismembered corpse is a reminder of the frailty of our bodies, and the ease with which exterior and interior are traversed. Julia Kristeva (1982) argues that abjection is resolutely a feminine condition and relates to the horror of the maternal entity. The bloody mess of Spoon's insides, strewn across the traditionally feminine domestic realm of the kitchen reiterates the concomitant triumph and horror of the maternal family. Furthermore, the visualisation of abject can be directly related to the masochistic spectatorship of the male body. Creed argues that the viewer re-establishes the boundaries of the established civilised order by looking away at moments when the images on screen become too horrific (1993b: 29). However, instead of looking away to eject the abject, there is a perverse masochistic pleasure in viewing the collapse of the body and dissolution of Spoon's identity.

The film concludes as Wells, turning into a werewolf, sacrifices himself and blows up the house, killing the werewolves. Hiding in the cellar, Cooper is forced to fight the newly resurrected werewolf Ryan at the film's close, and relive the antagonism made explicit in the prologue. Cooper discovers the *deus ex machina* silver knife, ostensibly recovered by the werewolf family from the campers in the prologue. Cooper stabs Ryan with the silver knife, and then finishes him off by shooting him in the head. Rather inconsistently, Megan was killed with a gunshot to the head using normal bullets, while Ryan requires a return to folkloric solutions. The film concludes as Cooper walks out into the morning light. It could be argued that the return of the phallus, symbolised by the knife, creates a contradictory conclusion to the proto-feminist narrative. This would accord with Klaus Rieser's reading of the slasher film. Rejecting Clover's feminist reading of such texts, Rieser argues that in the slasher film 'gender disruption is folded back into the hegemonic mold' and that the genre 'serves to reinforce the heterosexist matrix, despite – or even by way of – its break with mainstream gender forms' (2001: 375). However, the restitution of the phallus is short lived in *Dog Soldiers*, for the knife was given to the male camper by his girlfriend at the beginning of the film. As such, this act further emphasises the power of the woman, destabilises the possession of the phallus and undermines the power of the male body.

There is a distinct masochistic pleasure in viewing the dissolution of the male body on screen. Writing on the white, heterosexual male body in popular culture, Elizabeth Stephens suggests that 'the very dominance of male corporeality has come to elide its cultural specificity', and that 'whereas the bodies of women, children and "others" have traditionally been constructed as objects of analysis, the universalised male body has effaced itself as an invisible norm' (2007: 86). The contemporary British horror film *Dog Soldiers* offers a space, constructed through the destruction of the male body, in which fixed notions of gender, and the sanctity of the dominant body are subverted. The expectation of the lone woman Megan as the female victim is overturned as she becomes the creature they fear the most. In addition, in the tradition of horror's greatest Final Girls, Cooper emerges, bloodied, battered but triumphant.

VI. CONCLUSION

This chapter has aimed to elucidate how the British horror film *Dog Soldiers* has created a diachronic break between masculinity and the male body, suggesting that the male body as a single unified construct is dissolved by the female werewolf and her family. This idea also relates to Rieser's view that slasher films 'play with a "hot spot" of masculinity: the issue of control' (2001: 386). Despite their knowledge, Army training and phallic weaponry, the British squaddies lose all control, becoming forced to submit to the bestial power of the lycanthropic family. Following this, it has been argued that the undermining of the phallus and the dissolution of the male body leads to a mode of masochistic spectatorship. Broadly understanding masochistic spectatorship as a passive mode of looking that emphasises moments of shock, fear and horror, it has been suggested that the passivity evoked in masochistic looking is a result of the breakdown in the dominant hegemonic conceptions of the unified male body. Importantly, this chapter has moved away from widely accepted conceptions of gendered viewing practices, in terms of theorising the male or female spectator, to argue that the masochistic will to submission is available to all. Through its critical awareness of the horror genre, destruction of the male body and organisation of masochistic looking relations, *Dog Soldiers* challenges viewing expectations and generic conventions, thus representing an important intervention into British horror cinema.

NOTES

1 There has been much debate over the early and explicit reveal of the fire demon. For a detailed discussion of the tension between *Night of the Demon*'s producer Hal E. Chester, who favoured the outright shock of display, and director Jacques Tourneur who preferred a more subtle and suggestive presentation, see Earnshaw (2005).

2 For a discussion of Scottish national identity in *Dog Soldiers*, see Martin-Jones (2007).

Part 3

The Body, Sex and Sexuality

11

When 'Macho' Bodies Fail: Spectacles of Corporeality and the Limits of the Homosocial/sexual in Mexican Cinema

Vek Lewis

This chapter forges connections between three etymologically linked terms: spectacle, inspections and speculations. The male body, as visualised in two very different Mexican films, *Y tu mamá también/And Your Mother Too* (dir. Alfonso Cuarón, 2001) and *Zapata: el sueño del héroe/Zapata: Dream of a Hero* (dir. Alfonso Arau, 2004), joins the terms conceptually beyond their mere sound-alike similarity. In the limits of this chapter I will ask some central questions that relate to these terms: How is the male body positioned as *spectacle* in these two films? How does each film offer its male protagonists' corporeality up to *inspection* by the audience and what kind of *speculations* about the sexual and gendered tendencies of these bodies have been subsequently made by audiences and might also be available to the critic?

I. MALE BODIES ON FILM: THEORETICAL CONSIDERATIONS

Cinema would appear well disposed to the heightened visibility and spectacularisation of bodies given the very structural properties of the visual apparatus. The roving eye of the camera registers depth, contour, shadow, properties of light and differences between objects. Film is inevitably material and optical. Its materiality is not just the effect of optics but also the manipulation of visual content via selection, placement, contrast and contiguity. If film makes bodies into spectacles, thus making bodies into objects, it can only do so with the presence of a viewer who consumes the image. Thus filmic bodily spectacles are quite logically subject to inspections of another eye, that of the viewer. This implies a set of looking relations, which is not altogether unsurprising, given that the terms spectacle and inspection, like speculation, derive from the Latin *specere*, that is, to look. Looking relations concern who occupies the position of viewer and who is the object of the gaze. Steve Neale (1993) holds that Mulvey's thesis on woman as object of the male gaze in Hollywood cinema can, in essence, be applied to the relation between the cinematic male as object and the male viewer, who is brought into a relation of both identification and eroticisation of the male object. Neale flags this dynamic especially with respect to the male body on show in epics and action films.

The films examined in this chapter are not Hollywood-style epics in which the naked or semi-naked male body is placed on display as a site of bravery or phallic mastery, and, for this reason, they are not offered as spectacles in the classic sense as outlined by critics who follow Neale's analysis. And yet, all the male characters in the films discussed in this chapter must perform certain acts to make them men; masculinity is, in both films, viewed as a rite of passage. Macho bodies assert themselves but also risk failure because of 'the terrifying permeability of masculinity to femininity' (Silverman, 1992: 348). Such permeability – referred to by Kaja Silverman in the context of nineteenth-century sexological discourses on homosexuality – is linked in the Mexican cultural imaginary to the stigma of being open to penetration. The open body as the nightmarish sign of a descent into femininity and homosexuality is an important structuring element in the visualisation of male bodies, how they may be said to 'pass muster' and hence pass convincingly as masculine, and how they may fail. This is a central axis running through the present chapter, and as such, will be invoked at several points of the analysis of each film. The spectacular nature of the films' visualisation of male bodies is, moreover, underlined by the gendering and (homo)eroticisation of these bodies, and the looking relations established between the viewer and the objects of the gaze. Male bodies in both *Y tu mamá también* and *Zapata: el sueño del héroe* are offered up as spectacles for inspection, and subsequently, they generate a series of speculations.

Homoeroticism as subtext in seemingly heterosexual narratives has been studied at length by several generations of scholars, from the foundational works of Vito Russo (1981) and Richard Dyer (1990), to work on Hollywood cinema conducted within masculinity studies by Peter Lehman (1993), Yvonne Tasker (1993), Steven Cohan and Ina Rae Hark (1993), and Robert Lang (2002), as well as criticism that examines the encoding of the male body and sexuality in Spanish film by Chris Perriam (2003) and Santiago Fouz-Hernández and Alfredo Martínez

Expósito (2007). All critics highlight the ways in which homosocial entanglements can cue the viewer to homoerotic readings of the main characters in mainstream, especially Hollywood, productions. The potential of the generation of so-called 'queer readings' of male-on-male friendships has been critically foregrounded by Alexander Doty (1993). Most of this work assumes that the decoding of the homoerotic dynamic constitutes an alternative entry into the filmic text, wherein sexual interest between two males on the screen, though subliminated, may be activated by the viewer attentive to the dynamic. A key text in the explicit visualisation of the boundary between homosociality and homoeroticism, *Y tu mamá también* makes very conscious the tension between identification with and contemplation of male bodies, as well as between voyeurism and erotic fetishisation. It brings to the surface a tension that lay deep in previous Mexican cinematic productions of the male body, and challenges audiences to think and inhabit the ideational lines of same-sex desire in ways previously unheard of, reforming practices of spectatorship in the process.

Zapata, released three years after *Y tu mamá*, uncomfortably offers the body of its male protagonist, a fictional incarnation of the historical national hero Emiliano Zapata, represented by Alejandro Fernández, to its viewers. Its presentation of the male body, here most pointedly and mythically national, unconventionally cites alternative codes of masculinity normally screened out of Mexican cinema, particularly heroic cinema. Both films are linked by the interest in the display of male bodies, and by their unconventional visions of masculinity that cite but also rewrite traditional codes, especially as established around the figure of the *charro*, the Mexican rural cowboy. The very different fortunes of these films, both examples of the so-called New Mexican Cinema, suggest that their spectacles of male bodies were subject to vastly different forms of inspection, forming the ground of widely differing speculations around masculinity and homosexuality. The connections between masculinity and homosexuality as mediating axes will be fleshed out in the analysis of the two films in what follows. First, however, a brief history of the visualisation of male bodies and masculinity in Mexican cinema is necessary in order to understand how the two films reiterate and diverge from the historical pattern of depiction of male bodies in Mexican cinema.

II. THE MALE BODY IN MEXICAN CINEMA: AN OVERVIEW

In his study of Mexican film from the early days of the talkie (1910–20) through the Golden Age (1935–59), Sergio de la Mora speaks of 'the particular self-conscious form of national masculinity and patriarchal ideology articulated via the cinema and vigorously promoted by the revolutionary state as official ideology' (2006: 2). The name of this concept gives his book its title, cinemachismo. As an ideology, it marries machismo to national identity; *mexicanidad* and masculinity become synonymous. Realised in film, cinemachismo is traceable in the four main genres that form the focus of his study: the revolutionary melodrama, the musical comedy/'buddy movie', the prostitution melodrama, and *cabaretera* and *fichera* films.[1] For the purposes of this chapter, the first two genres are the most relevant. They also represent landmarks in filmic production of the Golden Age. Mexican Golden Age cinema, in particular, is known not only as the source of roughly hewn masculine bodily and behavioural ideals, but also as the wellspring of mythologies of Mexican national identity. It is in the cinema of this era that the principal motifs of the collective imagined community were forged, and the connection between masculine bodily economies and nation is by no means incidental. The post-revolutionary male hero is emblematic of the idealised collective, whose bonds are sealed via male homosocial relations and whose identity is asserted via the spectacle of masculinity.

The *charro* figure has its origin in films from the Golden Age. The *charro*, as de la Mora observes, is 'the quintessential symbol of masculine *mexicanidad*' (2006: 83). The films in which he appeared are full of 'mariachis and trios, and fierce women and fighting roosters' (Monsiváis 1995: 118). The legendary Jorge Negrete and Pedro Infante appeared, among other actors, in a chain of films that spectacularise the male body as a national one, including *¡Ay Jalisco, no te rajes!/Jalisco, Don't Backslide* (dir. Joselito Rodríguez, 1941), *No basta ser charro/Being a Charro is Not Enough* (dir. Juan Bustillo Oro, 1946), *Los tres García/The Three Garcías* (dir. Ismael Rodríguez, 1946), *Soy charro de Rancho Grande/I'm a Charro from the Big Ranch* (dir. Joaquín Pardavé, 1947), *Nosotros los pobres/We the Poor* (dir. Ismael Rodríguez, 1947), *Allá en el Rancho Grande/Out on the Big Ranch* (dir. Fernando de Fuentes, 1949), and *Dos tipos de cuidado/Two Careful Fellows* (dir. Ismael Rodríguez, 1953). Such films were nostalgic and pointed to 'the idea of a paradise lost located in an indefinite time where men were strictly male and women definitely female' (118).

III. *Y TU MAMÁ TAMBIÉN*

Y tu mamá también, although set in contemporary Mexico, partakes of the genre of the comic road/buddy movie and is arguably conscious of the tradition of the cinematic deployment of male bodies and archetypal Mexican masculinity as described above. Although its two young male protagonists, Julio, played by Gael

García Bernal, and Tenoch, played by Diego Luna, are far from rural men – in fact, they are primordially urban, specifically *chilango* in their Mexico City-derived use of slang and city lifestyles – they call each other '*charolastras*', a phrase they coin that mixes the word '*charro*' with '*astra*', that is, space cowboy. As *charolastras* they share a ten-point code of honour. These codes relate to how they perform their masculinity and their relations with other men. Women figure to the extent that they are sexual objects that cannot be shared between two *charolastras*. Their codes bind them homosocially in a boys' club; the first code enunciated by the protagonists while they are on the road in the company of their lust object, the Spanish traveller, Luisa (Maribel Verdú), states that 'There's no greater honour than being a charolastra'.[2] An urban update of the old, mythic Mexican cinematic ideal of the macho, codes of *charolastra* masculinity are cited in the embodied gender routines of the two protagonists and are also evident in the sexual contract on sharing women (a sublimated text about sharing each other's bodies) that lies behind its comic surface claims to honour and bravery.

Bodies, sex, sexuality, masculinity and machismo are all figured from the first few frames of *Y tu mamá también*. And yet as male bodies proffered up to the viewer's inspection, they are bodies that have barely reached 'manhood' as it is traditionally spectacularised in Golden Age cinema. The bodies, in all their liminality, seem very real, and form the site of viewer identification. As the critic Gustavo Geirola notes, 'the bodies and their speech offer themselves to the naturalness (and even realism) of the film [...] they allow themselves to be taken over by a voluptuousness that, on occasion, makes the presence of the cinematographic apparatus disappear' (2002: 173). Their adolescent, hairless bodies, supple, prone, are intimately shown. The primacy of filmic homoeroticism over heterosexuality in *Y tu mamá también* is marked by the fact that, as Paul Julian Smith notes, 'most of the film's frequent and graphic nudity is male' (2002: 16). Moreover, the sexual pursuit of Luisa that the boys ostentatiously flaunt pales in significance to the intensification in the film of what Andrea Noble labels the 'homoerotic charge' that exists in the friendship between Julio and Tenoch, who are inseparable and often shown naked together (2005, 123–24). On the rare occasions that the boys' penises are revealed they are never erect, but, rather, flaccid. When their bodies are completely naked they are mainly shot from behind; even as the protagonists engage in heterosexual coitus, they are coded visually for the voyeuristic and fetishistic (eroticising) gaze as open to penetration. This is also the case in a notable shower scene early in the film (see Figure 24). Such a subversive move up-ends the historical dynamic that demands of macho bodies a closed-ness, an impenetrability, the kind of intactness performed by Negrete and Infante in the Golden Age films, even as the film insistently Mexicanises and

Figure 24: Diego Luna and Gael García Bernal in *Y tu mamá también*. Anhelo Producciones.

masculinises its protagonists, whose eventual homoerotic union becomes part of their rite of passage into adult masculinity.

In the introduction to this chapter reference was made to the stigma of open bodies that suggest the permeability of masculinity to femininity. Given its stated centrality in Mexican cinematic visualisations of male bodies, it is necessary to elucidate the ways in which bodies and their (im)penetrability are linked in Mexican cultural logics to the performance of masculinity and (hetero)sexuality, as exposed by critics and thinkers such as Octavio Paz (1961), Roger Bartra (1996) and Marit Melhuus (1996). In his work *El laberinto de la soledad/The Labyrinth of Solitude* (1961), Paz famously claims that open bodies, or bodies that might be rent open by an outside, penetrating force, are quintessentially and historically aligned in Mexico with the figure of the raped Indian woman, Malinche, colloquially known as *La Chingada*. Mexican masculinity, in its much-touted flight from femininity, refuses the vulnerability of this openness, equated to violence, abjection and passivity (1961: 77). The macho's sense of self is founded on the desire for bodily integrity; all threats to this closed, 'intact' or hermetic state, to use Paz's terms, are repelled (31). The violence of colonial invasion of the people and the land is overwritten in sexual terms. Penetration enacts a feminisation that macho bodies must avoid. Paz sees this dynamic as deeply impressed in the Mexican psyche, and formative of its sense of the national. The macho is *chingón*, the one who wounds and penetrates. His aggressiveness assures he is not open (77).

The inspection of bodies by the camera in *Y tu mamá también*, with its emphasis on filming the protagonists' naked bodies from behind, is suggestive of this penetrability and potential loss of masculinity, and yet that depends largely on the viewer's decoding of the homoerotic subtext that does not come into full view until the film's finale. As if to compensate for the potential slide into openness and abjection, the two protagonists – in their youthful bodily vulnerability – invoke homophobic epithets, challenging the other's authority to masculinity by way of the insistent use of the word '*puto*' (faggot) and denigrating the other's (off-screen and unsighted) genitals. This sparring and play enacts a deferral of the homoerotic interest already well-established by the early scenes which feature Julio and Tenoch lying side by side overlooking a swimming pool, stimulating themselves sexually and mentally with fantasies of real and idealised women. This masturbation scene is not without precedent in Hispanophone film. Fouz-Hernández and Martínez Expósito see it as something of a homoerotic motif in recent Spanish cinema (2007: 42). The homoeroticism at this point simply underlines their *cuatismo*, the peculiarly Mexican form of homosociality. Later this muted conjunction of the homosocial and sexual is given an explicit name by the two *charolastras*, who dub themselves '*hermanitos de leche*' (cum brothers). Their sexual display in fact writes their bodies as masculine. In Mexico, as in other parts of Latin America, according to the most traditional models, the binary 'male/female' sits at the heart of understandings of both sex and sexuality, as critics such as Sylvia Chant and Nikki Craske (2003) point out. Men are as they are because of biological drives, possessive of an overt sexuality that can barely be reined in. Apart from its manifestation via tactics of aggression and homophobic disavowal, Mexican (hyper)masculinity is spectacularised via a sexual showiness and bravado typical of the two protagonists in *Y tu mamá también*.

Public knowledge of the two stars' heterosexuality also aids to defer speculation as to the full import of the potential penetrability of the protagonists' bodies and their (temporarily forestalled) homosexual desires. The profile of a widely admired star's private life and 'inclinations' undoubtedly participates in their reception of their on-screen personae. This is the case for both García Bernal and Diego Luna (and also Alejandro Fernández, as we shall see later in connection to *Zapata*), whose popularity in Mexico, especially among the younger generation, was prominent at the time of the film's release and has grown exponentially since. García Bernal and Luna have firm reputations as leading men both nationally and internationally. As de la Mora notes, tracing lines of contention around nation, masculinity and identification, Pedro Infante also secured an impressive profile that influenced viewer inspections of his body and speculations about his sexuality and masculinity (2006: 84). This provides an antecedent to Mexican audience modes of inspection and speculation about filmic masculine embodiments. Extratextual details of Infante's real-life voracious sexual appetite and conquests support the myth of his macho image and make him the prime site of collective identifications of Mexicanness and masculinity (84). It should be noted that García Bernal and Luna, although increasingly transnational in their personae, are also very much associated with Mexicanness, something that *Y tu mamá también*, with its very graphic and colloquial title phrase, constantly underlines, especially in contrast to the Spanishness of the character of Luisa, who is taken on a tour of regional Mexico as the trio make their way to the fictional 'Boca del cielo' beach. The film's visual tourism and ironic omniscient voice-over commentary on the nation simultaneously asserts its Mexicanness and deconstructs it.[3]

The risks of macho bodies and their potential failure to secure (heterosexual) masculinity fully and unambiguously are brought to bear in the sequences that culminate in the trio between Luisa, Julio and Tenoch once their bodies and inhibitions are relaxed after several days of the liberation of being at 'Boca del cielo' beach (an invented paradise), far from Mexico City and the usual social-sexual demands of the sprawling metropolis. The famous scene in which, in the midst of tequila-induced *ménage-à-trois* with Luisa, the two boys kiss and off camera have sex, diegetically echoes the earlier statement by Luisa to Julio and Tenoch that 'all you guys would like to do is fuck each other'. This scene, the first of its kind in Mexican cinema, caused an audible uproar wherever the film was screened, even as the mooted 'sex' happens off camera.[4] Although indeed a culmination of all the sexual tension behind the sparring and competitiveness of the two friends, many Mexican viewers did not speculate that the bravura display of masculinity on the attractive bodies of the young protagonists and the continual physical contact between them – Tenoch with his arm around Julio, pointing out a poster of Michelangelo's *David*, for instance, and grabbing his crotch – could be homoerotic. The very Mexicanness of the protagonists' homosociality, as well as their involvement with and lust for Luisa, among a range of fantasised female sex objects, perhaps all but discounted this possibility for audiences who saw García Bernal and Luna as resolutely heterosexual, where the slippage between the actors' real-life personae and their screen ones asserts itself. The scene of homoerotic initiation itself is an opening into a measure of privacy usually mentioned merely in undertones, and, at its most shrill in real life, the subject of informal scandal and gossip. Cuarón brings the configuration of his actors' bodies in direct alignment with non-heterosexual desire, and this proves to be too much (at least temporarily) for some audiences, and yet at the same time is voyeuristically fascinating. The popularity of the film suggests that this scene, although ostensibly discomforting to many a (heterosexual) male viewer, is somehow fundamental to many a macho's (disavowed) lived experience, or fantasy. The characters themselves disavow their encounter and its import, that is, the potential risk to their masculinity, by terminating their friendship once the trio separates, Julio and Tenoch returning to Mexico City, and Luisa to an uncertain fate that is tied up with the knowledge of her death. What might have risked the status of their masculine bodies becomes a half-remembered (dreamt?) and yet vivid fugue of memory, as the boys return to their heterosexual lives, somehow matured into men by the experience. *Y tu mamá también* inserts a new narrative into the Mexican myth-making process of machos and masculine bodies, one that offers codes to an audience perhaps lulled previously into the belief in the traditional notion that the macho and the *maricón* are mutually exclusive. As Paul Julian Smith observes, *Y tu mamá también* 'subtly revises models of gender and national identity for a new Mexico' (2002: 16).

De la Mora notes elsewhere in his study that 'flawed' masculinities are not necessarily erased from cinematic representation in Mexican film, and that indeed many of the most memorable embodiments of archetypal maleness by Mexican stars historically have embodied excess and do not depend, necessarily, on restraint, unlike the silent and stoic masculinities of many Anglo films (2006: 12). This underlines the importance of understanding Mexican filmic visualisations of masculinities and male bodies in their own socio-cultural peculiarity. If *cinemachismo*, to reiterate the use of this critic's phrase, is first born out of the revolutionary programme of modern patriarchal nation-state formation and collective identity, films made in more recent times should, and will, with all the attendant socio-cultural changes, map male bodies and masculinities in perhaps different ways, even as traditional gender discourses continue to circulate alongside emergent ones. *Y tu mamá también*'s citing of historical models and its new visualisation of masculinity and erotic bodily economies might be explained this way. So, too, the fictional presentation of the real-life revolutionary leader, Emiliano Zapata in the second film for analysis.

IV. *ZAPATA: EL SUEÑO DEL HÉROE*

Zapata, whose life and death continue to inspire many Mexicans, and whose name latterly lends itself to the *Ejército Zapatista de Liberación Nacional* (EZLN), counts as a sacred mythic symbol of revolutionary Mexico, alongside the other famous rural revolutionary outlaw, Pancho Villa.[5] Mexican film critics, according to de la Mora, have long argued that Pancho Villa was the nation's first macho superstar, being 'the epitome of the macho' (2006: 6). Even though Zapata himself fought against the *hacendado* (estate) system of land dispossession and rural peonage that defines the *charro* phenomenon, in the filmic imaginary he, like Pancho Villa, is identified with that kind of masculinity.

Zapata: el sueño del héroe is not the first biopic to chronicle the adventures of the revolutionary. Others who have portrayed the famous '*Caudillo del Sur*' include Marlon Brando in Elia Kazan's *Viva Zapata!* (1952) and Antonio Aguilar (known popularly as 'el charro de México') in Felipe Cazal's *Emiliano Zapata/ Zapata* (1970). In these films, we return to the incarnation of the *charro* in his rural and equestrian glory. The *charro* is never without his horse, a force of nature, unbridled and indomitable like the man himself. One star who has made his living by performing and embodying the Mexican macho *charro* is the singer, recently turned actor, Alejandro Fernández. Fernández's video clips cite endlessly the embodied masculine ideals inaugurated by Negrete and Infante in the Golden Age.

According to Alberto Batista (2004), director Arau chose Alejandro Fernández as the lead in his film because, impressed by his videography, he saw him as representative of *mexicanidad* and possessive of a strong physical resemblance to Zapata. Further, the director sees his film as part of the push for a global audience for Mexican films that still retain their *mexicanidad* (Caballero 2004). Reportedly the most expensive film ever made in Mexico, in spite of its touted faithfulness to national values, it was a dismal box office failure. The film was also thoroughly savaged by critics, several of whom barely contained their distaste for its depiction of their nation's beloved hero. Arau's *Zapata*, many argued, was an example of an unrealistic and ahistorical portrait of Mexico, in all its faux magical realist glory, proffered up to US audiences. In spite of its imprint of Mexicanness, then, Mexicans by and large rejected the film as false and artificial. As Batista observes:

> Mexicans have been tough critics of the film of their countryman Arau. And they have apparently been so fair in their judgments that Arau has not even been able to defend historically one iota of his film. And this fact [the lack of the film's historical defensibility], not the desire to film following Hollywood models in all their political correctness, contributed to the half-effeminate Zapata [of the film]. (2004)

I find this observation interesting because of the explicit connection it makes between lack of historical veracity (and therefore 'true' representative function of a vital period of Mexican national experience) and a compromised or 'failed' masculinity in the way Zapata is portrayed by Fernández. Believability in a truly Mexican story is implicitly linked to a believable and authentic masculinity. This reinforces the paradigm that was commonly found in post-revolutionary Golden Age cinema, especially in those films that fit in the revolutionary period genre. As Gutmann argues, by the time of the Mexican Revolution 'Mexico came to mean *machismo* and *machismo* came to mean Mexico' (1996: 224). One, presumably, cannot be had without the other; Mexicanness is synonymous with masculinity. And yet, why, if Fernández was so widely recognised as a prototypical embodiment of the macho *charro* in his musical career, and if, given previous comments about the complexity of recent cinematic masculinities, does this film fail to measure up? Eduardo Martínez Soto Alessi, for instance, declaims that the film shows 'a dressy and cloying hero that, among other things, never shoots a bullet' (2004). The language of this critic is also interesting for its intimations of affectation, symptomatic, again, of the perceived failure of the expectation of a 'pure' macho embodiment of Zapata. It is worth giving some consideration, then, to exactly how Fernández embodies Zapata on the screen, or rather, what kind of versions and visions of the male body Arau as director offers up for inspection in his film. We might then anchor some of the critical speculations on this body in the materiality of the film. To account for the audience rejection of the film, which many dismissed outright even before they had seen it, further discussion of the wider speculations about its star, Alejandro Fernández will also be undertaken, to the degree that any actor brings intertextual elements from previous productions, as well as talk about his or her private life, to bear on receptions of their bodies and performances.

From the first sequence of frames of *Zapata*, Fernández is shown in full *charro* regalia and mounting a horse. The scene could easily be spliced from one of his myriad film clips. The sumptuous cinematography of renowned Italian maestro Vittorio Storaro lends the mise-en-scene an ornate and studied quality. Historical melodrama turns into a mystic passion play under the visual design of Storaro and direction of Arau; Fernández's performance is hence concentrated and ponderous.

His Zapata is one that endures both spiritual and bodily trials, tellingly, (feminised?) under the guidance of three Indian women, ghosts from the past in a multi-dimensional universe where the time of the Conquest overlaps with the revolution and the future liberation of the poor, indigenous and popular rural folk. Zapata is paralleled to Cuauhtémoc, the legendary Aztec ruler tortured and finally executed by Hernán Cortés. Fernández's Zapata undergoes gruelling forms of bodily suffering and punishment at the hands of his oppressors, namely the General Huerta, but also as a test to draw out the mettle of his spirit and set him on the path to leadership of an insurrectional army. In the film, the revolutionary hero is depicted as constantly wavering and unsure of this path. The tortures of his body, like the pains of the suffering Christ (see Figure 25) outweigh any (masculine) glories. His body is lacerated and beaten, rained upon, burnt and made vulnerable. Only Mel Gibson's film *The Passion of the Christ* (2004) outdoes the gestures to bodily suffering and martyrdom of the cinematic male body. Although Fernández's famous taut frame and golden skin are placed on display, they offer little eroticism. The body offered to viewing inspection in these sequences is an open body, and hence risks a loss of masculinity, remembering traditional Mexican cultural logics

Figure 25: Alejandro Fernández in *Zapata: el sueño del héroe*. Zapata Dreams, Plethora Media Works, Hamsa, Angel Isidoro Rodríguez Productions and Zapata Productions.

around open and closed bodies. In the moments of battle, Zapata is quite bodiless, such is his remove from the proceedings at hand. Tellingly, as well, in the film's few love scenes, he is not the gallant, impassioned pursuer or lady's man that former cinematic *charros* Pedro Infante and Jorge Negrete so memorably incarnated. The one extended post-wedding moment of erotic union and marital consummation is a subdued affair, full of gestures and caresses and the chaste kisses that typify any and every other romantic dalliance featured between Zapata and his love interests in the rest of the film, and itself is reminiscent of a perfume commercial, replete with soft lighting, pensive pauses and longing looks. Zapata's transformation from rural hard man to urban dashing but polite gentleman occurs with little explanation, and conscripted army life does not detract from the aura of moral rectitude and removal that come to be among his defining features.

This is not the first film of Arau's that has framed its male romantic leads in a soft light. *Como agua para chocolate/Like Water for Chocolate* (1993) similarly depicted strong and hearty women and boyish, pliant men who become the object of women's gaze, in a thoroughly *novela rosa* hue. The permissibility of this kind of re-visioning of masculinities would seem to be very context-dependent. After all, as we have seen by the example of *Y tu mamá también*, liminal male bodies – at the threshold of 'manhood', still in the glow of adolescence – still offer the potential for eroticisation and audience identification. Such a space seems refused in *Zapata*. Indeed, when performing the revolutionary macho body, one so preciously anchored in the mythic history of a real-life national hero, the leeway open to a director to play with this liminality would appear to be in doubt. Such visions were rejected critically, as we have seen, on the grounds of failing to invoke and tally with the discourses of Mexicanness and also machismo.

And yet, would not audiences, already prepared by the highly popular *Y tu mamá también* that preceded *Zapata* by some three years, be able to accommodate this kind of non-traditional masculinity and re-visioning of the revolutionary macho body, even as it tests the limits of the genre as established in the Golden Age? Here I would suggest that macho bodies do not fail in the first film, in spite of the homoerotic encounter so vividly depicted and talked about, as the stars' own reputations as heterosexual allow audiences to suspend judgements and treat the film as *story*. As we have seen, the demands of *history* prove too heavy for *Zapata*; but there is also another element that may have been at work in the wholesale dismissal of Fernández's incarnation of Zapata, and that is, the perception of the actor and his own sexual liminality.

Around the time of the debut of the film, Fernández, whose career trajectory as a credible *ranchera* singer and much-loved macho idol seemed untouchable, was assailed by multi-sourced and widespread rumours of his purported sexual relations with other men. Although the film's colossal box office failure is often attributed to narrative continuity problems, bad direction and an unintentionally kitsch series of wardrobe and prop changes, wherein, as Martínez Soto Alessi notes, one hardly can even believe the lines when they are said by the actors (2004), the corroborating revelations about the lead's reputed 'inclinations' may have been a factor for the film's simultaneous and overwhelming critical and popular rejection.

Such rumours began to circulate on the internet as early as 1998, in spite of the actor's well-publicised marriage and more recent relationship with the Colombian model Ximena Díaz and his image as a masculine idol. Fernández is, of course, hardly the first and last star of his stature to have become the source of such rumours. His subsequent break with Díaz around the time of the film's release only added fuel to the speculation as to his sexuality. The star was rumoured to be engaged in an affair with footballer Rafa Márquez, among others (see, for example, Univisión 2006).

Rumours such as these imply a kind of unofficial folk knowledge, that while subject to firm and frequent official denials and counter-publicity, still have the potential to impact on a star's career and the way he or she is perceived on screen, and consequently, how his or her body and its tendencies are read. Moreover, regardless of a star's real desires, personality and alliances, members of the public engage with celebrities in such a way that each individual collates their own particular image of a star, as DeAngelis has shown (2001). The kind of comments found on weblogs during and after the film's release over 2004–5 evince a level of speculation that discounts the ability of Fernández to properly embody masculine Mexican revolutionary ideals, linking this failure to reputed sexuality.[6] Such was the intensity of speculation around the real-life (but always mediated) body of Fernández that the actor himself began a counter-defence citing his interest in clothing and personal appearance as proof of his metrosexuality more than anything else (Gómez 2004).

V. CONCLUSION

In conclusion, while the looking relations that film spectacles of bodies offer to viewer inspection depend to a great degree on how the possibilities of perception, identification and objectification are semiotically structured in cinematic discourse, the speculation that may arise from visual encounters with celluloid male corporealities depend, as well, on what pertains outside the threshold of the text. As I have sketched out in this chapter, the way in which both fictional and literal bodies are understood and talked about in the site(s) of production and reception informs the perception of filmic male bodies. In Mexico, the dialectic of closed and open bodies has a long history and still holds traction. I have foregrounded this dialectic as particular to Mexican cultural logics of gendered and sexualised bodies and bodies placed on display and hence offered to speculation in film.

Speculations, after all, are not simply about unmediated ways of looking; they also imply judgements, which in turn are shaped and informed by cultural discourses in circulation. If bodies in filmic discourse in general are commonly placed on show, the case of the failure of revolutionary macho embodiment in *Zapata* demonstrates that in Mexico male screen bodies can also be placed on trial. The shifting kaleidoscope of visual male embodiments is an unfinished affair, wherein spectacles of male corporeality are guaranteed neither full closure nor cultural authorisation. While the vision of liminal youthful bodies in *Y tu mamá también* appears to have been permissible in spite of its notable explicitness in linking homosociality to homoeroticism, the spectre of homosexuality outside the bounds of the fictional universe invalidates the potential of the same space being granted to Fernández's embodiment of revolutionary macho corporeality from the start; bodies too open to gossip and the incursion of homosexuality from 'the real', then, would appear to present too much to bear for the national body, especially when celebrated 'real-life' legends are involved in representational practices of the male.

NOTES

1 *Fichera* films were the most common genre of films in Mexico from the early 1970s to the mid-1980s. These films borrow themes from the *cabaretera* films of the 1940s, which explored urban nightlife and featured musical numbers.

2 This is my translation, as are all others featured in this chapter.

3 That the film both underlines and problematises Mexicanness as a unitary concept, as well as underlining and challenging traditional notions of masculinity, is an important point that, due to the limitations of this chapter, is not explored in depth here.

4 I was privy to this kind of audience reaction on seeing the film in a packed movie house in the *Zona Rosa* district of Mexico City within the first few days of its national release. On watching this scene, many among the audience not only expressed shock and surprise, but a visceral rejection of what they were watching. Combined with audience hooting and booing, several people threw objects at the screen. Tellingly, however, no one left the cinema.

5 The EZLN, or the Zapatista Army of National Liberation, is an armed revolutionary group based in the southern Mexican state of Chiapas. It is centred on the land and livelihood claims of the indigenous Mayan people of the region. The group's most visible spokesperson is the famous Subcomandante Marcos.

6 As one commentator who responded to a post about *Zapata: el sueño del héroe* featured on the Mexican blog site Bluecat colourfully addressed the issue, eliciting a notable degree of homophobia: 'I saw the movie Zapata and the truth is that Arau really fucked things up. Alex looks like a little fag when he acts. [...] Someone said that if in the movie they were going to bring out the homo side of Zapata [...] then the role would've fit Alejandro Fernández pretty damn well' (canek1 2005).

12

Cinematic Cruising: Tsai Ming-liang's *Bu san* and the Strangely Moving Bodies of Taiwanese Cinema

D. Cuong O'Neill[1]

Tsai Ming-liang's *Bu san/Goodbye, Dragon Inn* (2003) is a film that presents itself as a conspicuous constellation of minimalist images, sounds and actions. With almost no camera movement, the film unfolds as an elegy for a certain shared cinematic experience. In the first sequence following the opening credits, we are introduced to the kinaesthetic world of King Hu's martial arts film *Long men ke zhan/Dragon Gate Inn* (1967) as it is being screened in the auditorium of a grand movie palace to a capacity crowd united in what seems to be their single-minded regard for the film. Even the dramatic opening score of the film seems to have little effect in distracting from their focused appreciation. The screen images, however, open with a telling texture, marred by all the scratches and pops of an old celluloid film, as if to evoke the increasingly archaic projection apparatus itself, if not to anticipate its death. Moments later, we learn that the passage of time has indeed transformed the film into something of a relic, and the movie palace into a dilapidated space in Taipei on its closing night. We now see a near-empty auditorium screening the same film, but this time to a handful of patrons more interested in cruising the cavernous spaces of the movie palace.

In transforming the auditorium space of movie-going into one of brief exchanges and sexual encounters, Tsai's film seems again to speak to a sense of melancholic disconnection that pervades his earlier works; here, however, the specific homage paid to Hu's martial arts classic also triggers unexpected echoes and connections, especially in regards to questions of desire and mobility. Tsai's film seems supremely invested in the moving male body, as well as in the desire to arrest such a body, to submit it to another type of motion, affording another view, as if in the act of looking again the desiring gaze can reorient itself for a glimpse of what was first missed, perhaps creating an opportunity for reconnection. This homage focuses on a certain kind of vision in which we are invited to participate as yet another audience.

As a loving tribute, the film consigns, through Hu's *Long men ke zhan*, the martial arts genre to a past refracted through nostalgic melancholy as well as a recognition of inexorable change. The screening of Hu's film thus becomes a cryptic pretext for Tsai to reconsider the kinaesthetic male bodies of the martial arts film as both a cinematic inheritance and as a site of reinvention. Insofar as it is implicated in the body politic of Asian cinema, Tsai's film can be said to participate in a broader discussion of how the production and circulation of martial art films is shaping the contours of transnational cultural politics. Though not unrelated, my main concern will be to trace the movements and placements of the male body as glimpsed in Hu's *Long men ke zhan* as well as to explore the performative powers of such a codified body as recalled, remembered and transformed in the interstitial resonances embedded within Tsai's film. I am interested in the ways in which *Bu san* takes leave of the masculinist body of the martial arts film and alights on the juxtaposed figure of the cruising male to derive an explanatory circuit for the evasive mobility of the film's cultural import. This superimposition may explain how the viewer connects (or does not) with the film, even as the film lingers on in the hope of reconnection by always affording us a second glance within a bonded set of dual meanings.

As this chapter aims to show, *Bu san* establishes, through a minimalist aesthetics, a self-reflexive and intertextual perspective, one which calls our attention to a specific and highly codified form of the male body, whose underlying masculinist ethos is revealed and critiqued, though the perspective may be one that is unable to relinquish its attachments to such a body. As a compound minimalist work, the film takes up the task of capturing, through its attempts to memorialise Hu's martial arts epic, the moving sensuousness of a different cinematic body – one that not only opens itself up to unanticipated theoretical reckonings, but also reorients our understanding of Tsai's strangely moving bodies in contemporary Taiwanese cinema. *Bu san* produces, through this improbable relation to its object of representation, a specific tension between stasis and movement, between loving tribute and obligatory forgetting, perhaps doubling along the way as both a repetition in cultural memory and a trenchant anatomy of the transnational futures of Taiwanese cinema.

I. TSAI MING-LIANG: BETWEEN FATHERS AND SONS

It is almost a truism that the films of Tsai Ming-liang helped launch the second wave of 'Taiwanese New Cinema' and played a key role in defining a transnational film aesthetic that was embraced widely.[2] Responding to the stylistic minimalism of his works, scholars have coined the phrase 'emptied-out family-home' to describe a fundamental change in the cinematic representations of contemporary Taiwan society (Berry and Farquhar 2006: 98–99).[3] Seen to be embracing an iconoclastic spirit that will later develop into an ambivalent critique of patriarchal authority, Tsai's early films have been located within a cultural matrix of rebellion and alienation specific to Taiwan's recent political and social milieu. In these films, the anxiety of having to reconcile rapid socioeconomic change with a new cultural identity in a post-boom Taiwan is manifested through individual alienation and disconnection from family and tradition. Vandalism and delinquency, in Tsai's *Ch'ing shaonien na cha/Rebels of the Neon God* (1992), become telling symptoms of a society thrust into change when the rebellious energy of an emergent youth culture comes into conflict with established authority and values of tradition. Acutely oriented around political and social taboos, *He liu/The River* (1997) explores the depredations of patriarchal order through the homoerotic lens of sexual transgression; and, in *Ni neibian jidian/ What Time Is It There?* (2001), the death of the father figure becomes an event that both marks the collapse of family structure and reflects more broadly on contemporary insecurities about loss of tradition amidst increasing demands for more radical social reforms after the lifting of martial law in 1987. Locating in Tsai's ambivalent critique of patriarchal culture a potent allegory for Taiwan's troubled relationship with China, critics have linked the existential rootlessness of Tsai's protagonists to a crisis in Taiwan's national identity, one precipitated by the country's layered colonial past as well as its uncertain future with China's encroaching influence.

Tsai's stylistic minimalism has thus been richly allegorised as an 'emptying out' of home, a spirited critique of tradition and patriarchy, and, for some, a symbolic expression for Taiwan's strained relationship with China. Following and deviating somewhat from these allegorical readings, I argue that within Tsai's oeuvre, lie a homoerotic modality and a Taiwanese specificity yet to be disclosed, a liaison of sorts poised at the very edge of semantic availability.

II. KING HU'S HEROES AND MOBILE BODIES

Though the Tsai oeuvre bespeaks an ambivalent disconnection with the past and the masculinist ethos that gives the past expression, the elegiac overtures Tsai makes to Hu's *Long men ke zhan* trigger some unexpected resonances. If the earlier films of Tsai's oeuvre identify a problematic male structure of feeling by placing into crisis the established authority of the father, then *Bu san* can be seen as an attempt to re-inhabit this feeling and to explore the past as an anxious form of erotic longing. Hu's 1967 classic film is a touchstone of sorts for martial arts films and continues to exert an important influence on the present. Such influence, with its cinematographic evocations of the time-honoured codes of heroism, has been much richer and more varied than its relative obscurity at present would suggest. The first film Hu directed after relocating to Taiwan and breaking with the Hong Kong-based Shaw Brothers, *Long men ke zhan* enriched the martial arts genre, reinvigorating tropes, such as the woman warrior sidekick and the all-powerful evil eunuch, as well as enhancing the performative powers of the male body with its glorified physical prowess and moral virility.[4]

Drawing from the resources of martial arts fiction and Peking opera, Hu's film aesthetic engenders a specific type of male hero, whose moral worth is made legible in the dexterity of action, a body celebrated not so much for its musculature as for its mobility. Though the natural athleticism of actors contributed to the dynamism of motion, it was Hu's choreography and editing techniques that fashioned a more dynamic sense of movement, energy and conflict. In addition to the conventional use of trampolines and wire works, Hu's sword fighting sequences are orchestrated as a series of dance-like movements and pauses. The energy of the choreography is amplified by Hu's editing technique, a tactic of allowing deliberate 'imperfections' by staging and cutting the action so that it becomes 'too quick, too distant, or too sidelong for us to register fully' (Bordwell 1998: 33). Through this treatment of action, the audience is afforded only 'glimpses' of the moving body, with the suggestion that the heroic body in action moves faster than the eye can record. Rather than shooting the action sequences statically with the motionless camera placed at a distance from the action where the actors would improvise a fight, Hu's choreography and editing techniques extended the kinaesthetic possibilities of the martial arts genre, altering the viewer's cinematic perceptions of the ways bodies move through space. Hu's achievements amplified the kinaesthetic effect of the choreographed body on the celluloid screen. In this regard, the influence of his aesthetics has been decisive.

The virtually enhanced masculine ethos of Hu's film – a structure of feeling inscribed by the movement of the male body on screen – expresses a nearly supernatural power that is, nevertheless, linked naturally to the male body to reaffirm the cultural coherence of patriarchal order. Though there may be variations, Hu's warriors are known more for their lyrical balance of physical prowess and moral rectitude.[5] With the historical setting of an ancient China, Hu's warriors fight not for blind vengeance but to preserve community and moral values, and can, even in combat, manage to display a Zen-like serenity of perfectly judged physical movements. Behind the emphasis on achieving a balance of physical and moral strength is the gravitas of Confucian order as one of the fundamental values grounding the martial hero to this world and structuring the ideological and value system of *wu xia*.[6] Berenice Reynaud argues that the *wu xia* world, as rendered in literature and film, is an ambivalent space, and while that world accommodates itself to instances of 'rebellious disorder', it eventually 'abides with the Confucian respect of the master, father and traditional authority' (2003: 4).[7] Following Reynaud's observation, Gomes argues that this ambivalence arises ultimately as a reaction to the 'patriarchal politics of Confucian society where the father, husband and son are the dominant figures of the family' and 'where the power of subjugation by the patriarchal order persists throughout' (Gomes 2005: 51).[8] Under such a perspective, although the male-impersonating swordswoman in Hu's films may have strong martial skills, we would expect her to be subjugated by Confucian values that maintain patriarchal order. In his formalist analysis of the genre, David Bordwell stresses the importance of 'stasis' in the 'pause-thrust-pause' pattern of fight choreography (2000: 221–31). Following this observation, we can argue that the narrative trajectory of Hu's film is organised around the figure of the male body mobilised through a dialectic of movement and stasis, a narrative tension which finds its closure on either moral victory or heroic sacrifice, and ultimately in the re-inscription of order, normalcy and hierarchy. The masculine power made legible by the supernatural mobility of the male body on screen can be seen as a virtual creation, a hyper-masculinity, as it were, produced by modern filmic effects and yet reaffirmed on a presumed naturalness of male power and authority.

The implication of this thematic and structural emphasis on normalcy and order for the gender politics of the martial arts film, both past and present, seems obvious; yet any passing evaluation of the genre's power to contain difference or to reaffirm the normative must take into consideration the libidinal circuits evoked from the patchwork of homosocial bonding and cross-dressing common in *wu xia* films.[9] Without simplifying the complex desires and identifications depicted in *Bu san*, one can argue that Tsai's film draws explicitly on this patchwork to put under scrutiny the masculinist ethos of the genre. Yet, at the same time, I want to suggest that the critique of patriarchy does not fully explain Tsai's sentimental regard for Hu's *Long men ke zhan*. As part of Tsai's homage, the two main actors who played the role of enemy swordsmen in Hu's classic film make a special appearance: sitting in the auditorium, both Shih Chun and Miao Tien are watching their younger and more robust selves battling on screen. With the camera focused on their now wrinkled faces, marking a certain passage of time, the viewer is afforded a lengthy, but tender close-up of Shih Chun's face as a tear trickles down his face. The presence of these men does not provoke scorn. In the same way, King Hu's work, for Tsai, does not provoke an 'anxiety of influence' but rather inspires recognition of how desire and mobility stipulate each other through the oblique counterpoints of memory and of strangely moving bodies.

III. THE MINIMALISM OF SOUNDS AND ANGLES

In Tsai's homage, the kinaesthetic pleasures afforded by Hu's heroic bodies are not reclaimed or realigned under the authority of moral order or patriarchal power, but refracted throughout to encourage an ironic engagement with the homoerotic subtext of Hu's film. In contrast to the lavish kinaesthetic movements displayed on screen, we learn that some of the patrons in the auditorium are more interested in a movement that transforms the anonymous hallways and corners of the movie palace into an undifferentiated space of sexual possibilities. Through an ensemble of minimalist images and sounds, *Bu san* provides a platform for unorthodox representations of the moving male body.

As an element of the repository of special effects, sounds in Hu's film are equally aggressive as the pictorial composition of the frame. Hu's orchestration of sound and image often transforms the action sequences of *Long men ke zhan* into a rousing echo chamber of the body in motion – whether that body is flying, rolling or colliding into another body. This fullness of sound that marked the force of each strike or kick with a distinct thud, however, echoes through Tsai's nearly empty auditorium without any visual analogue. The non-diegetic music that synchronises Hu's action sequences to the robust percussive beat of Peking Opera registers merely as ambient noise. Relegated to background noise, the disembodied soundtrack takes a whimsical turn in the dark auditorium as it ventriloquises for the silent strangers cruising for sex. With the ominous music of Hu's film ringing in the background, a young man moves in slowly to engage the attention of a stranger (played by Shih Chun, the actor who plays the protagonist role in Hu's classic). The tense musical interlude – used typically to prepare the viewer for a dramatic turn of event – opens out in Tsai's film to announce the sudden entrance of a pair of feet from an unconcerned patron draping his legs over the seat next to the young man. The somewhat unsightly image of feet inserted into the centre of the frame not only impedes our view of the 'action', but also blocks the young man's line of sight to his intended target. As the scene progresses, the repeated shouts of 'Halt!' from Hu's on screen heroes coincide with the young man's startled reaction to the unsolicited touch of a neighbour. He jumps from his seat, as if acting in direct response to the injunction on screen. Moments later, as the young man finds another opportunity for an approach and moves in with an expectant look, we hear a dialogue between two enemy swordsmen attempting to extract information about their mutual identities. Here, the young man's sexual overtures – what is in fact, his second attempt at cruising the same person – are choreographed against the two swordsmen's guarded exchange. As he moves closer to the stranger, stopping to wait for a response, we hear the following:

> Hu – 'What name do you go by?'
> [He moves closer to meet the man's gaze, his face almost caressing the seat separating him and the man]
> Hu – 'You come here for what purpose?'
> [He stares at his unresponsive partner]
> Hu – 'Ah, we are here on a secret mission'
>
> The young man sits up indignantly, stands up and leaves the auditorium as a line from Hu's film cues in with the question
>
> – 'Are you asking me to leave?'

In linking the displaced dialogue to a new set of actions, Tsai provides an ironic commentary on the goings-on in the auditorium, as the moral struggle between good and evil in Hu's film is displaced and transformed into a form of sexual adventure.[10]

Not only are Hu's sounds disembodied (and yet sexualised), his images are reoriented to destabilise the secured coherence of their gender and sexual orientations. Displacing the image of the moving body from its hyper-masculine context, Tsai transforms the scenes of heroic combat into a chiaroscuro of light and darkness. In one scene, the projections of Hu's moving bodies are represented as a luminous mosaic of white dots shifting over a woman's face. We are not sure what to make of the woman's amorous gaze: whether she is identifying with the cross-dressing woman warrior on screen or she is looking through the screen for a glimpse of the elusive male projectionist. In another, with the sound of the movie reel clicking, the disassembled images of another combat scene, as they are reflected on the back wall of the projection room, appear in the form of a ghostly palimpsest rotating on a surface where the sounds of masculine struggle are suggestively left without any clear visual analogue. At various points throughout *Bu san*, Tsai dislodges Hu's vast and spectacular fight scenes from the central axis of the opening sequence and positions them on the periphery of his own film's diegetic space. One dramatic scene is tilted diagonally, giving us a perspective of Hu's film at a slant, returning us to the high-flying warriors only to have them emerge as distorted images repositioned from varying distances. These slanted perspectives and acute angles reduce the acrobatic bodies of Hu's heroes and assassins, once made dynamic and exciting by the use of the widescreen frame, to misshapen images, as if to expose their cinematic origin as moving objects of light projected on a flat screen.

The interplay of light and darkness continues to play a central role in pictorially framing the cruising scenes as the lighting from Hu's film, diffused and refracted over the auditorium, simultaneously illuminates bodies and extends spaces for secret encounters. Tsai's sloping frame and lighting effects displace the moving body from its widescreen presence, relocating it to a darker space in which the act of pursuing one's foes takes on new meanings. Submitted to a different kind of motion, the cruising body wanders methodically and strategically within the auditorium looking for a match, moving with a performative alertness to emphasise neither speed nor direction. Governed by a strangely incalculable pattern of movement, each cruiser's distinctive way of moving is absorbed by everyone else in the cast of live 'players'. Once triggered by desire, the body of those who feign indifference comes to life and seems invested in its own presence. Compelled as such, some move across the auditorium to survey the territory, while others simply sit in place and wait. In contrast to the kinaesthesia of the high-flying bodies projected on screen, Tsai's own action sequences at ground are designed to revolve around the unexceptional acts of sitting, standing and walking; and it is in the brief moments of diffused lighting tracing the subdued, almost imperceptible forms of social kinetics that we are afforded an ancillary kind of 'thrill'. Critical to this thrill is Tsai's exploration of mobility and the male body within the theatre overlaid upon Hu's played out on the screen.

IV. SECOND GLANCES AND THE IMPERMANENCE OF PLACE

Tsai's long static takes are for the most part contained within the space of the theatre; the cruisers' elliptical process of seduction, however, leads us deeper into the cavernous spaces of the movie palace where the desire to connect and the failure to do so often lead to a lingering second glance and a desire to retrace the same path. Much of the significance of Tsai's medium and long shot compositions is derived from how characters enter or exit a frame, how they are situated in space. Though Tsai's minimalism favours such extended takes with virtually no camera movement, the labyrinthine backroom of the movie palace, with its shadowy corners and meandering passages, invites a different treatment: under the rarefied environment of one backroom scene, the camera is mobilised methodically and strategically to follow and align the moving body against a backdrop of vertical lines created by the vast walls of storage boxes. As a cruiser navigates through the maze of boxes, moving through a plane of intersecting lines, we see the camera holding its gaze on his body as if wanting to provide a photographic documentation of movement, thus echoing Muybridge's famous photo sequences recording the sequential strides of trotting horses (and, later, human locomotion). In another scene, we follow the paths of various bodies drifting in and out of shadows, making their ways through the labyrinthine backroom whose sloping floors seem to tilt the action at an angle towards the viewer. One man walks past another; he pauses with a turn of the head towards the stranger whose body he had brushed against in passing. The lack of response from the latter is not registered; and within the continuum of this second glance, the man is already moving on into another patch of darkness. Here in these moments, we are often left with a view of an empty room – a marker of an unsuccessful attempt at cruising – as Tsai's long shots often linger over the uninhabited space, even after a character leaves it. Though the cruiser may have left the frame of the shot, we, the viewers, nevertheless inherit his second glance, a sidelong glance functioning as both a reminder of the failure to connect (the room is empty) and the lingering hope of a reconnection (that there the glance lingers).

As Tsai's camerawork continues to follow the elliptical path of cruising, these movements gradually reveal themselves to be a figuration of temporality as well. Not to invite any unwanted advance, a young man squeezes himself into a passageway, hoping for a more preferred intimate encounter. Keeping his eyes locked on a man who has piqued his interest, he moves closer. The medium deep-focus shot of this approach seems to retain the integrity of a private space where the smallest movement within the frame can communicate with a wordless significance, but the tight framing of the shot also reminds us that other bodies can drift easily into the frame as an element of surprise, as if to suggest that the promise of privacy can be betrayed at any moment. In this tight quarter, the anxious but hopeful young man squeezes past the stranger, pausing long enough to show interest. Without receiving any encouragement from the stranger, he finally takes leave of this space. Still, he hovers around similar passageways, finally returning to the same passageway as if retracing the memory in movement. With the setting of the dilapidated movie palace, Tsai is bidding farewell to a certain kind of cinematic experience, but what is revealed and explored in the repeated movements and second glances is a lingering attachment to the fulfilling promise of such an experience as well as a recognition of its elusiveness.

Functioning as a tribute to the martial arts film genre through Hu's *Long men ke zhan*, Tsai draws from the kinaesthetic pleasure of the moving body and reinvests mobility itself with an erotic charge drawn from the contingency of impulse, rather than from romantic preparedness. On one level, the nature of cruising reveals the different ways people survive change, how they may re-inhabit the old and adapt to the new, regarding change as inevitable. In a sense, cruising, by relishing in the impermanence of urban space, rearticulates Tsai's vision of the modern city as a privileged site where people must accommodate themselves to the contingency of disposable space, a theme that runs through Tsai's oeuvre, as buildings – like theatres – and roadways and bridges are transformed to make way for new developments.[11] Yet Tsai's depiction of cruising in the derelict movie palace possesses a lingering sensuality that betrays the anonymous emptiness of modern life and bears the promise of unanticipated intimacies. The old movie palace on its final night may appear for some a decrepit space serving as an elegy for a loss of 'tradition' or standing in for a certain lost communal movie-going experience. This much is suggested in the opening sequence by the rows of attentive viewers lined up in stiff regulation seating. But for others, this space becomes a place of transgression where viewers may roam about the auditorium under a permissive play of light and darkness, where a stranger's feet (or hands) may assert themselves into the space of another, breaking that established line of seating. With the ensemble of slanted perspectives, acute angles and disjointed lines, Tsai turns the movie palace, initially a space of melancholic reflection, into a space of perverse desire and possible reconnections. Though darkness may be preferred, the act of cruising does not depend on a permanence of space or a specificity of identity, since the space of cruising seems to 'never endure beyond the sexual act' (Betsky quoted in Leung 2001: 440).[12] The design of space or architecture, thus, does not contain nor determine relations between people, but rather, in the impermanence of space, those relations may just appear where they are least expected or wanted.

Tsai's nostalgic yet playful engagement with Hu's film engenders a distracted mode of perception by turning our attention to the periphery as we try to make sense of the disorienting mobility of his filmic subjects. Tsai's long shots play on the viewer's potential inattention, luring the viewer into the belief that nothing will take place within the frame; yet this focus is set up in contrast to the interpretive wakefulness demanded of the cruising male.[13] By extending the frame of reference to include the peripheral goings-on in the theatre, *Bu san* creates a suggestive homology between our own practice of viewing and the act of cruising depicted on screen, drawing an analogy between our reading strategies, as sexually motivated readers of Tsai's film, when we pursue and track the various sounds, images and subtexts for analysis as well as those of the hermeneutically driven cruisers when they scan the cavernous backrooms for bodies and gestures with which to interpret and engage. In creating the homology between cruising and our own reading practice, Tsai reveals the different ways we may rehearse the logic of cruising itself as we try to understand and interpret the film, though the elliptical perspectives afforded by Tsai's aesthetic ensemble do not bear the promise of clarity. We are initiated to the nonverbal protocols for seduction that do not necessarily position us any closer to the 'true meaning' of *Bu san*, but rather continue to open up the body politics of Hu's film (and by extension, the martial arts genre) to possibilities of identifying with and enacting different sexual identities and fantasies.

Tsai's reconfiguration of Hu's film displaces the male body outside its hyper-masculine context, a (queer) body rearticulated primarily in and through a visual language of the slanted and the elliptical. At the same time, the act of cruising – the intermingling of body, desire and movement that is articulated in and through a language of sexual deviance or perversion – is also a space that provides opportunities for loss of identity. In one of the more notable cruising sequences, the same young man, whose earlier courtship was unceremoniously terminated by a pair of intrusive feet, attempts to recast his failed attempt at seduction as a narrative of cultural misunderstanding. Perhaps believing that his failure to connect is due to his inability to decipher signs that might be otherwise comprehensible to those sharing the same cultural codes, the young man declares in Mandarin that he is Japanese ('*wo shi riben ren*') hoping for a more hospitable reception. This declaration of one's identity in the language of another strikes us as an odd linguistic act, as if the declaration of one's foreign status would compensate, given the context of cruising where everyone is rendered a stranger to one another. Perhaps in the claim to foreignness, the tourist is merely hoping to renew the possibilities of connection. In this strange moment of self-identification, however, the image of the body is for a brief moment marked as a contested terrain of competing identities, as we are provided with a sudden but fleeting glimpse of a world shaped by another form of mobility: the cross-cultural encounters, colonisation, migration patterns that continue to shape Taiwan's layered past, historical patterns of domination and adaptation that blur the distinction between foreign and native, even as contemporary ideologues continue to mine them for the many acts of nation building.[14] The Japanese tourist's declaration is met with no success because, in the act of cruising, connections are built on anonymity where the negotiation of sexual transactions is predicated on a complex and shifting set of codes and practices. In its will to preserve anonymity, cruising then becomes not only a space where all identity is lost, but one where the body performs its own denial of the category of identity, where sexuality becomes not a type of identity but a type of loss of identity. Tsai's film introduces the pleasures of cruising to promote and to imagine the possibility of contact with non-identity. Rather than determined by identity, the body becomes a conjunction of forces endowed with a certain capacity for being affected, an anchoring point for the articulation of unanticipated passions and desires.

V. CONCLUSION

In its understated manner, Tsai's film is an engagement (albeit an oblique one) with contemporary changes to Asian cinema. Perhaps like Ang Lee's *Wo hu cang long/Crouching Tiger Hidden Dragon* (2000) and Zhang Yimou's *Ying xiong/Hero* (2002), Tsai's *Bu san* can be seen to have benefited from the resurgence of the martial arts genre in the international arena, a genre so thoroughly engrossed in the kinaesthesia of the male body, in which heroes fight or die for historical nationalist causes, that its violent masculinist ethos has become iconographic, serving as a symbolic resource for the Chinese film industry's current global celebrity.[15] As its critical reception indicates, however, the translation of this ethos into a transnational idiom has brought not only popular attention, but also new scrutiny to the genre's underlying patriarchal centrism and heteronormative views of family and cultural identity.

Though it is not without ambivalence that films such as *Ying xiong* continue to resuscitate a codified form of masculinist self-understanding, *Bu san*, in summoning the kinaesthetic figure of the male body, expands and radicalises the concept of the 'moving body' to not only rehearse the liberating possibilities that the rhetoric of transnational capital supposedly presents, but to also track the elusive mobility of perverse identifications and deviant desires that is not finally determined by or contained within such rhetoric. Through the elliptical perspectives afforded by Tsai's film, the movement of the male body is submitted to a rather strange logic, one in which the queer cruising male body not only reproduces itself as contingency, but also exposes, through translation and adaptation, the heteronormative notions of 'masculinity' to be inhabited by a comparable level of contingency. In doing so, *Bu san* opens up the body politics of King Hu's celluloid epic to renewed scrutiny as well as anxiously anticipates new virtual forms of apprehending the moving body in an increasingly globalised and deterritorialised environment of Taiwanese film.

NOTES

1 Thanks to Andrew Jones, Bao Weihong, Lin Yuting David Averbach and Paula Varsano for readings and invaluable comments.
2 This second generation of filmmakers, which included Ang Lee, Tsai, Yee Chih-yen and Stan Yin, came onto the international scene in the wake of Hou Hsaio-hsien and Edward Yang, whose works in Taiwanese New Cinema were known in Western film criticism for their neo-realist representations of Taiwanese identity. For a discussion of Taiwanese New Cinema, see Yip (2004: 54–60).
3 For a critical reading of Tsai's films in relation to Taiwan's changing historical position, see Yeh and Davis (2005: 217–48) and Liu (2001).
4 For a discussion of Hu's aesthetics and filmic contributions, see Rayns (1976: 8–13) and Teo (2001, 2002).
5 Li (2001) provides a brief discussion of the impact of Zhang Che's contrasting style on the martial arts/kung fu genre. For an informative study of the history of the martial arts film, see Teo (1997: 87–110) and Bordwell (2000: 199–261).
6 Tsai recognises the immense influence of Confucian ideas on traditional Chinese society and remains ambivalent about their ideological reach into contemporary society. See his interview with Rivière (1999: 79–80).
7 For a similar perspective, see Teo (2005b).
8 For a discussion of the woman warrior's status in martial arts films and the gender politics of the genre, see Sek (1996: 26–33), Cai (2005) in addition to Reynaud (2003) and Gomes (2005).
9 Stephen Teo (1997: 97–109), for example, has commented on the persistent homoeroticism of martial arts film.
10 Yeh and Davis (2005: 235–38) attribute such aural and visual displacements of Hu's original meanings a 'subversive' function in which the homophobic conflict of the martial arts tradition is exposed and criticised.
11 Through a reading of Tsai's short film *Tianqiao bu jianle/The Skywalk is Gone* (2002), Hu (2003) shows how Tsai's nostalgia functions as a defence mechanism against the continuous technological forces driving modern city life.
12 Leung (2001) provides an excellent discussion of the 'queer undercurrent' of Hong Kong cinema.
13 Chris Wood (2007) demonstrates how Tsai draws intertextually from Hu's film in order to destabilise the boundary between the viewers in the auditorium and we, as viewers of *Bu san*.
14 Leo Ching (2001) provides a critical overview of the Japanese occupation of Taiwan from 1895 to 1945. For a discussion of Taiwanese cultural sense of self in relation to China, Japan and the West, see also Yip (2004: 210–48).
15 For an account of the globalisation of *wu xia*, see Chan (2004). In the interview with Wang and Fujiwara (2006: 219–41), Tsai discusses the transnational status of his films in terms of financing, marketing and distribution.

13

Exposing the Body Guy: The Return of the Repressed in *Twentynine Palms*

Peter Lehman and Susan Hunt

The 1990s saw the emergence of a genre in which a working-class 'man of the earth' is romanticised and celebrated as a phenomenal lover who awakens and fulfils the repressed sexuality of a beautiful woman from a higher socio-economic class. Most of these films serve an ideology of anti-intellectualism in that the 'body guy', as we have named this character type, is exalted at the expense of an educated, cultured and/or upper-class male – the 'mind guy' – to whom the beautiful woman is somehow attached. The pattern is found in films such as *The Piano* (dir. Campion, 1993), *Legends of the Fall* (dir. Zwick, 1994), and *Titanic* (dir. Cameron, 1997), and persists to this day with films as diverse as *The Notebook* (dir. Cassavetes, 2004) and *Asylum* (dir. Mackenzie, 2005). Various forms of the pattern have even found their way to television in shows such as *Desperate Housewives* (ABC) and *Lost* (ABC).

This genre revives the myth of masculinity epitomised by D. H. Lawrence's *Lady Chatterley's Lover* from the 1920s. Many traits attached to the body guy are portrayed as favourable, but, as with the gamekeeper in *Lady Chatterley*, the body guy's most salient attribute is his lovemaking style – a trait to which his power is intrinsically tied. This sex style is vigorous and athletic with penis-centred intercourse and represented in a variety of ways from the 'do-it-all-night-in-multiple-positions' montage of *Legends of the Fall* to the 'pound-against-the-wall/shake-plaster-from-the-ceiling' imagery graphically simulated or blatantly suggested in films such as *Killing Me Softly* (dir. Chen, 2002) and *Fight Club* (dir. Fincher, 1999). Even when intercourse and explicit foreplay are elided for ratings purposes, the notion of 'wild' lovemaking is implied. In *Titanic*, the lovers end up in the back seat of a car in a freezing cargo hold as they hide from a man who has chased them with a gun, yet their first-time sex is so intense that it steams the car window, allowing the woman to smear it as she braces herself in ecstasy. In *Enemy at the Gates* (dir. Annaud 2001), the woman seduces the body guy in a chilly cavern as he lies amid rows of filthy, coughing and snoring soldiers who may awaken at any moment, yet their first-time sex is so satisfying he must stifle the woman's orgasmic screams.

The body guy's stellar sexual performance is contrasted with the intellectual male's lack of skill or appeal as depicted in films such as *Sirens* (dir. Duigan, 1994) and *I.Q.* (dir. Schepisi, 1994), among myriad others. So formidable is the body guy's sexuality and sensitivity to women that he is literally labelled a 'saviour' in several films. On the other hand, in addition to being poor lovers, the cultured or intellectual men are often depicted as controlling, manipulative, violent or even homicidal (recall the prolonged chase scene in *Titanic* when the cultured Cal tries to kill his fiancée and her body guy lover).

We focus on mind/body films from roughly the late 1980s to the present, although related films in the pattern have occurred throughout film history. Several significant films from classic Hollywood include *Morocco* (dir. Sternberg, 1930), *Red Dust* (dir. Fleming, 1932), *Casablanca* (dir. Curtiz, 1942), *Duel in the Sun* (dir. Vidor, 1946) and *The Man Who Shot Liberty Valance* (dir. Ford, 1962). Due to the ratings system in place during those years, such films of necessity differ from those we concentrate on since they could not depict explicit lovemaking or nudity including, of course, representing the penis. We have catalogued the panoply of films in the pattern, however, and we have discovered that the contemporary discourse of the exciting, sexually potent body guy and the boring, sexually incompetent intellectual in cinema is international and global in scope. In fact, the contemporary revival of the pattern can most likely be traced to Brazil and Bruno Barreto's 1976 film *Dona Flor e Seus Dois Maridos* /*Dona Flor and Her Two Husbands*, which was re-made as *Kiss Me Goodbye* in 1982 by Robert Mulligan.

In 1988 Zalman King's *Two Moon Junction* virtually defined the contemporary genre, marking a milestone in its American development. *Two Moon Junction* is to this mind/body genre as a film like *Little Caesar* (dir. LeRoy, 1932) is to the classic gangster genre: it puts all the key elements into place at the beginning of the cycle. Revealingly, however, the American-produced *At Play in the Fields of the Lord* (1991) was directed by Argentinean Hector Babenco and filmed entirely in Brazil and the next crucial films in the pattern came from Australia: *Hammers Over the Anvil* (1993) directed by Ann Turner, and John Duigan's Australian/British production *Sirens* from 1994. The year1993 also offered what might be the quintessential international film of the genre, Jane Campion's *The Piano*, a New Zealand/Australia/France co-production. The release of Dutch director Marleen Gorris's *Antonia's Line* – a Dutch/Belgian/British co-production – and Philip Haas's *Angels and Insects*, a British/USA co-production were seen in 1995. The British production of *The Governess*, directed by Sandra Goldbacher, followed in 1998.

It is within this global context that we analyse the contemporary mind/body narrative, *Twentynine Palms* – a French/German production released in 2002 and directed by Frenchman Bruno Dumont. In the film, David, an American photographer played by American actor David Wissak, scouts locations in the California desert with his Russian/French girlfriend Katya (Yekaterina Golubeva). David's status as a body guy is immediately established: his scouting links him to the land, he has a buff body and rugged good looks, wears jeans and drives a Hummer. His style of lovemaking resembles other body guy representations as he pounds Katya in a motel swimming pool, eliciting moans of pleasure from her even as her body is arched awkwardly over the concrete pool edge.

As a photographer, David is positioned within a sub-set of the mind/body paradigm in which the body guy is an artist seen in films such as *Henry & June* (dir. Kaufman, 1990) and *The End of the Affair* (dir. Jordan, 1999). The artist would seem to deviate from the earthy body guy in that artists are associated with the world of the mind and even intellectual circles. But for narratives set in the city, artists are the logical analogous figures to the rural body guys in that they are linked to the working class through the trope of 'artist as Bohemian'; and they are also outsiders in touch with their bodies and feelings. Artists can also be more readily represented as stellar lovers in that stereotypically they are disdainful of bourgeois morality and sexual constraints imposed by society. David is both a body guy and an artist, but *Twentynine Palms* deviates from the classic mind/body paradigm in that there is no rival 'mind guy'. Dumont's use of this variation, however, undercuts the usual body-guy-saviour/mind-guy-destroyer pattern. In the typical pattern, the woman in between is enlightened and impassioned by the artist, but the lovers part in the end. Their parting endows the body guy and his sex style with further mythic potency in that the lovers separate with regretful longing or one of them dies tragically from illness or accident. In *Twentynine Palms*, however, instead of liberating the beautiful woman, David ends up killing her in a brutal manner, and then apparently commits suicide. The body guy is the destroyer, not the saviour.

Twentynine Palms also subverts the mythic quality of the body guy's sexual performance style by linking it to aggression and ultimately violence; signalling the return of a repressed representation: the body guy as brute, a character type that can be traced to the Victorian era before mass industrialisation and urbanisation relegated the man of the earth to a figure of nostalgia (a la 'Lady Chatterley'). This beast-like body guy is described by Wilkie Collins in his 1886 novel *The Evil Genius* in a chapter aptly titled 'The Brute':

> The man [...] was one of the human beings who are grown to perfection on English soil. He had the fat face, the pink complexion, the hard blue eyes, the scanty yellow hair, the smile with no meaning in it, the tremendous neck and shoulders, the mighty fists and feet, which are seen in complete combination in England only. Men of this breed possess a nervous system without being aware of it; suffer affliction without feeling it; exercise courage without a sense of danger; marry without love; eat and drink without limit; and sink (big as they are), when disease attacks them, without an effort to live. (63)

Hardly a description of the blue-eyed, yellow-haired Brad Pitt of *Legends of the Fall* or *A River Runs Through It* (dir. Robert Redford, 1992). Note how Collins ties this figure to having been 'grown' from the 'soil' and how the muscular buff features admired in present time here suggest a violent coarseness: 'the tremendous neck and shoulders, the mighty fists and feet'. Instead of the sexy handsome faces of contemporary body guys, Collins describes his brute's face as having 'no meaning in it'. Indeed he goes so far as to suggest that such a man lacks *all* self-awareness, let alone possess a special sensitivity and insight to the erotic or innermost feelings of women. Also in 1886, Robert Louis Stevenson presents an even more brutish character in Mr Hyde, the infamous body guy alter ego of the brilliant Dr Jekyll. Like David of *Twentynine Palms*, Hyde also murders his victims with a horrific intensity. The body guy discourse at the time of Collins and Stevenson was not tied to a denigration of the intellect as it is constructed today; on the contrary it elevated the world of the mind.

Films featuring brutish body guys have paradoxically also proliferated from the 1990s to the present. Some of these films form a mind/body sub-genre in that the brutish body guys are constructed in opposition to intelligent men with a beautiful woman placed between them in some manner as in *Kalifornia* (dir. Sena, 1993), *The River Wild* (dir. Hanson, 1994) and *Derailed* (dir. Håfström, 2005), to name a few. In all of these films, the body guy is depicted as curiously charismatic, but is revealed to be, at best, potentially violent and at worse a psychopathic serial killer. What all of the brute body guy films make clear is that these male characters specifically pose a potential threat to women. In the typical pattern, the intellectual male ultimately defeats the brute body guy, but he must become a brute himself in order to do so, thus validating violent behaviour in the guise of saving the family or a woman. The mind guy learns something valuable about himself by becoming a body guy. He is in a sense empowered by the body guy and moves towards the film's definition of ideal masculinity through what he learns from him, as in the graphic climactic battle between Brad Pitt and David Duchovny in *Kalifornia* or Kevin Bacon and David Strathairn in *The River Wild.*

Twentynine Palms provides an incisive critique of even this sub-set of mind/body narratives in that the body guy's violent behaviour is not validated in any manner and it is also linked to his sexual performance style in a disturbing and revealing way. As noted above, David's appearance at first sight is like that of the conventional body guy and at first glance so is his style of lovemaking as he pounds Katya to her ostensible delight in the motel swimming pool. Later in bed, their graphic pounding leaves David screaming with animalistic yelps. In another sexual encounter they have stripped while hiking among rocks in the desert and they make love.

The desert lovemaking scene here directly references another important international film of the genre, Michelangelo Antonioni's *Zabriskie Point* (1970), also named after an actual place in Death Valley, California. The reference is central to an understanding of the global context of the mind guy/body guy films and serves to remind us of the longstanding tradition of European filmmakers and writers coming to America to comment upon its national character (e.g. Alexis de Tocqueville's *Democracy in America* published in 1835 and Jean Baudrillard's *America* published in 1988). Indeed, *Zabriskie Point* may be the overlooked precursor to the entire genre. It places Daria, a young woman, between Mark, a college dropout 'body guy' and Lee, a highly successful upper-class businessman for whom she works and who either has a relationship with her or designs upon her. The body guy is a classic type – he has been expelled from college for all kinds of disruptive mischief, he works as a forklift operator, drives a pickup truck, and wears nothing but jeans and a T-shirt. Although he aligns himself with student revolutionaries, he is 'the man of action' who has no patience for too much talk and theorising. The business man, on the other hand, deals in high-end land development, wears expensive suits, has offices and meetings either at the top of high-rent L.A. high-rise office buildings or in beautiful, secluded mansions in the desert near Phoenix.

The plot of the film unites Mark and Daria in the desert. She is on her way to meet Lee at the mansion where he is closing a business deal. She immediately falls under his spell, they have fun together followed by an epic lovemaking session which Antonioni films in a surreal style, inter-cutting countless images of the lovers in the desert with those of imaginary figures coupling alongside them. As soon as they are done making love, the other figures disappear and Mark and Daria lie in the desert fully sated. Although they have just met, the images of their intertwined bodies along with the imagined couplings surrounding them all suggest a perfectly fulfilling first-time sexual experience in keeping with the performance expectations of the body guy. Indeed, Daria is so transformed by her powerful sexual encounter with Mark in the desert that by the time she gets to the desert mansion she is appalled by the upper-class lifestyle and the film ends with her fleeing the home and imagining its destruction. After sex in the desert with the fork lift operating, truck driving, jeans wearing, college dropout body guy, everything Lee stands for is repulsive to the point of needing destruction. Daria's encounter in the desert is nothing short of nirvana. By contrast, Katya's encounter in the desert in *Twentynine Palms* is far from heavenly.

David pounds Katya from behind, the sounds of their body impact greatly amplified. David's penis is prominent in several shots in the sequence, as is common in the genre (a la Harvey Keitel in *The Piano*, Figure 26 and Mark Gerber in *Sirens*, Figure 27), further marking him as a body guy, but *Twentynine Palms*'s narrative development centres on David and Katya's increasingly problematic sexuality, and the problems seem to stem from his masculinity. In the sex among the rocks scene, Katya says that she is too dry and begins giggling. The next encounter has them back in the pool where David pushes Katya's head underwater for oral sex, but this time she becomes enraged after he insensitively begins to drown her. By this point a clear pattern of extremely aggressive sex has emerged on David's part, an aggressive behaviour bordering on hostility, and moments in their earlier lovemaking now take on added significance. While David has pounding intercourse with her in the hotel swimming pool the first time he repeatedly asks her 'Can you feel [that]', implying some fear that he is somehow inadequate. On the rocks in the desert, he shows no sensitivity to her need for

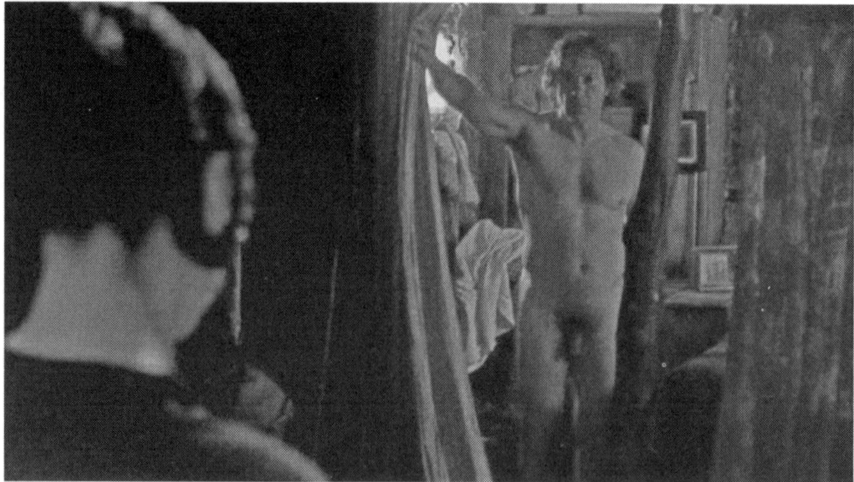

Figure 26: Harvey Keitel in *The Piano*. Jan Chapman Productions PTY Limited.

Figure 27: Mark Gerber in *Sirens*. Australian Film Finance Corp., WMG Film, British Screen Finance Limited, Samson Productions Two Ply, Sarah Radclyffe Productions.

foreplay, leading to the failed lovemaking with her giggling and complaining of being dry. Finally, back in the pool she becomes outraged that he would dare to hold her underwater.

Far from fulfilling a fantasy of the body guy as gifted lover a la *Zabriskie Point*, David emerges as aggressive to the point of violence as well as self-centred to the point of near total disregard for his lover's feelings, or sexual responsiveness, causing her physical discomfort and even fear instead of a blissful orgasm. Far from awakening any sexuality within her, a trope of the genre, he seems to be forcing his highly physical thrusting style upon her. In one sense, then, David is a critique of the body guy and his pounding style of penile centred thrusting so crucial to the genre's depiction of good sex. Here pounding intercourse crosses over into something ugly and frightening. But it is just a hint of what is to come.

When David and Katya are in the town of Twentynine Palms a truck drives by and someone hurls a crude insult at them. They ignore what seems to be a fleeting, if unpleasant, moment but later notice a truck following close behind them. The truck is filmed in an ominous manner with a dark, impenetrable windshield hiding its occupants. Then the unthinkable happens. David and Katya are forced off the road by the truck and the men inside pull them from their vehicle. Stripped of her clothing, Katya is forced to watch as David is beaten with a club and anally raped with the same aggressive thrusting techniques and animalistic howling we had observed between David and Katya.

The scene is extraordinary in its critique of the body guy and his style of sex: now David, the normally romanticised body guy, is brutally victimised by other body guys whose sexual techniques and style recall his own, but they are as far removed from a romanticised ideal as possible; they represent what we term the return of the repressed in the body guy narrative tradition. Lawrence in *Lady Chatterley*, of course, was in part reacting against the Victorian repression of sexuality and the body, celebrating what had been forbidden and unrepresented in its mainstream literary tradition. By the last quarter of the twentieth century, however, that which began with E. M. Forster and Lawrence had evolved into something quite different. The realities of being close to actual body guys who were uneducated, worked the land, or worked closely with animals as gamekeepers or cowboys were now in the distant past. The body guys in the dominant movie tradition are completely sanitised, lacking any sweat, smell or crudeness – they just possess wonderful 'natural' bodies, physically coordinated, perfectly equipped sexually (more on that below) and an intuitive gift for masterful sexual performance that awakens true desire in women whose previous mind guy lovers have been clueless about such deep sexual responsiveness.

The rape scene in *Twentynine Palms* is as if Wilkie Collins's Brute and Stevenson's Hyde suddenly erupted into the late twentieth and early twenty-first century narrative paradigm. The body guy becomes the recipient of his own pounding sex style and it is safe to say, he does not like it. Furthermore the body guys that perpetrate this upon him are in general appearance and behaviour what can only be termed 'brutes'. Crude, insensitive, uncaring, violent – they are the mirror opposite of body guys like Robert Redford in *The Horse Whisperer* (dir. Redford, 1998). They even make Katya watch, heightening David's humiliation. It is hard to imagine how Dumont could present a more shocking eruption of the return of the repressed in relation to the body guy.

But he does, and in the very next sequence. After David's brutal rape, it seems that we have seen it all and, in classic narrative terms, the climax has occurred, leaving only the denouement. But in fact the climax occurs when David, apparently traumatised by his rape, suddenly dashes naked from the bathroom of their motel room and repeatedly stabs Katya with a large knife while screaming in the same animalistic way we heard at his earlier sexual climax with Katya, *and* at his rapist's climax. This surprising turn of events involving Katya's murder exceeds the graphic rape we have just seen and now the critique of the body guy as romanticised, ideal, great lover has been taken to the final level – he has become a psychotic killer. The denouement is equally significant in rounding out the critique. We see David's dead nude body lying in the desert, stripped of a potent sexuality on the land once linked to sex and romance. Even the position of the body is telling – David lies on his stomach, his penis not visible as it had been earlier but, rather, fused with the land which, in this genre, normally gives it magical potency. But here it is more like the genre's magical penis is on a journey of 'ashes to ashes, dust to dust' – dead and impotent like the seemingly vibrant body guy myth that Dumont has brilliantly deconstructed as being at the heart of American culture.

In ending the film with an assault, rape, murder and apparent suicide Dumont invokes another core aspect of American national identity: violence. In charting the characters' trajectory, the film links violence with two other American obsessions: masculinity and penis size. In addition to their deteriorating sexual relationship, Dumont impels Katya and David's *personal* relationship on a downward spiral towards violence, and masculinity issues lie at the centre of this decline. With each rift in their relationship, Katya's behaviour is so emotionally extreme that she seems mentally unstable: she sobs uncontrollably because David will not talk with her about what is on his mind; she has a tantrum when David glances at an attractive woman in a restaurant; she laughs hysterically when David is upset that she scratched his Hummer; she cries while watching a tabloid talk show where a man confesses to his wife that he slept with their daughter and asks David if he would do that; she screams at him for not stopping the car when she has to urinate, and she screams hysterically that David 'has no heart' when he doesn't immediately help a dog he injured with the Hummer. In each case, Katya's emotional outbursts are related to what might be deemed stereotypical masculine behaviours: stoicism, sexual appetite, insensitivity and so on.

Their personal deterioration culminates in a scene in which Katya emerges after locking herself in the motel bathroom and announces that she's 'splitting'. Her anger has no immediate narrative motivation. She wanders aimlessly along the side of the highway, but evades David when he eventually looks for her. After a cat-and-mouse chase, David finally pins her to the ground, slaps her face and body while repeatedly saying 'I hate you'. He then drags her towards the motel. A sparring match ensues while David taunts her, but they ultimately reconcile and return to their room. The climactic sequence follows, in which David masochistically tells Katya to again drive the Hummer and they end up on an impassable road where they are attacked. Katya is the dethroning thorn in the side of David's masculinity (and alongside David's scratched Hummer, as it were). This trajectory perhaps explains the question, why does David kill Katya instead of the men who raped him. From the moment he appears driving a Hummer, David's masculinity is linked to 'over-compensation'. He strives to be part of the normative spectacle of masculinity but he fails in all regards: his Hummer is forced off the road, and as we'll see momentarily his forceful lovemaking style fails to satisfy his partner and his penis fails to live up to the normative spectacle of representation. All these failures find their culmination in the rape scene where Katya is forced to watch as another man uses his penis/phallus on David in a manner that makes his body the centre of spectacle in the exact opposite way that David intends. He is a centred sexual spectacle precisely at the moment that he is a passive victim of powerful, phallic male sexual violence. That his girlfriend watches this spectacle is his ultimate humiliation. Added to the fact that, as we shall see in a moment, he fears that his penis is inadequately small and that his style of thrusting during intercourse is ineffective, this pushes him over the top and his entire façade of phallic masculinity collapses. The target of his wrath is not the men who rape him but the woman who scratches his Hummer, wants 'more' from his coital techniques, laughs at his inadequate attempt to clumsily penetrate her in the desert and finally watches him 'take it from behind'.

But we find the central manner in which Dumont links David's penis size to masculinity issues and violence disturbing.[1] A series of posts on Celebrity Nudity Database (cndb.com) is very revealing in this regard. The website enables users to search under film titles or actor's names for comments about nude scenes posted by other users. Three of the four posts under David Wissak's name (the actor who plays David) refer to his penis size, body and sexual desirability, something that in itself demonstrates how noticeable this aspect of the film is to some viewers. One reviewer gets right to the point in a brief post: 'David is very lean and nice-looking. During a rock-climbing scene, he shows off a short, plump weenie; very nice. It has almost no shaft, just a head. Brave guy. Kudos.' His description is unusually graphic in noting that the penis is 'short' and 'has almost no shaft, just a head'. But he likes it and the courage it takes for an actor with a penis like that to do a nude scene. Another reviewer is equally graphic, 'we see david's (sic) little dickhead among his long, dense black pubic hair. pretty and tiny, it's no wonder Katya wants to put her hand on it to protect it from the sun. when she takes her hand away it's lying back slightly, no bigger than a nut, pretty much just a head'. Again what jumps out here is the need to describe his smallness in such an explicit and even vivid manner: 'little dickhead', 'tiny', 'no bigger than a nut, pretty much just a head'. Obviously the two reviewers agree on what they are seeing and it strikes them enough to go into unusual detail. But a third reviewer forgoes the detail in favour of a general reaction, including voicing disbelief at the first commentator quoted above: 'This is a very ordinary guy, face and body. I am stunned that another reviewer gave him such a positive review. We do see a lot of him, back [and] front. But it is unlikely that any of what you see will make you hot.'

A close analysis of the film in relation to these comments raises two different issues. It is in fact true that the actor who plays David has a penis that shows little shaft before erection (Figure 28), something that deviates from the norm of other body guys in the genre and male nudity in films in general. But the detailed comments we have just quoted in fact reveal a form of hysteria not borne out by the film: It is not true that his penis is 'tiny' or that it has no shaft and is 'just a head' and 'no bigger than a nut' when she removes her hand from covering his genitals (Figure 29). This hysteria shows the profound impact that the careful regulation of the representation of the penis has had on some within our culture. Two of these commentators seem to simply long for a normative, 'impressive' spectacle surrounding the penis. Even if it were true that Wissak's penis showed no shaft, revealed only a head and looked like a 'nut' we would welcome such a departure from the clichéd assumption that for a man's sexuality to be worth looking at or be able to bear the burden of masculine representation, the shaft of his penis has to be prominently visible, ensuring that the penis dangles on full display at all times. Indeed, in standard representation the flaccid penis is a stand-in for the erect penis, which it resembles. Instead of the head being the prominent feature, the long, hanging shaft dominates. All the penis has to do is get hard; we need not worry that it will be small or disproportionate. On the other hand, a penis like Wissak's that shows little or no shaft before erection, may be perceived as being incapable of expanding normatively, thus accounting for the strong reaction on the website. The good-sized flaccid penis seems to offer a guarantee of the good-sized erection.

For us the problem lies elsewhere. Unfortunately if, initially, David's penis may seem a refreshing departure from the usual clichés, in fact it becomes another cliché due to the manner in which David's character is developed through both dialogue and visual imagery. As we noted, we hear him earlier frantically and repeatedly ask Katya, 'Do you feel [that]?' while he's pounding her during sex in the pool. Thus, his aggressive sexual behaviour appears linked to being so small that he fears she doesn't feel him when he is inside her. His attack on Katya at the end of the film seems to reinforce his perceived need for a larger penis in that he wields a classic phallic-looking knife which he plunges into Katya an excessive fifteen times while howling in the same manner we heard during his earlier lovemaking. Attention is drawn to the knife-as-phallus in that it is filmed in close-up in a manner resembling the stabbing of Marion Crane in Hitchcock's *Psycho* (1960). After the stabbing, David sits nude on Katya's dead body in a composition that rhymes with their earlier lovemaking.

David's apparent penile inadequacy also relates to an earlier scene in which David and Katya are dining near a US Marine whose head is closely shaven in the typical manner. The following conversation ensues:

- David: 'You wouldn't want me to shave my head like them?'
- Katya: 'If you do, I'll leave you'
- David: 'You don't like Marines?'
- Katya: 'I do. They're really handsome'

David then becomes angered by Katya's seemingly contradictory statement.

In the scene prior to her murder, we see Katya comforting David who appears battered, but with a full head of hair. Katya then leaves the motel to buy food and is murdered upon her return. When David charges from the bathroom to stab her, we see that his head is now mostly shaven, recalling their previous conversation about the phallic Marine. Fashion commentators have noted that the bald

Figure 28: Yekaterina Golubeva and David Wissak in *Twentynine Palms*. 38 Productions, Thoke Moebius Filmcompany.

Figure 29: Yekaterina Golubeva and David Wissak in *Twentynine Palms*. 38 Productions, Thoke Moebius Filmcompany.

look for men transforms the entire male body into a phallus, the bald head resembling the head of a penis. While David does not sport the bald, shiny fashion look, clearly he has attempted to transform his entire body into a penis, in this case by referencing the Marine-style haircut.

Thus both the violence of his sexual performance style and his homicidal violence intersect with a cultural discourse that men with a small penis aggressively overcompensate (by doing such things as driving Hummers), another cliché which far from being a refreshing departure ties the usually unrepresented penis – a penis that shows little or no shaft before erection – to an undesired and even dangerous smallness, implying, perhaps, that the true body guy with the mythic penis is out there waiting to awaken and fulfil a woman's every desire.

NOTE

1 The following discussion does not depend upon the circumstances of the film's production. We do not know, nor do we care, whether Dumont asked the actors to audition for the part nude. Either he cast Wissak in the lead role knowing that his penis is smaller than the norms of the average size in representation or he cast him without knowing. If it is the former, the narrative trajectory and visual patterns we analyse were in some sense determined at the outset. Even if Dumont and no one associated with the production saw Wissak nude before they filmed the nude scenes, this in no way hurts our analysis since what matters is how they incorporated his body into the film as it was being made. They chose various camera angles, cutting patterns, actions, dialogue etc., which emphasise his penis size in a certain manner. Katya, for example, puts her hand over David's genitals as he lies down, removes it and then sits up next to him, while looking at him. All of the actions in this sequence – covering his genitals, removing her hands, and then sitting up and looking – bring the viewers' attention to David's penis in a manner that could easily have been avoided. Whether in advance or while making the film, Dumont made choices to foreground David's comparatively small penis in relation to the norms of representation in a manner that embedded it within the film's ideological project, which in this case ties his size to a terrible insecurity that finds an outlet in overcompensation that progresses from aggression, to violence, to homicidal rage.

Bibliography

Abbas, Ackbar (1997) *Hong Kong: Culture and the Politics of Disappearance*. Minneapolis: University of Minnesota Press.

Ageron, Charles-Robert (1984) 'L'Exposition Coloniale de 1931: mythe républicain ou mythe impérial?' in Pierre Nora (ed.) *Les lieux de mémoire, tome I. La République*. Paris: Gallimard, pp. 561–91.

Aguilar, Pilar (1998) *Mujer, amor y sexo en el cine español de los 90*. Madrid: Fundamentos.

Ahmad, Aijaz (1992) *In Theory*. New Delhi: Oxford University Press.

Alloula, Malek (1981) *L'Harem colonial. Images d'un sous-érotisme*. Paris: Atlantic-Séguier.

Amiel, Vincent (1998) *Le corps au cinema: Keaton, Bresson, Cassavetes*. Paris: Presses universitaires de France.

Anderson, Benedict (1994) *Imagined Communities: Reflections on the Origin and Spread of Nationalism*. London: Verso.

Ang, Ien (2001) *On Not Speaking Chinese: Living Between Asia and the West*. New York: Routledge.

Ang, Ien (2003) 'From White Australia to Fortress Australia: The Anxious Nation in the New Century' in Laksiri Jayasuriya, David Walker and Jan Gothard (eds) *Legacies of White Australia*. Perth: University of Western Australia Press, pp. 51–69.

Appadurai, Arjun (1996) *Modernity at Large: Cultural Dimensions of Globalization*. Minneapolis: University of Minnesota Press.

Arenas, José E. (1998) 'Ventura Pons presenta hoy en Madrid la película *Caricias*', *ABC* (12 July), 94.

Baguley, David (1990) *Naturalist Fiction: The Entropic Vision*. Cambridge: Cambridge University Press.

Bancel, Nicolas, Pascal Blanchard and Francis Delabarre (1997) *Images d'Empire 1930–1960*. Paris: Editions de la Martinière/La Documentation française.

Baron, Lawrence (2003) '*X-Men* as J Men: The Jewish Subtext of a Comic Book Movie', *Shofar* 22 (1), 44–52.

Bartchy, S. Scott (2006) 'Where is the History in Mel Gibson's *The Passion of the Christ*?' in Zev Garber (ed.) *Mel Gibson's Passion: The Film, the Controversy, and Its Implications*. West Lafayette, IN: Purdue University Press, pp. 76–92.

Bartky, Sandra (1990) *Femininity and Domination: Studies in the Phenomenology of Oppression*. New York: Routledge.

Bartov, Omer (2005) *The 'Jew' in American Cinema: From the Golem to Don't Touch My Holocaust*. Bloomington and Indianapolis: Indiana University Press.

Bartra, Roger (1996 [1987]) *La jaula de la melancolía*. Grijalbo: México.

Batista, Alberto (2004) 'Historias mexicanas a la pantalla', *El diario* <http://www.eldiariony.com/noticias/especiales/detail.aspx?especialid=11&id=986355&date=09/16/2004> Last consulted in December 2007.

Baudrillard, Jean (1988) *America*. New York: Verso.

Beasley, Chris (2005) *Gender & Sexuality: Critical Theories, Critical Thinkers*. Thousand Oaks and London: Sage.

Beasley, Chris (forthcoming) 'Re-thinking Hegemonic Masculinity in a Globalising World', *Men & Masculinities*.

Beasley, Chris and Carol Bacchi (2007) 'Envisaging a New Politics for an Ethical Future: Beyond Trust, Care and Generosity Towards an Ethic of Social Flesh', *Feminist Theory* 8 (3), 279–98.

Beasley, Chris and Juanita Elias (2006) 'Situating Masculinities in Global Politics', Refereed Conference Proceedings, *Oceanic Conference on International Studies* (5–7 July). Melbourne: University of Melbourne <http://www.politics.unimelb.edu.au/ocis/Beasley_Elias.pdf> Last consulted December 2007.

Benthien, Claudia (2002) *Skin: On the Cultural Border Between Self and the World*. New York: Columbia University Press.

Benwell, Bethan (2003) 'Introduction' in Bethan Benwell (ed.) *Masculinities and Men's Lifestyle Magazines*. Oxford: Blackwell, pp. 6–30.

Bergougniou, Jean-Michel, Rémi Clignet and Philippe David (2001) *'Villages Noirs' et visiteurs africains et malgaches en France et en Europe (1870–1940)*. Paris: Karthala.

Berry, Chris (2000) 'Happy Alone? Sad Young Men in East Asian Gay Cinema' in Andrew Grossman (ed.) *Queer Asian Cinema: Shadows in the Shade*. New York: Haworth Press, pp. 187–200.

Berry, Chris (2006) 'Stellar Transit: Bruce Lee's Body or Chinese Masculinity in a Transnational Frame' in Fran Martin and Larissa Heinrich (eds) *Embodied Modernities: Corporeality, Representation, and Chinese Cultures*. Honolulu: University of Hawaii Press, pp. 218–34.

Berry, Chris and Mary Farquhar (2006) *China on Screen: Cinema and Nation*. New York: Columbia University Press.

Betsky, Aaron (1997) *Queer Space: Architecture and Same-Sex Desire*. New York: William Morrow.

Block, Bruce (2001) *The Visual Story: Seeing the Structure of Film, TV, and New Media*. Boston: Focal Press.

Bogdal, Klaus-Michael (2001) 'Hard-Cold Fast: Imagining Masculinity in the German Academic, Literature, and the Media' in Roy Jerome (ed.) *Conceptions of Postwar German Masculinity*. Albany, NY: SUNY Press, pp. 13–42.

Bonitzer, Pascal (1981) 'Partial Vision: Film and the Labyrinth', trans. Fabrice Ziolkowski, *Wide Angle* 4 (4), 56–63.

Bordo, Susan (1999) *The Male Body: A New Look at Men in Public and Private*. New York: Farrar, Straus and Giroux.

Bordwell, David (1979) 'The Art Film as A Mode of Film Practice', *Film Criticism* 4 (1), 56–64.

Bordwell, David (1998) 'Richness through Imperfection: King Hu and the Glimpse' in Law Kar (ed.) *Transcending the Times: King Hu and Eileen Chang*. Hong Kong: Urban Council, pp. 32–39.

Bordwell, David (2000) *Planet Hong Kong: Popular Cinema and the Art of Entertainment*. Cambridge: Harvard University Press.

Boyarin, Daniel (1997) *Unheroic Conduct: The Rise of Heterosexuality and the Invention of the Jewish Man*. Berkeley: University of California Press.

Bresson, Robert (1986) *Notes on the Cinematographer*. London: Quartet Books.

Brett, Judith (2003) *Australian Liberals and the Moral Middle Class: From Alfred Deakin to John Howard*. Melbourne: Cambridge University Press.

Brienes, Paul (1990) *Tough Jews: Political Fantasies and the Moral Dilemma of American Jewry*. New York: Basic Books.

Brockmann, Stephen (2006) '"Normalization": Has Helmut Kohl's Vision Been Realized?' in Stuart Taberner and Paul Cooke (eds) *German Culture, Politics, and Literature into the Twenty-First Century: Beyond Normalization*. Rochester, NY: Camden House, pp. 17–31.

Burns, James (2006) 'The African Bioscope: Movie House Culture in British Colonial Africa', *Afrique et histoire* 5 (1), 65–80.

Butler, Judith (1993) *Bodies That Matter: On the Discursive Limits of Sex*. London: Routledge.

Butler, Judith (1999a) *Gender Trouble: Feminism and the Subversion of Identity*. New York and London: Routledge.

Butler, Judith (1999b) 'From Interiority to Gender Performatives' in Fabio Cleto (ed.) *Camp: Queer Aesthetics and the Performing Subject – A Reader*. Ann Arbor: University of Michigan Press, pp. 361–69.

Butler, Judith (2004) *Undoing Gender*. New York and London: Routledge.

Caballero, Jorge (2004) 'Con Zapata…violé la historia, pero le hice un hijo muy bonito: Arau', *La Jornada* <http://www.jornada.unam.mx/2004/04/28/08an1esp.php?origen =espectaculos.php&fly=2> Last consulted in December 2007.

Cai, Rong (2005) 'Gender Imaginations in *Crouching Tiger, Hidden Dragon* and the *Wuxia* World', *positions: east asia cultures critique* 13 (2), 441–71.

Campo Vidal, Anabel (2004) *Ventura Pons: La mirada libre*. Madrid: SGAE.

canek1 (2005) Comment on 'Zapata, un intro', *Bluecat Reloaded* http://bluecat.blog.com.mx/?p=20>.Last consulted in December 2007.

Celebrity Nudity Database <http://cndb.com/movie.html?title=Twentynine+Palms+%282003%29> Last consulted April 2007.

Chan, Jachinson (2001) *Chinese American Masculinities: From Fu Manchu to Bruce Lee*. New York: Routledge.

Chan, Kenneth (2004) 'The Global Return of the *Wu Xia Pian*: Ang Lee's *Crouching Tiger, Hidden Dragon*', *Cinema Journal* 43 (4), 3–17.

Chant, Sylvia and Nikki Craske (2003) *Gender in Latin America*. New Brunswick, NJ: Rutgers University Press.

Ching, Leo (2001) *Becoming 'Japanese': Colonial Taiwan and the Politics of Identity Formation*. Berkeley: University of California Press.

Chow, Rey (1993) *Writing Diaspora: Tactics of Intervention in Contemporary Cultural Studies*. Bloomington: Indiana University Press.

Chow, Rey (1998) *Ethics After Idealism: Theory, Culture, Ethnicity, Reading*. Bloomington: Indiana University Press.

Chow, Rey (2000) *Reimagining a Field: Modern Chinese Literary and Cultural Studies in the Age of Theory*. Durham: Duke University Press.

Clancy-Smith, Julia and Frances Gouda (eds) (1998) *Domesticating the Empire: Race, Gender and Family Life in French and Dutch Colonialism*. Charlottesville and London: Virginia University Press.

Clover, Carol (1992) *Men, Women and Chainsaws: Gender in the Modern Horror Film*. London: British Film Institute.

Cohan, Steven and Ina Rae Hark (eds) (1993) *Screening the Male: Exploring Masculinities in Hollywood Cinema*. New York: Routledge.

Collen, Anthea (1998) 'Ideal Masculinities: An Anatomy of Power' in Nicholas Mirzoeff (ed.) *The Visual Culture Reader*. London and New York: Routledge, pp. 603–16.

Collins, Wilkie (1994[1886]) *The Evil Genius*. Orchard Park, NY: Broadview Press.

Connell, R. W. (2000) *The Men and the Boys*. Cambridge: Polity Press.

Connell, R. W. (2002) *Gender*. Oxford: Polity.

Connell, R. W. (2005) 'Globalization, Imperialism and Masculinities' in Michael Kimmel, Jeff Hearn and R. W. Connell (eds) *Handbook of Studies on Men and Masculinities*. Thousand Oaks and London: Sage, pp. 71–89.

Connell, R. W. and Messerschmidt, James (2005) 'Hegemonic Masculinity: Rethinking the Concept', *Gender & Society* 19 (6), 829–59.

Cooke, Paul (2006) 'Abnormal Consensus? The New Internationalism of German Cinema' in Stuart Taberner and Paul Cooke (eds) *German Culture, Politics, and Literature into the Twenty-First Century: Beyond Normalization*. Rochester, NY: Camden House, pp. 223–37.

Coombes, Annie and Steve Edwards (1989) 'Site Unseen: Photography in the Colonial Empire: Images of Subconscious Eroticism', *Art History* 12, 511–17.

Creed, Barbara (1993a) 'Dark Desires: Male Masochism in the Horror Film' in Steven Cohan and Ina Rae Hark (eds) *Screening the Male: Exploring Masculinities in Hollywood Cinema*. London: Routledge, pp. 118–33.

Creed, Barbara (1993b) *The Monstrous-Feminine: Film, Feminism, Psychoanalysis*. London: Routledge.

Creed, Barbara (2004) *Pandora's Box: Essays in Film Theory*. Victoria: Australian Centre for the Moving Image.

Cross, Alice (1993) 'Portraying the Rhythm of the Vietnamese Soul: An Interview with Tran Anh Hung', *Cineaste* 20 (3), 35–37.

Dargis, Manohla (2007) 'A Mighty Heart; Using the Light of a Star To Illuminate Ugly Truths', *The New York Times* online <http://query.nytimes.com/gst/fullpage.html?res=9F07EEDD153EF931A15755C0A9619C8B63> Last consulted in November 2007.

Davis, Bob (2001) 'A Midsummer Vision of Vietnam', *American Cinematographer* 82 (9), 24–29.

De la Mora, Sergio (2006) *Cinemachismo: Masculinities and Sexuality in Mexican Film.* Austin: University of Texas Press.

de Tocqueville, Alexis (2003 [1835]) *Democracy in America*, trans. Garald Bevan. New York: Penguin.

DeAngelis, Michael (2001) *Gay Fandom and Crossover Stardom: James Dean, Mel Gibson, Keanu Reeves.* Durham, N.C.: Duke University Press.

Deleuze, Gilles (1986) *Cinema 1: The Movement-Image*, trans. Hugh Tomlinson and Barbara Habberjam. Minneapolis: University of Minnesota Press.

Deleuze, Gilles (1989) *Cinema 2: The Time-Image*, trans. Hugh Tomlinson and Robert Galeta. Minneapolis: University of Minnesota Press.

Deleuze, Gilles (1991) *Masochism: Coldness and Cruelty*, trans. Jean McNeil, New York: Zone Books.

Deleuze, Gilles and Félix Guattari (1987) *A Thousand Plateaus: Capitalism and Schizophrenia*, trans. Brian Massumi. Minneapolis and London: University of Minnesota Press.

Deleuze, Gilles and Félix Guattari (2000) *Anti-Oedipus: Capitalism and Schizophrenia.* 10th ed. Minneapolis: University of Minnesota Press.

Dennis, Kelly (1994) 'Ethno-Pornography: Veiling the Dark Continent', *History of Photography* 18, 22–29.

Desser, David (2001) 'Jews in Space: The "Ordeal of Masculinity" in Contemporary American Film and Television' in Murray Pomerance (ed.) *Ladies and Gentlemen, Boys and Girls: Gender in Film at The End of The Twentieth Century.* Albany: State University of New York Press, pp. 267–81.

Doane, Mary Ann (2003) 'The Close-Up: Scale And Detail In The Cinema', *Differences* 14 (3), 89–111.

Doty, Alexander (1993) *Making Things Perfectly Queer: Interpreting Mass Culture.* Minneapolis: University of Minnesota Press.

Du Coudray, Chantal Bourgault (2006) *The Curse of the Werewolf: Fantasy, Horror and the Beast Within.* London: I. B. Tauris.

Dyer, Richard (1982) 'Don't Look Now: The Male Pin-Up', *Screen* 23 (3/4), 61–73.

Dyer, Richard (1990) *Now You See It: Studies on Lesbian and Gay Film.* London: Routledge.

Earnshaw, Tony (2005) *Beating the Devil: The Making of* Night of the Demon. Sheffield: Tomahawk Press.

Elder, Catriona (2007) *Being Australian: Narratives of National Identity.* Sydney: Allen and Unwin.

Elsaesser, Thomas (1992) 'The New German Cinema's Historical Imaginary' in Bruce A. Murray and Christopher J. Wickham (eds) *Framing the Past: The Historiography of*

German Cinema and Television. Carbondale, IL: Southern Illinois University Press, pp. 280–307.

Emeagwali, Gloria (2004) 'Nigerian Film Industry', *African Update* 11 (2) <http://www.ccsu.edu/Afstudy/upd11-2.html> Last consulted in March 2007.

Eng, David (2001) *Racial Castration: Managing Masculinity in Asian America.* Durham: Duke University Press.

Eribon, Didier (2004) *Insult and the Making of the Gay Self.* Durham: Duke University Press.

Faulkner, Sally (2003) 'Catalan City Cinema: Violence and Nostalgia in Ventura Pons's *Carícies*', *New Cinemas* 1 (3), 141–48.

Fehrenbach, Heide (1998) 'Rehabilitating Fatherland: Race and German Remasculinization', *Signs* 24 (1), 107–27.

Fernández, Josep-Anton (2004) 'The Authentic Queen and the Invisible Man: Catalan Camp and its Condition of Possibility in Ventura Pons's *Ocaña, Retrat Intermitent*', *Journal of Spanish Cultural Studies* 5 (1), 83–99.

Flood, Michael (2002) 'Between Men and Masculinity: An Assessment of the Term "Masculinity" in Recent Scholarship on Men' in Sharyn Pearce and Vivienne Muller (eds) *Manning the Next Millennium: Studies in Masculinities.* Perth: Black Swan Press, pp. 203–14.

Fotis, Georgiatis (2007) 'White Sometimes Black', *The Athens Contemporary Review* 12 (April 2007), 12–20.

Fouz-Hernández, Santiago and Alfredo Martínez-Expósito (2007) *Live Flesh: The Male Body in Contemporary Spanish Cinema.* London and New York: I.B.Tauris.

Fouz-Hernández, Santiago (2005) 'Phallic Matters: Ewan McGregor and the Representation of the Male Body in Peter Greenaway's *The Pillow Book* (1996)', *Men and Masculinities* 8 (2), 133–47.

Freud, Sigmund (1979 [1919]) 'A Child is Being Beaten' in *Pelican Freud Library 10: On Psychopathology*, ed. Angela Richards. London: Pelican, pp.159–93.

Freud, Sigmund (1991 [1924]) 'The Economic Problem of Masochism' in Penguin Freud Library 11: *On Metapsychology: The Theory of Psychoanalysis*, ed. Angela Richards. London: Penguin, pp. 409–26.

Fung, Richard (1996) 'Looking for My Penis: The Eroticized Asian in Gay Video Porn' in Russell Leong (ed.) *Asian American Sexualities: Dimensions of the Gay and Lesbian Experience.* New York: Routledge, pp. 181–98.

Gabler, Neal (1988) *An Empire of Their Own: How the Jews Invented Hollywood.* London: W. H. Allen.

Geirola, Gustavo (2002) 'Y tu mamá también', *Chasqui* 31 (1), 170–74.

Gerschick, Thomas (2005) 'Masculinity and Degrees of Bodily Normativity in Western Culture' in Michael Kimmel, Jeff Hearn and R. W. Connell (eds) *Handbook of Studies on Men & Masculinities.* Thousand Oaks and London: Sage, pp. 367–76.

Gertel, Elliot B. (2003) *Over the Top Judaism: Precedents and Trends in the Depiction of Jewish Beliefs and Observances in Film and Television.* Lanham, MD: University Press of America.

Gibson, Mark (2007) *Culture and Power: A History of Cultural Studies*. Oxford and New York: Berg.

Gilman, Sander (1991) *The Jew's Body*. London and New York: Routledge.

Göktürk, Deniz (2002) 'Beyond Paternalism: Turkish German Traffic in Cinema' in Tim Bergfelder, Erica Cater and Deniz Göktürk (eds) *The German Cinema Book*. London: BFI, pp. 248–56.

Goldstein, Laurence (1997) *The Male Body: Features, Destinies, Exposures*. Ann Arbor: University of Michigan.

Gomes, Catherine (2005) 'Crouching Women, Hidden Order: Confucianism's Treatment of Gender in Ang Lee's *Crouching Tiger, Hidden Dragon*', *Limina* 11, 47–56 <http://www.limina.arts.uwa.edu.au/current_volume?f=79246> Last consulted in May 2007.

Gómez, Carlos (2004) 'Alejandro Fernández se reconoce como metrosexual', *Anodis* <http://www.anodis.com/nota/2541.asp> Last consulted in December 2007.

Gotteri, Nicole (2005) *Le Western et ses mythes: les sources d'une passion*. Paris: Giovanangeli.

Gould, Carol (2006) 'Women's Human Rights in a Culturally Diverse World', unpublished paper presented at the Experts Meeting of the Social Trends Institute (STI) 'Gender Identity in a Globalized Society', Barcelona, Spain (13–14 October).

Graham, Helen and Jo Labanyi (eds) (1995) *Spanish Cultural Studies: An Introduction*. Oxford: Oxford University Press.

Grossman, Andrew (ed.) (2000) *Queer Asian Cinema: Shadows in the Shade*. New York: Haworth.

Grosz, Elizabeth (1994) *Volatile Bodies: Towards a Corporeal Feminism*. Sydney: Allen and Unwin.

Gutmann, Matthew C. (1996) *The Meanings of Macho: Being a Man in Mexico City*. Berkeley: University of California Press.

Hake, Sabine (2001) *Popular Cinema of the Third Reich*. Austin, TX: University of Texas Press.

Halberstam, Judith (2007) 'Neo-splatter: *Bride of Chucky* and the Horror of Heteronormativity' in Benjamin A. Brabon and Stéphanie Genz (eds) *Postfeminist Gothic: Critical Interventions in Contemporary Culture*. Hampshire: Palgrave Macmillan, pp. 30–42.

Hamamoto, Darrell (2000) 'The Joy Fuck Club: Prolegomenon to an Asian American Porno Practice' in Darrell Hamamoto and Sandra Liu (eds) *Countervisions: Asian American Film Criticism*. Philadelphia: Temple University Press, pp. 59–89.

Hanke, Robert (1999) 'Jon Woo's Cinema of Hyperkinetic Violence: From *A Better Tomorrow* to *Face/Off*', *Film Criticism* 24 (1), 49–96.

Hanson, Ellis (2007) 'Cinema A Tergo: Queer Theory And Gus Van Sant' (unpublished presentation) *Screen Studies Conference*, University of Glasgow.

Harries, Dan (2000) *Film Parody*. London: BFI Publishing.

Hayward, Susan (2006) *Cinema Studies: The Key Concepts*, third edition. London and New York: Routledge.

Hearn, Jeff (1998) Book Review: '*The Swimsuit Issue and Sport: Hegemonic Masculinity in "Sports Illustrated"* by Laurel R. Davis', *The American Journal of Sociology* 103 (6), 1749–51.

Heinrich, Larissa and Fran Martin (eds) (2006) *Embodied Modernities: Corporeality, Representation, and Chinese Cultures*. Honolulu: University of Hawaii Press.

Hißnauer, Christian and Thomas Klein (eds) (2002) *Männer, Machos, Memmen: Männlichkeit im Film*. Mainz: Bender.

Holmlund, Chris (2002) *Impossible Bodies: Femininity and Masculinity at the Movies*. London and New York: Routledge.

Hopkins, Susan (2002) *Girl Heroes: The New Force in Popular Culture*. Sydney: Pluto Press.

Hu, Brian (2003) 'Goodbye City, Goodbye Cinema: Nostalgia in Tsai Ming-liang's *The Skywalk is Gone*', *Senses of Cinema* <http://www.senseofcinema.com/contents/03/29/skywalk_is_gone.html> Last consulted in May 2007.

Hughes, Bryn (2004) 'Political Violence and Democracy: Do Societal Identity Threats Matter? The Security and Politics of Identity', unpublished conference paper presented at the Australasian Political Studies Association Conference, University of Adelaide, South Australia (29 September–1 October).

Hung, Natalia Chan Sui (2000) 'Rewriting History: Hong Kong Nostalgia Cinema and Its Social Practice' in Poshek Fu and David Desser (eds) *The Cinema of Hong Kong*. Cambridge: Cambridge University Press, pp. 252–72.

Hunt, Leon (2002) 'Necromancy in the UK: Witchcraft and the Occult in British Horror' in Steve Chibnall and Julian Petley (eds) *British Horror Cinema*. London: Routledge, pp. 82–98.

Hunter, Latham (2003) 'The Celluloid Cubicle: Regressive Constructions of Masculinity in 1990s Office Movies', *The Journal of American Culture* 26 (1), 71–76, 79–86.

Hutchings, Peter (1993a) *Hammer and Beyond: The British Horror Film*. Manchester: Manchester University Press.

Hutchings, Peter (1993b) 'Masculinity and the Horror Film' in Pat Kirkham and Janet Thumin (eds) *You Tarzan: Masculinity, Movies and Men*. London: Lawrence and Wishart, pp. 84–94.

Inness, Sherrie (1996) *Tough Girls: Women Warriors and Wonder Women in Popular Culture*. Philadelphia: University of Pennsylvania Press.

Jacquemin, Jean-Pierre (2001), '"Chemise jaune et pantalon bleu": entretien avec Barly Baruti', *Notre Librairie* 145, special issue, *La bande dessinée* <http://www.adpf.asso.fr/librairie/derniers/pdf/nl145_6.pdf> Last consulted in March 2007.

Jagose, Annamarie (1999) Interview with Judith Halberstam, 'Masculinity without Men', *Genders* 29 <http://www.iiav.nl/ezines/web/GendersPresenting/2006/No45/genders/g29_halbesstam.html#fig9> Last consulted December 2007.

Jeffords, Susan (1994) *Hard Bodies: Hollywood Masculinity in the Reagan Era*. New Brunswick, NJ: Rutgers UP.

Jerome, Roy (ed.) (2001) *Conceptions of Postwar German Masculinity*. Albany, NY: SUNY Press.

Johnson, Carol (2006) 'Shaping the Culture: Howard's "Values" and Australian Identity', unpublished paper presented at Politics Discipline Seminar Series, University of Adelaide (20 March).

Johnston, Anna and Alan Lawson (2000) 'Settler Colonies' in Henry Schwarz and Sangeeta Ray (eds) *A Companion to Postcolonial Studies*. Oxford: Blackwell, pp. 360–76.

Kasander and Wigman Productions (1996) *The Pillow Book* press book. Alpha Films.

Khoo, Olivia (2006) 'Love in Ruins: Spectral Bodies in Wong Kar-wai's *In the Mood for Love*' in Fran Martin and Larissa Heinrich (eds) *Embodied Modernities: Corporeality, Representation, and Chinese Cultures*. Honolulu: University of Hawaii Press, pp. 235–52.

Kiernan, Brian (2000) 'Australia's Postcoloniality', *Antipodes* 11, 14 (1) (June), 11–16.

Kimmel, Michael (1997) 'Integrating Men into the Curriculum', *Duke Journal of Gender, Law and Policy* 4 <http://www.law.duke.edu/journals/djglp/articles/gen4p181.htm> Last consulted in March 2006.

Kimmel, Michael (2001) 'Gender Equality: not for Women Only', Lecture prepared for International Women's Day Seminar, 'Men and Gender Equality – What Can Men Gain?', Committee on Women's Rights and Equal opportunities, Seminar organised by the European Parliament and the Swedish Presidency, Brussels (8 March).

Kimmel, Michael (forthcoming) *Guyland: The Inner World of Young Men*, 18–27, Chapter 5, 'Boys and Their Toys', unpublished manuscript cited with author's permission.

Kimmel, Michael, Jeff Hearn and R. W. Connell (2005) 'Introduction' in Michael Kimmel, Jeff Hearn and R. W. Connell (eds) *Handbook of Studies on Men and Masculinities*. Thousand Oaks and London: Sage, pp. 1–11.

Kirkham, Pat and Janet Thumin (eds) (1993) *You Tarzan. Masculinity, Movies and Men*. London: Lawrence & Wishart.

Kitses, Jim (2004) *Horizons West. Directing the Western from John Ford to Clint Eastwood*. London: BFI Publishing.

Kraicer, Shelly (2005) 'Tracking the Elusive Wong Kar-wai', *Cineaste* 30 (4), 14–15.

Kristeva, Julia (1982) *Powers of Horror: An Essay on Abjection*. New York: Columbia University Press.

Lang, Robert (2002) *Masculine Interests: Homoerotics in Hollywood Film*. New York: Columbia University Press.

Laplanche, Jean and Jean-Bertrand Pontalis (2004) *The Language of Psychoanalysis*, trans. Donald Nicholson-Smith. London: Karnac Books.

LaSalle, Mick (2002) 'Review *Food of Love*', San Francisco Chronicle (8 November), D–5.

Lawrence, D.H. (1928) *Lady Chatterley's Lover*. New York, NY: Bantam Books.

Lehman, Peter (1993) *Running Scared. Masculinity and the Representation of the Male Body*. Philadelphia: Temple University Press.

Lehman, Peter (2001a) (ed.) *Masculinity: Bodies, Movies, Culture*. London and New York: Routledge.

Lehman, Peter (2001b) 'Crying over the Melodramatic Penis: Melodrama and Male Nudity in Films of the 90s' in Peter Lehman (ed.) *Masculinity: Bodies, Movies, Culture*. London and New York: Routledge, pp. 25–41.

Lehman, Peter (2007) *Running Scared: Masculinity and The Representation of the Male Body*, new edition. Detroit: Wayne State University Press.

Lehman, Peter and Susan Hunt (2007) 'The Naked and the Dead: The Jewish Male Body and Masculinity in *Sunshine* and *Enemy at the Gates*'. in Danel Bernardi (ed.) *The Persistence of Whiteness: Race and Contemporary Hollywood Cinema*. New York: Routledge, pp. 157–64.

Lessing, Gotthold Ephraim (2005 [1766]) *Laocoon: An Essay Upon the Limits of Painting and Poetry*, trans. Ellen Frothingham. Mineola, New York: Dover.

Leung, Helen Hok-sze (2001) 'Queerscapes in Contemporary Hong Kong Cinema', *positions: east asia cultures critique* 9 (2), 423–47.

Li, Siu Leung (2001) 'Kung Fu: Negotiation Nationalism and Modernity', *Cultural Studies* 15 (3), 515–42.

Liu, Kate (2001) 'Family in the Postmodern "Non-Places" in the Films by Atom Egoyan and Ming-liang Tsai', *Fu Jen Studies: Literature and Linguistics* 34 <http://www.eng.fju.edu.tw/canada/paper/egoyan_tsai/et2.htm> Last consulted in May 2007.

Loomba, Ania (1998) *Colonialism/Postcolonialism*. London and New York: Routledge.

Lorcin, Patricia M. E. (1995) *Imperial Identities: Stereotyping, Prejudice and Race in Colonial Algeria*. London and New York: I.B.Tauris.

Lu, Sheldon H. and Emilie Yueh-yu Yeh (eds) (2005) *Chinese-Language Film: Historiography, Poetics, Politics*. Honolulu: University of Hawaii Press.

Lumby, Catherine (1997) *Bad Girls: The Media, Sex and Feminism*. Sydney: Allen and Unwin.

Lusted, David (2003) *The Western*. Harlow: Pearson Education.

Ma, Sheng-mei (2000) *The Deathly Embrace: Orientalism and Asian American Identity*. Minneapolis: University of Minnesota Press.

Mann, Michael (2001) 'Globalization and September 11', *New Left Review* 12, 51–72.

Marchetti, Gina and Tan See Kam (eds) (2007) *Hong Kong Film, Hollywood and the New Global Cinema: No Film is an Island*. London: Routledge.

Marks, Laura U. (2000) *The Skin of the Film: Intercultural Cinema, Embodiment, and the Senses*. Durham: Duke University Press.

Martin-Jones, David (2007) 'National Symbols: Scottish National Identity in *Dog Soldiers*', *Symbolism: International Annual of Cultural Aesthetics* 7, 169–200.

Martínez Soto Alessi, Eduardo (2004) 'Zapata, la pesadilla del héroe', Esmas.com <http://www.esmas.com/espectaculos/cine/360094.html> Last consulted in December 2007.

McClintock, Anne (1995) *Imperial Leather: Race, Gender and Sexuality in the Colonial Contest*. New York and London: Routledge.

McGee, Patrick (2007) *From Shane to Kill Bill: Rethinking the Western*. Oxford: Blackwell.

McKay, Jim, Janine Mikosza and Brett Hutchins (2005) '"Gentlemen, the Lunchbox Has Landed": Representations of Masculinities and Men's Bodies in the Popular Media' in Michael Kimmel, Jeff Hearn and R. W. Connell (eds) *Handbook of Studies on Men and Masculinities*. Thousand Oaks and London: Sage, pp. 270–88.

Melhuus, Marit (1996) 'Power, Value and Ambiguous Meanings of Gender' in Marit Melhuus and Kristi Anne Stølen (eds) *Machos, Mistresses, Madonnas: Contesting the Power of Latin American Gender Imagery*. New York: Verso, pp. 230–59.

Metz, Christian (1977) *The Imaginary Signifier: Psychoanalysis and the Cinema*. Bloomington: Indiana University Press.

Mira, Alberto (2004) *De Sodoma a Chueca: una historia cultural de la homosexualidad en España en el siglo XX*. Madrid: Egales.

Mitscherlich, Alexander and Margarete (1967) *Die Unfähigkeit zu trauern, Grundlagen kollektiven Verhaltens*. Munich: Piper.

Mitscherlich, Alexander and Margarete (1975) *The Inability to Mourn: Principles of Collective Behavior*, trans. Beverly Placzek. New York: Grove.

Monsiváis, Carlos (1995) 'Mythologies' in Paulo Antonio Paranaguá (ed.) *Mexican Cinema*. London: British Film Institute, pp. 117–27.

Morrell, Robert and Sandra Swart (2005) 'Men in the Third World: Postcolonial Perspectives on Masculinity' in Michael Kimmel, Jeff Hearn and R. W. Connell (eds) *Handbook of Studies on Men and Masculinities*. Thousand Oaks and London: Sage, pp. 90–113.

Morris, Meaghan, Siu Leung Li and Stephen Chan Ching-kiu (eds) (2005) *Hong Kong Connections: Transnational Imagination in Action Cinema*. Durham: Duke University Press.

Moser, Tilmann (2001) 'Paralysis, Silence, and the Unknown SS-Father: A Therapeutic Case Study of the Third Reich in Psychotherapy' in Roy Jerome (ed.) *Conceptions of Postwar German Masculinity*. Albany, NY: SUNY Press, pp. 63–91.

Mosse, George (1996) *The Image of Man: The Creation of Modern Masculinity*. Oxford, NY: Oxford University Press.

Mulvey, Laura (1975) 'Visual Pleasure and Narrative Cinema', *Screen* 16 (3), 6–18.

Mulvey, Laura (1989 [1981]) 'Afterthoughts on "Visual Pleasure and Narrative Cinema" Inspired by King Vidor's *Duel in the Sun* (1946)' in Laura Mulvey (ed.) *Visual and Other Pleasures*. Basingstoke and London: Macmillan, pp. 29–38.

Mulvey, Laura (2000 [1975]) 'Visual Pleasure and Narrative Cinema' in Robert Stam and Toby Miller (eds) *Film and Theory: An Anthology*. Oxford: Blackwell, pp. 483–94.

Naficy, Hamid (2001) *Accented Cinema: Exilic and Diasporic Filmmaking*. Princeton, NJ: Princeton University Press.

Neale, Steve (1981) 'Art Cinema as Institution', *Screen* 22 (1), 11–39.

Neale, Steve (1993 [1983]), 'Masculinity as Spectacle: Reflections on Men and Mainstream Cinema' in Steven Cohan and Ina Rae Hark (eds) *Screening the Male: Exploring Masculinities in Hollywood Cinema*. New York: Routledge, pp. 9–20.

Noble, Andrea (2005) *Mexican National Cinema*. New York: Routledge.

Norindr, Panivong (2006) 'Vietnam: Chronicles of Old and New' in Anne Tereska Ciecko (ed.) *Contemporary Asian Cinema*. Oxford: Berg, pp. 45–57.

O'Regan, Tom (1996) *Australian National Cinema.* London and New York: Routledge.

Pande, Alka (2004) *Ardhanarishvara: Probing the Gender Within.* New Delhi: Roli Books.

Pang, Laikwan (2005) 'Introduction: The Diversity of Masculinities in Hong Kong Cinema' in Laikwan Pang and Day Wong (eds) (2005) *Masculinities and Hong Kong Cinema.* Hong Kong: Hong Kong University Press, pp. 1–14.

Pang, Laikwan and Day Wong (eds) (2005) *Masculinities and Hong Kong Cinema.* Hong Kong: Hong Kong University Press.

Paz, Octavio (1961 [1950]) *The Labyrinth of Solitude.* New York: The Grove Press.

Peak, Wendy Chapman (2003) 'The Romance of Competence: Rethinking Masculinity in the Western', *Journal of Popular Film and Television* 30 (4), 206–18.

Perriam, Chris (2003) *Stars and Masculinities in Spanish Cinema: From Banderas to Bardem.* Oxford: Oxford University Press.

Pinedo, Isabel Cristina (1997) *Recreational Terror: Women and the Pleasures of Horror Film Viewing.* Albany: State University of New York Press.

Poiger, Uta (1998) 'A New, "Western" Hero? Reconstructing German Masculinity in the 1950s', *Signs* 24 (1), 147–62.

Pons, Ventura (2005) *Guión* Amor idiota. Madrid: Ocho y Medio.

Powrie, Phil, Ann Davies and Bruce Babington (eds) (2004) *The Trouble with Men: Masculinities in European and Hollywood Cinema.* London and New York: Wallflower Press.

Pratt, Mary Louise (1992) *Imperial Eyes: Travel Writing and Transculturation.* London and New York: Routledge.

Radhakrishnan, Sarvapalli (1918) *The Philosophy of Rabindranath Tagore.* London: MacMillan.

Raymond, Janice (1996) 'The Politics of Transgenderism' in Richard Ekins and Dave King (eds) *Blending Genders: Social Aspects of Cross-Dressing and Sex-Changing.* London: Routledge, pp. 215–24.

Rayns, Tony (1976) 'Director: King Hu', *Sight and Sound* 45 (1), 8–13.

Rees-Roberts, Nick (2007) 'Down And Out: Immigrant Poverty and Queer Sexuality in Sébastian Lifshitz's *Wild Side*', *Studies in French Cinema* 7 (2), 143–55.

Reich, June L. (1992) 'Genderfuck: The Law of the Dildo', *Discourses* 15 (1), 112–27.

Reik, Theodor (1941) *Masochism in Modern Man.* New York: Grove Press.

Rentschler, Eric (1996) *The Ministry of Illusion: Nazi Cinema and Its Afterlife.* Cambridge, MA: Harvard University Press.

Reynaud, Berenice (2003) 'The Book, the Goddess and the Hero: Sexual Politics in the Chinese Martial Arts Film', *Senses of Cinema* <http://www.senseofcinema.com/contents/03/26/sexual_politics_chinese_marital-arts.html> Last consulted in May 2007.

Richter, Horst-Eberhard (2006) 'Die Helden sind ratlos', *Der Spiegel* 40, 150–54.

Rieser, Klaus (2001) 'Masculinity and Monstrosity: Characterization and Identification in the Slasher Film', *Men and Masculinities* 3 (4), 370–92.

Rivière, Danièle (1999) 'Scouting', trans. A. Rothwell in Jean-Pierre Rehm, Olivier Joyard and Danièle Rivière (eds) *Tsai Ming-liang.* Paris: Dis Voir, pp. 79–80.

Rogin, Michael (1998) *Independence Day*. London: BFI.

Russo, Vito (1981) *The Celluloid Closet: Homosexuality in the Movies*. New York: Harper & Row.

Saïd, Edward (1978) *Orientalism*. London: Routledge and Kegan Paul.

Saïd, Edward (1993) *Culture and Imperialism*. London: Chatto and Windus.

Sandell, Julian (1997) 'Reinventing Masculinity: The Spectacle of Male Intimacy in the Films of John Woo', *Film Quarterly* 49 (4), 23–34.

Santner, Eric L. (1990) *Stranded Objects: Mourning, Memory, and Film in Postwar Germany*. Ithaca: Cornell University Press.

Savarese, Éric (1998) *L'Ordre colonial et sa légitimation en France métropolitaine: oublier l'autre*. Paris: L'Harmattan.

Schneider, Tassilo (1998) 'Finding a New Heimat in the Wild West: Karl May and the German Western of the 1960s' in Edward Buscombe and Roberta E. Pearson (eds) *Back in the Saddle Again: New Essays on the Western*. London: BFI Publishing, pp. 141–59.

Schrader, Paul (1972) *Transcendental Style in Film: Ozu, Bresson, Dreyer*. New York: Da Capo Press.

Schulte-Sasse, Linda (1996) *Entertaining the Third Reich: Illusions of Wholeness in Nazi Cinema*. Durham, NC: Duke University Press.

Seem, Mark (1983) 'Introduction' in Gilles Deleuze and Felix Guattari *Anti-Oedipus: Capitalism and Schizophrenia*, trans. Robert Hurly, Mark Seem and Helen R. Lane. Minneapolis: University of Minnesota Press, pp. xv–xxiv.

Sek, Kei (1996) 'The War Between the Cantonese and Mandarin Cinema in the Sixties or How the Beautiful Women Lost to the Action Men' in Law Kar (ed.) *The Restless Breed: Cantonese Stars of the Sixties*. Hong Kong: The Urban Council, pp. 26–33.

Sen, Amartya Kumar (2005) *The Argumentative Indian: Essays: Writings on Indian History, Culture and identity*. London: Penguin.

Shandler, Jeffrey (1999) *While America Watches: Televising the Holocaust*. New York: Oxford University Press.

Shapiro, Michael J. (1999) *Cinematic Political Thought: Narrating Race, Nation and Gender*. New York: New York University Press.

Shaviro, Steven (1993) *The Cinematic Body*. Minneapolis: University of Minnesota Press.

Shaviro, Steven (2008) '*The Cinematic Body* REDUX', *Parallax* 14 (1), 48–54.

Shelton, Emily (2002) 'A Star is Porn: Corpulence, Comedy, and the Homosocial Cult of Adult Film Star Ron Jeremy', *Camera Obscura* 17 (3), 115–46.

Siegel, Marc (2001) 'The Intimate Spaces of Wong Kar-Wai' in Esther Yau (ed.) *At Full Speed: Hong Kong Cinema in a Borderless World*. Minneapolis: University of Minnesota Press, pp. 277–94.

Silverman, Kaja (1988) 'Masochism and Male Subjectivity', *Camera Obscura* 17, 31–68.

Silverman, Kaja (1992) *Male Subjectivity at the Margins*. New York: Routledge.

Simpson, Mark (1994) *Male Impersonators: Men Performing Masculinity*. London and New York: Routledge.

Sklar, Robert (2001) 'The Politics of Pure Emotion: Interview with Filmmaker Tran Anh Hung', *Cineaste* 26 (4), 69–70.

Slavin, David Henry (2001) *Colonial Cinema and Imperial France, 1919–1939. White Blind Spots, Male Fantasies, Settler Myths.* Baltimore and London: John Hopkins University Press.

Smith, Paul Julian (2002) 'Heaven's Mouth', *Sight and Sound* 12 (4), 16–20.

Smith, Paul Julian (2003) 'Catalan Independents? Ventura Pons's Niche Cinema', *Contemporary Spanish Culture: TV, Fashion, Art and Film.* Cambridge: Polity Press, pp. 113–42.

Sobchack, Vivian (2004) *Carnal Thoughts: Embodiment and Moving Image Culture.* Berkeley: University of California Press.

Sontag, Susan (1966a [1964]) 'Against Interpretation' in *Against Interpretation and Other Essays.* New York: Farrar, Straus & Giroux, pp. 3–14.

Sontag, Susan (1966b [1964]) 'Godard's *Vivre sa vie*' in *Against Interpretation and Other Essays.* New York: Farrar, Straus & Giroux, pp. 196–208.

Sontag, Susan (1966c [1963]) 'Resnais' Muriel' in *Against Interpretation and Other Essays.* New York: Farrar, Straus & Giroux, pp. 232–41.

Spivak, Gayatri Chakravorty (1997) 'Can the Subaltern Speak?' in Bill Ashcroft, Gareth Griffiths and Helen Tiffin (eds) *The Post-colonial Studies Reader*, second edition. London and New York: Routledge, 24–8.

Spurr, David (1993) *The Rhetoric of Empire: Colonial Discourse in Journalism, Travel Writing and Imperial Administration.* Durham and London: Duke University Press.

Stam, Robert (2002) *Introducing Film Theory.* London: Blackwell Publishing.

Stanfield, Peter (1998) 'Dixie Cowboys and Blue Yodels: The Strange History of the Singing Cowboy' in Edward Buscombe and Roberta E. Pearson (eds) *Back in the Saddle Again: New Essays on the Western.* London: BFI Publishing, pp. 96–118.

Stephan, Inge (2003) 'Im toten Winkel: Die Neuentdeckung des "ersten Geschlechts" durch *men's studies* und Männlichkeitsforschung' in Clauda Benthien and Inge Stephan (eds) *Männlichkeit als Maskerade: Kulturelle Inszenierungen vom Mittelalter bis zur Gegenwart.* Cologne: Böhlau, pp. 11–36.

Stephens, Elizabeth (2007) 'The Spectacularized Penis: Contemporary Representations of the Phallic Male Body', *Men and Masculinities* Special Issue on the Male Body 10 (1), 85–98.

Stephens, Elizabeth and Jørgen Lorentzen (2007a) *Men and Masculinities* Special Issue on the Male Body 10 (1).

Stephens, Elizabeth and Jørgen Lorentzen (2007b) 'Male Bodies: An Introduction', *Men and Masculinities* Special Issue on the Male Body 10 (1), 5–8.

Stevenson, Robert Louis (2002 [1886]) *The Strange Case of Dr Jekyll and Mr Hyde.* New York: W. W. Norton.

Still, Judith (2003) (ed.) *Male Bodies* (*Paragraph* 26 (1/2)). Edinburgh: Edinburgh University Press.

Stringer, Julian (1997) '"Your Tender Smiles Give Me Strength": Paradigms of Masculinity in John Woo's *A Better Tomorrow* and *The Killer*', *Screen* 38 (1), 25–41.

Studlar, Gaylyn (1984) 'Masochism and the Perverse Pleasures of the Cinema', *Quarterly Review of Film Studies* 9 (4), 267–78.

Studlar, Gaylyn (1992) *In the Realm of Pleasure: Von Sternberg, Dietrich, and the Masochistic Aesthetic*. New York: Columbia University Press.

Taberner, Stuart and Paul Cooke (2006) 'Introduction' in Stuart Taberner and Paul Cooke (eds) *German Culture, Politics, and Literature into the Twenty-First Century: Beyond Normalization*. Rochester, NY: Camden House, pp. 1–15.

Tambling, Jeremy (2003) *Wong Kar-wai's Happy Together*. Hong Kong: Hong Kong University Press.

Tasker, Yvonne (1993) *Spectacular Bodies: Gender, Genre and Action Cinema*. London and New York: Routledge.

Tasker, Yvonne (1997) 'Fists of Fury: Discourses of Race and Masculinity in the Martial Arts Cinema' in Harry Stecopoulos and Michael Uebel (eds) *Race and the Subject of Masculinities*. Durham: Duke University Press, pp. 315–36.

Teo, Stephen (1997) *Hong Kong Cinema: The Extra Dimensions*. London: BFI Publishing.

Teo, Stephen (2001) 'Love and Swords: The Dialectics of Martial Arts Romance', *Senses of Cinema* <http://www.senseofcinema.com/contents/00/11/crouching.html> Last consulted in May 2007.

Teo, Stephen (2002) 'King Hu', *Senses of Cinema* <http://www.senseofcinema.com/contents/directors/02/hu.html> Last consulted in April 2007.

Teo, Stephen (2005a) *Wong Kar-wai: Auteur of Time*. London: British Film Institute.

Teo, Stephen (2005b) '*Wuxia* Redux: *Crouching Tiger, Hidden Dragon* as a Model of Late Transnational Production' in Meaghan Morrow, Siu Li and Stephen Chan (eds) *Hong Kong Connections: Transnational Imagination in Action Cinema*. Durham, NC: Duke University Press, pp. 191–204.

Theweleit, Klaus (1977) *Männerphantasien I: Frauen, Fluten, Körper, Geschichte*. Frankfurt: Rowohlt.

Thomas, Nicholas (1994) *Colonialism's Culture: Anthropology, Travel and Government*. Cambridge: Polity Press.

Thompkins, Gwen (2007) 'Country Music in a Far Country', National Public Radio (NPR) broadcast, 7 April 2007, Weekend Edition Saturday.

Tompkins, Jane (1992) *West of Everything: The Inner Life of Westerns*. Oxford: Oxford University Press.

Ukadike, Nwachcukwu Frank (1994) *Black African Cinema*. Berkeley: University of California Press.

Univisión (2006) 'Rafa Marquez y Alejandro Fernández en pleno romance', *Foros Univisión* <http://foro.univision.com/univision/board/message?board.id=elgordoylaflaca&me sage.id=2191159&page=1> Last consulted in December 2007.

van Kriekan, Robert, Philip Smith, Daphne Habibis, Kevin McDonald, Michael Haralambos and Martin Holborn (2000) *Sociology: Themes and Perspectives*, second edition. Sydney: Pearson Education Australia.

Varma, Pavan Kumar (1999) *The Great Indian Middle Class*. New Delhi: Penguin.

Vincendeau, Ginette (2003) 'What She Wants', *Sight and Sound* (May), 20–22.

Wang, Shujen and Chris Fujiwara (2006) 'My Films Reflect My Living Situation. An Interview with Tsai Ming-liang on Film Spaces, Audience and Distribution', *positions: east asia cultures critique* 14 (1), 219–41.

Waugh, Thomas (1993) 'The Third Body: Patterns in the Construction of the Subject in Gay Male Narrative Film' in Martha Gever, John Greyson and Pratibha Parmar (eds) *Queer Looks: Perspectives on Lesbian and Gay Film and Video*. New York and London: Routledge, pp. 141–61.

Wayne, Mike (2001) *Political Film: The Dialectics of Third Cinema*. London: Pluto.

Whittle, Stephen (1996) 'Gender Fucking or Fucking Gender? Current Cultural Contributions to Theories of Gender Blending' in Richard Ekins and Dave King (eds) *Blending Genders: Social Aspects of Cross-Dressing and Sex-Changing*. London: Routledge, pp. 196–214.

Williams, Linda (1999) *Hard Core: Power, Pleasure and the 'Frenzy of the Visible'*. Berkeley, Los Angeles and London: University of California Press.

Wood, Chris (2007) 'Realism, Intertextuality, and Humour in Tsai Ming-liang's *Goodbye Dragon Inn*', *Journal of Chinese Cinema* 1 (2), 105–16.

Yau, Esther (ed.) (2001) *At Full Speed: Hong Kong Cinema in a Borderless World*. Minneapolis: University of Minnesota Press.

Yeh, Emilie and Darrell Davis (2005) *Taiwan Film Directors: A Treasure Island*. New York: Columbia University Press.

Yip, June (2004) *Envisioning Taiwan: Fiction, Cinema, and the Nation in the Cultural Imaginary*. Durham and London: Duke University Press.

Yosef, Raz (2004) *Beyond Flesh: Queer Masculinities and Nationalism in Israeli Cinema*. New Brunswick, NJ and London: Rutgers University Press.

Zecchi, Barbara (2006) 'Women Filming the Male Body: Subversions, Inversions and Identifications', *Studies in Hispanic Cinemas* 3 (3), 187–204.

Filmography

2046 (dir. Wong Kar-wai, 2003)
52 Pick-Up (dir. John Frankenheimer, 1986)
À la verticale de l'été/Vertical Ray of the Sun (dir. Tran Anh Hung, 2000)
A ma soeur/Fat Girl (dir. Catherine Breillat, 2001)
A toute vitesse/Full Speed (dir. Gäel Morel, 1996)
Achin Paki/The Unknown Bard (dir. Tanvir Mokammel, 1996)
Actrius/Actresses (dir. Ventura Pons, 1996)
A-Fei Zhengzhuan/Days of Being Wild (dir. Wong Kar-wai, 1991)
Agnes und seine Brüder/Agnes and His Brothers (dir. Oskar Roehler, 2004)
Allá en el Rancho Grande/Out on the Big Ranch (dir. Fernando de Fuentes, 1949)
Along Came Polly (dir. John Hamburg, 2004)
American Beauty (dir. Sam Mendes, 1999)
American Pie (dir. Paul Weitz, 1999)
American Pie 2 (dir. James B. Rogers, 2001)
American Wedding (dir. Jesse Dylan, 2003)
American Werewolf in London, An (dir. John Landis, 1981)
Amic/Amat/Beloved/Friend (dir. Ventura Pons, 1998)
Amor idiota/Idiot Love (dir. Ventura Pons, 2004)
Angels and Insects (dir. Philip Haas, 1995)
Antonia's Line (dir. Marleen Gorris, 1995)
Asylum (dir. David Mackenzie, 2005)
At Play in the Fields of the Lord (dir. Hector Babenco, 1991)
¡Ay Jalisco, no te rajes!/Jalisco, Don't Backslide (dir. Joselito Rodríguez, 1941)
Ballade des Dalton, La/The Dalton's Trip (dirs René Goscinny and Henri Gruel, 1978)
Bamako (dir. Abderrahamane Sissako, 2006)
Barcelona, un mapa/Barcelona, a Map (dir. Ventura Pons, 2007)
Ben Hur (dir. William Wyler, 1959)
Bhavantaran (dir. Kumar Shahani, 1996)
Big Lebowski, The (dir. Joel Cohen, 1998)
Black and White (dir. Craig Lahiff, 2002)

Black Hawk Down (dir. Ridley Scott, 2001)
Blood and Chocolate (dir. Katja von Garnier, 2007)
Boys Don't Cry (dir. Kimberly Pierce, 1999)
Braveheart (dir. Mel Gibson, 1995)
Breaker Morant (dir. Bruce Beresford, 1979)
Bride of Chucky (dir. Ronny Yu, 1998)
Brokeback Mountain (dir. Ang Lee, 2005)
Bu san/Goodbye, Dragon Inn (dir. Tsai Ming-liang, 2003)
Bugsy (dir. Barry Levinson, 1991)
Carícies/Caresses (dir. Ventura Pons, 1997)
Casablanca (dir. Michael Curtiz, 1942)
Casino (dir. Martin Scorsese, 1995)
Ch'ing shaonien na cha/Rebels of the Neon God (dir. Tsai Ming-liang, 1992)
Chatte à deux têtes, La/Porn Theatre (dir. Jacques Nolot, 2002)
Chongqing Senlin/Chungking Express (dir. Wong Kar-wai, 1994)
Chopper (dir. Andrew Dominik, 2000)
Chunguang Zhaxie/Happy Together (dir. Wong Kar-wai, 1997)
Clan, Le/The Clan (dir. Gäel Morel, 2004)
Como agua para chocolate/Like Water for Chocolate (dir. Alfonso Arau, 1993)
Company of Wolves, The (dir. Neil Jordan, 1984)
Confusion des genres, La/Confusion of Genders (dir. Illan Duran Cohen, 2000)
Cowboys sont noirs, Les/The Cowboys are Black (dir. Serge Moati, 1966)
Crash (dir. David Cronenberg, 1996)
Crocodile Dundee (dir. Peter Faiman, 1986)
Crossfire (dir. Edward Dmytryk, 1947)
Crustacés et coquillages/Cockles and Muscles (dirs Olivier Ducastel and Jacques Martinez, 2005)
Crying Game, The (dir. Neil Jordan, 1992)
Cursed (dir. Wes Craven, 2005)
Daayara/The Square Circle (dir. Amol Palekar, 1996)
Daisy Town (dir. René Goscinny, 1971)
Dalton en cavale, Les /The Daltons on the Run (dir. Hanna-Barbera, 1983)
Dalton, Les /The Daltons (dir. Philippe Haim, 2004)
Dead Heart (dir. Nick Parsons, 1996)
Dead of Night (dirs Alberto Cavalcanti, Robert Hamer, Charles Crichton, Basil Dearden, 1945)
Derailed (dir. Mikael Håfström, 2005)
Desperate Housewives (television series, ABC, 2004–)
Die Hard (dir. John McTiernan, 1988)

Die Hard 2 (dir. Renny Harlin, 1990)
Die Hard 3: With a Vengeance (dir. John McTiernan, 1995)
Dirty Deeds (dir. David Caesar, 2002)
Dog Soldiers (dir. Neil Marshall, 2002)
Dona Flor e Seus Dois Maridos/Dona Flor and Her Two Husbands (dir. Bruno Barreto, 1976)
Dongxie Xidu/Ashes of Time (dir. Wong Kar-wai, 1994)
Doppelte Lottchen, Das/Two Times Lotte (dir. Josef von Báky, 1950)
Dos tipos de cuidado/Two Careful Fellows (dir. Ismael Rodríguez, 1953)
Douches froids/Cold Showers (dir. Antony Cordier, 2005)
Duel in the Sun (dir. King Vidor, 1946)
E Dieu... créa la femme/And God Created Woman (dir. Roger Vadim, 1956)
Eating Out (dir. Q. Allan Brocka, 2004)
Elephant (dir. Gus Van Sant, 2003)
Emiliano Zapata/Zapata (dir. Felipe Cazal, 1970)
Emmanuelle (dir. Just Jaeckin, 1974)
End of the Affair, The (dir. Neil Jordan, 1999)
Enemy at the Gates (dir. Jean-Jacques Annaud, 2001)
Exodus (dir. Otto Preminger, 1960)
Face/Off (dir. John Woo, 1997)
Falling Down (dir. Joel Schumacher, 1993)
Fetten Jahre sind vorbei, Die/The Edukators (dir. Hans Weingartner, 2004)
Fiddler on the Roof (dir. Norman Jewison, 1971)
Fight Club (dir. David Fincher, 1999)
Fleuve, Le/The River (dir. Jean Renoir, 1951)
Fly, The (dir. David Cronenberg, 1986)
Food of Love (dir. Ventura Pons, 2001)
Freund von mir, Ein /A Friend of Mine (dir. Sebastian Schipper, 2006).
Friday the Thirteenth (dir. Sean S. Cunningham, 1980)
Freie Wille, Der/The Free Will (dir. Matthias Glasner, 2006)
Gallipoli (dir. Peter Weir, 1981)
Garçon stupide/Stupid Boy (dir. Lionel Baier, 2004)
Gentleman's Agreement (dir. Elia Kazan, 1947)
Ghoul, The (dir. T. Hayes Hunter, 1933)
Ginger Snaps (dir. John Fawcett, 2000)
Godfather II, The (dir. Francis Ford Coppola, 1974)
Goodbye, Lenin!/Goodbye Lenin! (dir. Wolfgang Becker, 2003)
GoodFellas (dir. Martin Scorsese, 1990)
Governess, The (dir. Sandra Goldbacher, 1998)

Halloween (dir. John Carpenter, 1978)
Hammers Over the Anvil (dir. Ann Turner, 1993)
He liu/The River (dir. Tsai Ming-liang, 1997)
Henry & June (dir. Philip Kaufman, 1990)
History Boys, The (dir. Nicholas Hytner, 2006)
History of the World, Part 1 (dir. Mel Brooks, 1983)
Horse Whisperer, The (dir. Robert Redford, 1998)
Hostel (dir. Eli Roth, 2005)
Howling, The (dir. John Dante, 1981)
Huayang Nianhua/In the Mood for Love (dir. Wong Kar-wai, 2000)
Hulk, The (dir. Ang Lee, 2003)
I.Q. (dir. Fred Schepisi, 1994)
Im Juli/In July (dir. Fatih Akin, 2000)
Independence Day (dir. Roland Emmerich, 1996)
Inside Man (dir. Spike Lee, 2006)
Irréversible/Irreversible (dir. Gaspar Noé, 2002)
Japanese Story (dir. Sue Brooks, 2003)
Jaws (dir. Steven Spielberg, 1975)
Jazz Singer, The (dir. Alan Crosland, 1927)
Jud Süß/Jew Suss (dir. Veit Harlan, 1940)
Jurassic Park (dir. Steven Spielberg, 1993)
Juste une question d'amour/Just a Question of Love (dir. Christian Faure, 2000)
Kalifornia (dir. Dominic Sena, 1993)
Khalnayak/The Villain (dir. Subhash Ghai, 1993)
Killing Me Softly (dir. Kaige Chen, 2002)
Killing Zoe (dir. Roger Avary, 1994)
Kini et Adams/Kini and Adams (dir. Idrissa Ouédraogo, 1997)
Kiss Me Goodbye (dir. Robert Mulligan, 1982)
L'homme blessé/The Wounded Man (dir. Patrice Chéreau, 1983)
Lady from Shanghai, The (dir. Wong Kar-wai, in production)
Leben der Anderen, Das/The Lives of Others (dir. Florian Henckel von Donnersmarck, 2006)
Legends of the Fall (dir. Edward Zwick, 1994)
Lepke (dir. Menahem Golan, 1975)
Lethal Weapon (dir. Richard Donner, 1987)
Lethal Weapon 2 (dir. Richard Donner, 1989)
Lethal Weapon 3 (dir. Richard Donner, 1992)
Lethal Weapon 4 (dir. Richard Donner, 1998)
Little Caesar (dir. Mervyn LeRoy, 1932)

Live Free or Die Hard (dir. Len Wiseman, 2007)
Lola rennt/Run Lola Run (dir. Tom Tykwer, 1998)
Lone Ranger, The (dir. Stuart Heisler, 1956)
Lone Ranger, The (TV series 1949–75) (Season 1 dir. George B. Seitz Jr; Hollingsworth Morse)
Lonesome Cowboys (dir. Andy Warhol, 1968)
Long Goodbye, The (dir. Robert Altman, 1973)
Long men ke zhan/Dragon Gate Inn (dir. King Hu, 1967)
Lost (television series, ABC, 2004–)
Lost World: Jurassic Park, The (dir. Steven Spielberg, 1997)
Lucky Luke (animated TV series) (dir. Hanna-Barbera, 1983–84; 1990–91)
Lucky Luke (dir. Terence Hill, 1991)
Lucky Luke (TV Series) (dir. Terence Hill, 1983)
Lucky Luke 2 (dirs Ted Nicolau and Richard Schlesinger, 1991)
Lucky Number Slevin (dir. Paul McGuigan, 2006)
Ma vraie vie à Rouen/My Life on Ice (dirs Olivier Ducastel and Jacques Martinez, 2002)
Maîtresse/Mistress (dir. Barbet Schroeder, 1976)
Man Who Shot Liberty Valance, The (dir. John Ford, 1962)
Meet the Fockers (dir. Jay Roach, 2004)
Meet the Parents (dir. Jay Roach, 2000)
Mighty Heart, A (dir. Michael Winterbottom, 2007)
Morocco (dir. Josef von Sternberg, 1930)
Mùi dud u xanh/The Scent of Green Papaya (dir. Tran Anh Hung, 1993)
Munich (dir. Steven Spielberg, 2005)
My Blueberry Nights (dir. Wong Kar-wai, 2007)
Mysterious Skin (dir. Greg Araki, 2005)
Ni neibian jidian/What Time Is It There? (dir. Tsai Ming-liang, 2001)
Nichts bereuen/No Regrets (dir. Benjamin Quabeck, 2001)
Night of the Demon (dir. Jacques Tourneur, 1957)
No basta ser charro/Being a Charro is Not Enough (dir. José Bustillo Oro, 1946)
North to Alaska (dir. Henry Hathaway, 1960)
Nosotros los pobres/We the Poor (dir. Ismael Rodríguez, 1947)
Notebook, The (dir. Nick Cassavetes, 2004)
Nouvelles aventures de Lucky Luke, Les/The New Adventures of Lucky Luke (animated TV series) (dir. Jean-Marie Olivier, 2001)
Ocaña, retrat intermitent/Ocaña, an Intermittent Portrait (dir. Ventura Pons, 1978)
Olympia (dir. Leni Riefenstahl, 1938)
Paheli/The Riddle (dir. Amol Palekar, 2005)

Pale Rider (dir. Clint Eastwood, 1985)
Passion of the Christ, The (dir. Mel Gibson, 2004)
Per un pugno di dollari /A Fistful of Dollars (dir. Sergio Leone, 1964)
Perquè de tot plegat, El /What's It All About (dir. Ventura Pons, 1995)
Piano, The (dir. Jane Campion, 1993)
Pillow Book, The (dir. Peter Greenaway, 1996)
Pink Cadillac (dir. Van Horn, 1989)
Pornstar: The Legend of Ron Jeremy (dir. Scott J. Gill, 2001)
Presque rien/Come Undone (dir. Sébastien Lifshitz, 2002)
Psycho (dir. Alfred Hitchcock, 1960)
¡Puta Miseria!/Bloody Pittance (dir. Ventura Pons, 1989)
Què t'hi jugues Mari Pili?/What's Your Bet, Mari Pili? (dir. Ventura Pons, 1990)
Rabbit Proof Fence (dir. Philip Noyce, 2001)
Red Dust (dir. Victor Fleming, 1932)
Reine Margot, La/Queen Margot (dir. Patrice Chéreau, 1994)
Retour d'un aventurier, Le/An Adventurer's Return (dir. Mustapha Alassane, 1966)
Ridicule (dir. Patrice Leconte, 1996)
River Runs Through It, A (dir. Robert Redford, 1992)
River Wild, The (dir. Curtis Hanson, 1994)
Rocky (dir. John G. Avildsen, 1976)
Rocky 2 (dir. Sylvester Stallone, 1979)
Rocky 3 (dir. Sylvester Stallone, 1982)
Rocky 4 (dir. Sylvester Stallone, 1985)
Rocky 5 (dir. John G. Avildsen, 1990)
Rocky Balboa (dir. Sylvester Stallone, 2006)
Romance (dir. Catherine Breillat, 1999)
Rossa del Bar, La /The Blonde at the Bar (dir. Ventura Pons, 1986)
Samba Traoré (dir. Idrissa Ouédaogo, 1992)
Schindler's List (dir. Steven Spielberg, 1993)
Scream (dir. Wes Craven, 1996)
Sebastian (dir. Derek Jarman, 1976)
Seinfeld (television series, NBC, 1990–98)
Serenity (dir. Joss Whedon, 2005)
Sex is Comedy (dir. Catherine Breillat, 2002)
Shane (dir. George Stevens, 1953)
Shining, The (dir. Stanley Kubrick, 1980)
Shortbus (dir. John Cameron Mitchell, 2006)
Sirens (dir. John Duigan, 1994)
Sitcom (dir. François Ozon, 1998)

Snatch (dir. Guy Ritchie, 2000)
Solino/Solino (dir. Fatih Akin, 2002)
Soy charro de Rancho Grande/I'm a Charro from the Big Ranch (dir. Joaquín Pardavé, 1947)
Spoilers, The (dir. Ray Enright, 1942)
Spotswood (dir. Mark Joffe, 1992)
Sunset Boulevard (dir. Billy Wilder, 1950)
Sunshine (dir. István Szabó, 1999)
Taxi Driver (dir. Martin Scorsese, 1976)
Temps qui reste, Le/Time to Leave (dir. François Ozon, 2005)
Ten Commandments, The (dir. Cecil B. DeMille, 1956)
Terminator 2: Judgment Day (dir. James Cameron, 1991)
Terminator 3: Rise of the Machines (dir. Jonathan Mostow, 2003)
Terminator, The (dir. James Cameron, 1984)
Testosterone (dir. David Moreton, 2003)
Texas Chain Saw Massacre, The (dir. Tobe Hooper, 1974)
There's Something About Mary (dirs Bobby and Peter Farrelly, 1998)
Tianqiao bu jianle/The Skywalk is Gone (dir. Tsai Ming-liang, 2002)
Tilaï/The Law (dir. Idrissa Ouédraogo, 1990)
Titanic (dir. James Cameron, 1997)
Tout va bien/All is Well (dir. Jean-Luc Godard, 1972)
Tracker, The (dir. Rolf De Heer, 2001)
Tres García, Los /The Three Garcías (dir. Ismael Rodríguez, 1946)
Trouble Every Day (dir. Claire Denis, 2001)
Troy (dir. Wolfgang Petersen, 2004)
Twentynine Palms (dir. Bruno Dumont, 2002)
Two Moon Junction (dir. Zalman King, 1988)
Untergang, Der/Downfall (dir. Oliver Hirschbiegel, 2004)
Valseuses, Les / Going Places (dir. Bertrand Blier, 1974)
Vicari d'Olot/The Vicar of Olot (dir. Ventura Pons, 1981)
Viva Zapata! (dir. Elia Kazan, 1952)
Werewolf of London (dir. Stuart Walker, 1935)
Weiße Rauschen, Das/The White Sound (dir. Hans Weingartner, 2001)
Wild Side (dir. Sébastian Lifshitz, 2004)
Wild Tigers I Have Known (dir. Cam Archer, 2006)
Wo hu cang long/Crouching Tiger Hidden Dragon (dir. Ang Lee, 2000)
Wolf (dir. Mike Nichols, 1994)
Wolf Man, The (dir. George Waggner, 1941)
Wunder von Bern, Das/The Miracle of Bern (dir. Sönke Wortmann, 2003)

Xich Lo/Cyclo (dir. Tran Anh Hung, 1995)
X-Men (dir. Bryan Singer, 2000)
X-2 (dir. Bryan Singer, 2003)
X-Men: The Last Stand (dir. Brett Ratner, 2006)
Y tu mamá también/And Your Mother Too (dir. Alfonso Cuarón, 2001).
Ying xiong/Hero (dir. Zhang Yimou, 2002)
Young Adam (dir. David Mackenzie, 2003)
Zabriskie Point (dir. Michaelangelo Antonioni, 1970)
Zapata: el sueño del héroe/Zapata: Dream of a Hero (dir. Alfonso Arau, 2004).

Index